FROM SCRUBS TO STARTUPS™

For Nurses Leaving the Bedside in search of Options,
Autonomy and a Better Life

Laurie A. Alves, LPN

ISBN: 979-8-9988567-0-9

Cover design by Laurie A. Alves

Interior design by Laurie A. Alves

Published by Sovereign Ink Press

Printed in the United States of America

www.sovereigninkpress.com

Acknowledgement

This book wasn't written in a café or with a circle of advisors by my side. It was written in real life. In between long days, hard decisions, and quiet, radical moments of clarity.

I didn't have a traditional support team, but I did have something just as powerful: *Purpose.*

That purpose was **you**.

To every nurse who has ever whispered "I can't do this anymore" This book was written in your honor.

Thank you for showing up every day.

Thank you for reading.

Thank you for *daring* to look for more.

Table of Contents

Part I: The Shift

1. The Real Deal on Bedside Nursing: (and Why You Might Be Ready for a Change)

2. Beyond the Bedside:
Discovering Your Nursing Superpowers

3. A Nurse Entrepreneur's Self-Assessment Guide:
Taking Stock of Your Value

4. The Nurse Entrepreneur Mindset: Overcoming Fears and Recognizing Your Potential

5. Transitioning to Autonomy:
Work-from-Home Opportunities in Nursing

Introduction: The Nurse Entrepreneur Revolution

As you pull into the parking lot for another shift, do you ever wonder if there's more to your nursing career? Do you find yourself bursting with ideas to improve patient care but feel no one is listening? If so, you're not alone – and I'll bet you don't even know that you're holding the key to unlocking a world of possibilities.

Welcome to "From Scrubs to Startups: Redefining Nursing Careers Through Entrepreneurship." I'm Laurie, a 30-year nurse, who once stood where you are right now, begging for more value to be placed on what I did every day. Looking for someone to realize that I was more than a warm body to do the things administration either couldn't or just plain didn't want to do. Nursing wasn't what I thought it was going to be, and I found a way to change its impact on my life. Unfortunately, I found the answer after working for more than 25 years in a broken system. Thankfully, you don't have to go through those struggles, because I did the work for you.

As nurses, we often find ourselves caught in an impossible balancing act. We're torn between the demands of our calling and the needs of our personal lives. The mental exhaustion that follows us home, the missed family events, the struggle to make simple decisions after a grueling shift, these are the hidden costs of our profession that are rarely discussed. We haven't even touched on politics, the cliques and the co-workers who rarely show up on time if they show up at all. I bet you're also thinking of 101 other reasons and about the fact that you never get PTO when you ask, you always have to beg, negotiate and compromise. Or, if you do get it, it's never long enough because just as you feel human again, it's time to go back to work.

These challenges aren't just anecdotal. A recent survey conducted by AMN Healthcare in January 2023, as reported by Becker's Hospital Review, reveals a stark reality:
85% of nurses in hospital roles said they planned to quit within the next 12 months.
There were double-digit decreases across satisfaction scores, and double-digit increases in emotional drain among nurses.

72% of nurse leaders reported feeling burnt out, with 31% considering leaving their hospital jobs.

These statistics are alarming, but they also represent an opportunity. Nurses are seeking alternatives, with many considering returning to school, seeking travel positions or part-time roles, or even leaving the profession entirely. What's particularly exciting is that nurses are becoming more empowered and are "willing (and able) to take control of their own destinies." This book is born from a deep understanding of these challenges. It's a roadmap to a nursing career that doesn't require sacrificing your personal life, your mental health, or your family time. There is another way, and it's time we explored it together.

This book is a result of my journey from bedside nurse to a successful author & entrepreneur, and it's designed to be your roadmap to the freedom to create the career you dreamed of when you were in nursing school.

From Scrubs to Startups™ is more than just a how-to guide. It's a call to action for nurses everywhere to re-imagine their roles in healthcare. As Nurse Entrepreneurs, we have the power to innovate, to fill gaps in patient care, and to shape the future of our profession while enjoying a fulfilled, successful independent life.

A Note to *All* Nurses: LPNs, RNs, and Beyond Before we dive in, I want to make something abundantly clear: when we talk about "nurses" and nurse entrepreneurship, we're talking about ALL nurses. LPNs, RNs, BSNs, MSNs APRNs - your specific credentials don't define your potential as an entrepreneur. What matters is your experience, your insights, and your passion. While your roles in traditional healthcare settings might differ, the world of nurse entrepreneurship offers opportunities for all. Throughout this book, you'll find that the principles, strategies, and opportunities we discuss apply across the nursing spectrum. Your unique perspective as a NURSE is valuable, and there are countless ways to leverage your specific skills and experiences in entrepreneurial ventures. So, whether you're an LPN working in a long-term care facility or an RN in a hospital ICU, know that this book - and the world of nurse entrepreneurship - is for you. In the pages that follow, we'll explore the exciting frontier of nurse entrepreneurship. You'll discover how your nursing skills – your compassion, critical thinking, and problem-solving abilities – are the perfect foundation for building a thriving business.

We'll delve into: The changing landscape of healthcare and the unprecedented opportunities it presents for nurses

How to identify your unique niche and develop a business concept that aligns with your passions and skills

The nuts and bolts of starting and growing a business, from creating a business plan to marketing your services

Real-life success stories of nurses who have made the leap into entrepreneurship Practical tools, resources, and strategies to support your entrepreneurial journey

Whether you're looking to start a side hustle while maintaining your nursing job, or you're ready to stand 10 toes down full-time into entrepreneurship, this book will provide you with the knowledge, inspiration, and practical steps to get started.

So, are you ready to trade in your scrubs for a startup? Let's begin this exciting journey together and unleash the Nurse Entrepreneur in you.

Chapter 1: The Real Deal on Bedside Nursing
(and Why You Might Be Ready for a Change)

Let's have a real conversation, just between us. When you first decided to become a nurse, the excitement, the calling to help others, the vision of making a real difference in people's lives. Meant something. The look of admiration and respect as soon as you told someone you were going to be a nurse? Now, fast forward to today. When someone asks you what you do, I bet you're still proud to say you're a nurse, but in the back of your mind you're saying, "if they only knew". If you're feeling a disconnect between that initial passion and your current reality, you're not alone. Those days when you're racing from patient to patient, barely have time to pee, let alone eat, and then come home feeling like you've been hit by a truck. Yeah, we're going to talk about that. But here's the thing – we're not just going to commiserate. We're going to look at how you can flip the script on these challenges.

In this chapter, we're going to get honest about what's really going on in bedside nursing today. No sugar-coating, no corporate speak – just the unvarnished truth about the challenges we face every day. We're talking about the stuff that keeps us up at night, the things we vent about in break rooms, and the issues that make us question if we can keep doing this job we once loved. We still love it, it's just that we love it like a partner we see potential in but have to fight for every aspect of enjoyment or benefit in the relationship.

We'll dive into three main areas that are hitting nurses hard:

Burnout: We're going beyond just feeling tired. We'll talk about that bone-deep exhaustion that follows you home and that state of "Functional Freeze" where you're just going through the motions.

Emotional Toll: Let's discuss the weight of dealing with human suffering day in and day out, the fears for our own safety, and the emotional roller coaster that comes with the job.

Lack of Control: We'll get real about feeling powerless in a system that often seems to value profits over patients and staff wellbeing.

As we go through this, I want you to know something important: if you're struggling with these issues, it's not because you're a bad nurse or because you're not tough enough. These are big, systemic problems that affect nurses across the board.

Why are we talking about all this heavy stuff? Because understanding these challenges is the first step to finding a way out. Whether you're just starting to feel the strain or you're at your wit's end, recognizing these issues can help you see that there might be a different path forward – one where you can use your nursing skills and passion in a way that doesn't drain you dry. So, grab a coffee (or something stronger – no judgment here), and let's dive into the real truth about bedside nursing today. It might get a bit uncomfortable, but I promise you, there's hope on the other side.

Common Frustrations and Challenges

As nurses, we enter the profession with high hopes of making a difference in people's lives. However, the reality of bedside nursing often presents challenges that can leave even the most passionate healthcare professionals feeling drained and disillusioned. Let's explore some of the most common frustrations and challenges faced by nurses today.

Burnout

Burnout is perhaps the most pervasive issue in nursing, affecting professionals at all levels of experience. It's more than just feeling tired after a long shift; it's a state of physical, emotional, and mental exhaustion that can have serious consequences for both nurses and their patients.

Causes of burnout include:

- ➤ Chronic understaffing that leads to heavy workloads
- ➤ Long and irregular hours, including night shifts and mandatory overtime
- ➤ Consistent High-stress environments with life-or-death decisions
- ➤ Lack of support from management or administration
- ➤ Constant exposure to human suffering and loss

Symptoms of burnout may include:

- ➤ Feeling overwhelmed and emotionally drained

3

➤ Decreased job satisfaction and performance
➤ Physical symptoms like headaches, insomnia, fatigue and weight gain
➤ Detachment from patients and colleagues
➤ Increased absenteeism or thoughts of leaving the profession
➤ Functional Freeze: A state where you're physically present but mentally disconnected, going through the motions without truly engaging. A state where you're able to perform your nursing duties effectively, but once you leave work, you're mentally and emotionally paralyzed, checked-out unable to fully engage with your personal life.

Scenario: It's the end of your 12-hour shift. You've given every medication on time, responded to every call light, and managed every crisis flawlessly. But as you sit in your car in the parking lot, the world is silent. The only thing you hear is the buzzing in your ears from the whirring in your mind. The drive home is a blur. You find yourself in your driveway, not realizing how you got there. You sit there for a moment in silence, mustering up the courage to move. Once inside, you're met with the expectation to engage with family or make decisions about dinner, but your mind is still racing and replaying the day's events. You retreat to the shower, seeking a few more moments of solitude before facing the rest of your day. On your days off, you sleep for as many hours as possible, your body and mind desperately try to recover.

Aha Moment: If you find yourself living for your job/paycheck and merely existing on your days off, it's time to reevaluate. Nursing shouldn't cost you your ability to enjoy your personal life.

The impact of burnout and Functional Freeze extends beyond the individual nurse. It affects our relationships, our ability to care for ourselves, and ultimately, the quality of care we can provide for our patients. It's a cycle that's difficult to break within traditional nursing roles, which is why exploring alternative career paths becomes so crucial.

You're running on empty, going through the motions, and maybe even wondering if you chose the right career. Sound familiar?

There's a silver lining: Here's where being a nurse entrepreneur can be a game-changer. Imagine being able to choose your projects, set your own schedule, and focus on the aspects of nursing you're truly passionate about. Sarah, a nurse I know, was on the verge of leaving the profession entirely. Instead, she started a wellness coaching business for healthcare workers. Now she's helping other nurses avoid burnout while reigniting her own passion for healthcare by working with healthcare professionals' she calls it her "joy business". It was the light at the end of a dark tunnel for her. Can't wait to hear what your light will be. No worries we'll get there.

Emotional Toll

Let's talk about something we don't discuss enough –
the emotional rollercoaster of nursing.

Nursing is inherently an emotional profession. We
connect with patients during some of the most
vulnerable moments of their lives. While this can be
incredibly rewarding, it also takes a significant
emotional toll.

Key aspects of the emotional challenge include:

> Dealing with patient suffering and loss on a
regular basis
> Balancing empathy with professional
boundaries
> Managing the expectations and emotions of
patients' families
> Coping with traumatic events or difficult cases
> Compassion fatigue, which can lead to
decreased empathy over time

Scenario: You've just finished comforting a family
whose loved one didn't make it despite your team's
best efforts. As you step out of the room, you see a
new admission rolling in - a child with severe injury.
You take a deep breath, push down your emotions,
and paste on a smile to greet the frightened child and
anxious parents. Later, at home, a friend asks how
your day was. You say "fine" because you don't have
the energy to explain or relive the emotional
rollercoaster you've just experienced.

6

Sometimes we're celebrating a patient's recovery, the next minute you're comforting a family who just lost their loved one. It's like emotional whiplash, right? And this is real life, some days it feels like you're leaving a piece of your heart at the facility when you clock out.

This is where being a nurse entrepreneur can be a breath of fresh air. You get to choose how and when you engage with patients. Maybe you decide to focus on health education, where you're empowering people to take charge of their wellness. Or perhaps you will create a support network for nurses dealing with compassion fatigue. Or you work with patients, but now because you make your own schedule you have the time to process, feel and recover. Being a Nurse Entrepreneur doesn't necessarily mean you have to leave your patients. They can be the reason we love what we do. We just have to balance the toll they take on us and Nurse Entrepreneurship can help with that.

For example, take Lisa, she was a Hospice nurse for 15 years and felt like she was drowning in constant emotional demands. Now, she runs a successful consulting business teaching mindfulness and stress management techniques to healthcare workers. She went straight to the source. Created a niche where she knew there was a need and brought it to the CEOs and Corporations who need to offer these types of programs to retain their employees. She's still making a difference, but on her own terms.

The best part? You're not leaving your compassion behind — you're channeling it in a way that's sustainable for you. It's like putting on your own oxygen mask first, you know?

What about Fear and Safety Concerns?

> ➤ Fear and Safety Concerns: The constant threat of physical or verbal abuse from patients or family members, especially in high-stress environments.

> ➤ Unsafe Working Conditions: The anxiety of entering potentially dangerous situations, particularly in home care settings.

The cumulative effect of these emotional stressors can lead to anxiety, depression, and even post-traumatic stress disorder (PTSD) in some nurses. It's not just about being "tough" or "professional" - it's about finding a sustainable way to care for others without losing ourselves in the process.

Scenario (Hospital Setting): You're working in the ER when a patient under the influence becomes violent and hits you in the back of your head while you're trying to insert their IV. As you try to remain calm and professional, you're acutely aware of the potential for harm to yourself, your colleagues, and other patients. Even after you call security to intervene, your heart races for hours, your head hurts to remind you that this is healthcare, and everyone deserves quality patient care, but now you find yourself flinching at sudden movements for the rest of your shift.

Scenario (Home Care): As you approach your next patient's home, you see a stranger on the patient's doorstep you've never seen before. You hesitate before approaching and knocking, wondering if you should call for backup or risk entering alone. This isn't the first time you've felt unsafe; you've been in homes where med-seeking relatives are hanging out waiting for the nurse to arrive and you know it won't be the last.

Scenario (Hospice): You've been caring for a terminally ill patient for weeks, forming a bond with them and their family. As you arrive for your shift, you learn the patient is imminent. Your day has completely changed. Now, you must support the grieving family, try to be present in supporting the family and the patient; while trying to reschedule your other patients, and oh yeah you need to process your own sense of loss, all before moving on to care for your next patient.

Aha Moment: How often have you felt fear about your personal safety at work? How often have you given yourself a moment to process your grief? How has this affected your job satisfaction and overall well-being? Is this level of stress sustainable in the long term? Let me give you a hint. The answer is No. Something has to give.

The emotional toll of nursing extends far beyond the compassion fatigue we often discuss. It encompasses a complex web of emotions - from fear for our safety to the deep sense of loss when we lose patients, we've grown close to. While we can't eliminate these emotional challenges entirely, we can seek ways to manage them more effectively or explore nursing paths that align better with our emotional well-being.

Acknowledging these emotional challenges isn't a sign of weakness. It's a crucial step in addressing the very real mental health impacts of our profession. By recognizing these issues, we can begin to explore solutions that allow us to continue providing excellent care without sacrificing our own well-being.

While we've talked about some heavy stuff when it comes to safety concerns, let's look at how one nurse flipped the script on this challenge.

Meet Rachel, a former addiction nurse who spent years doing in-home testing. She'd seen her fair share of dicey situations – from aggressive patients to unsafe neighborhoods. But instead of letting fear hold her back, Rachel decided to take control.

"I realized that many of us in healthcare felt unprepared for potentially dangerous situations," Rachel says. "So, I thought, why not change that?"

Rachel took her experience and turned it into a business opportunity. She got certified as a self-defense instructor and created "Safe Hands, Healing Hearts" – a specialized self-defense course for healthcare workers.

Her classes don't just teach physical techniques. Rachel incorporates de-escalation strategies, situational awareness, and even tips for advocating for safer workplace policies. She now travels to hospitals, addiction centers, and nursing schools, empowering healthcare workers to feel confident and safe on the job.

"The best part," Rachel shares with a grin, "is that I'm still using my nursing skills every day. I'm just applying them in a way that helps protect and empower my fellow healthcare workers."

Rachel's story shows us that even our challenges can become opportunities. By addressing a need she saw in the healthcare community, she created a thriving business that allows her to make a difference on her own terms.

So, the next time you feel unsafe or uncertain at work, think about Rachel. Your experiences – even the scary ones – could be the foundation for your next great idea. Who knows? You might just find your calling in helping make healthcare a safer place for everyone.

Lack of Control

Despite being the backbone of patient care, nurses often find themselves at the mercy of corporate healthcare decisions that prioritize profits over patients and staff well-being. This systemic lack of control can lead to frustration, burnout, and a sense of powerlessness.

Key aspects of this lack of control include:

> ➤ Chronic short-staffing due to budgetary constraints
> ➤ Unsafe workloads that threaten nurses' licenses and patient safety
> ➤ Limited input on scheduling, despite being the primary care providers
> ➤ Lack of say in benefit packages and promotion tracks
> ➤ Minimal influence on workplace policies that directly affect patient care

Scenario: It's Nurses Week, and you've just received an email about a pizza party to celebrate. Ironically, you're reading this while working your third consecutive 16-hour shift due to short-staffing. You know the CEO just flew in on the corporate jet for a 30-minute appearance, while your request for an additional nurse on your unit was denied due to "budget constraints."

Or maybe, You submitted a PTO request months ago for your child's graduation. Two weeks before the event, it was denied due to "staffing issues." You're told that as a senior nurse, you need to be "available". Meanwhile, you notice that the facility has spent thousands on new artwork for the lobby.

Aha Moment: When was the last time you felt your expertise was truly valued in decision-making processes that affect your daily work life? How often are you asked for input on policies that directly impact patient care and your professional satisfaction?

The impact of this corporate-driven lack of control extends beyond individual job satisfaction:

➢ Increased risk of burnout and turnover
➢ Compromised patient safety due to overworked staff
➢ Stifled innovation as nursing input is overlooked
➢ Decreased overall quality of care

As Nurse Entrepreneurs, we have the opportunity to reclaim control over our professional lives. By creating our own businesses or working independently, we can:

➢ Set our own schedules and workload
➢ Prioritize patient care over corporate profits
➢ Design our own benefit packages
➢ Implement innovative care practices that align with current standards on our terms
➢ Ensure safe working conditions that protect our licenses and our patients

While we can't change the entire healthcare system overnight, we can create our own environments where our expertise is valued, our schedules are flexible, and our impact on patient care is direct and meaningful.

Where Do We Go from Here?

Alright, fellow nurses, we've just taken a deep dive into some pretty heavy stuff. We've talked about the burnout that leaves us running on empty, the emotional toll that weighs on our hearts, and the lack of control that makes us feel like cogs in a machine rather than the skilled professionals we are.

If you're sitting there thinking, "Wow, this hits close to home," know that you're not alone. These challenges aren't just your personal struggles – they're symptoms of a healthcare system that often prioritizes profits over people, including its own staff.

But here's the thing: recognizing these issues is the first step toward change. You've spent long hard hours studying for your degrees and took a national board exam to get your license, it took years to hone your skills, and to develop your compassion. You have learned how to navigate truly complex situations and hold it all together. Those abilities don't disappear just because the current system isn't serving you well.

So, where *do* we go from here?

Well, that's what the rest of this book is about. We're going to explore how you can take those incredible nursing skills and use them in new ways – ways that don't leave you drained, frustrated, and questioning your career choice.

In the coming chapters, we'll dive into the world of Nurse Entrepreneurship. We'll look at how nurses like you and me are carving out new paths, creating businesses that align with our values, and reigniting our sense of purpose so we can reclaim the satisfaction we once felt in our work.

Before we move on, I want you to take a moment to reflect. Think about which of these challenges resonates most with you. What aspects of nursing still light you up, despite the difficulties? Hold onto those thoughts – they'll be your compass as we navigate the exciting possibilities ahead.

You became a nurse because you wanted to make a difference. That hasn't changed. What we're going to do now is explore how you can make that difference in a way that's sustainable for you.

So, take a deep breath. You've made it through the tough part – acknowledging the problems. Now, let's roll up our sleeves (like we always do) and start talking about solutions. The best part? This time, we're calling the shots.

Ready to reimagine your nursing career? Let's go!

Scan to Access Tools for Chapter One

Chapter 2: Beyond the Bedside: Discovering Your Nursing Superpowers

Introduction:

When you first put on your scrubs, full of excitement about the difference you were going to make in people's lives, that passion that drive to help others, it's still there. It's just waiting to be channeled in new and exciting ways.

Welcome to the world of Nurse Entrepreneurship, where your nursing skills become superpowers in the realm of business and innovation. In this chapter, we're going to explore how the very qualities that make you an excellent nurse can also make you a successful entrepreneur.

You might be thinking, "Me? An entrepreneur? I'm just a nurse." But here's the thing – you're not "just" anything. You're a healthcare professional with a unique set of skills that are in high demand far beyond the hospital walls.

Think about it. Every day, you:

- Solving complex problems under pressure
- Communicate effectively with a wide range of people
- Adapt to rapidly changing situations
- Pay meticulous attention to detail
- Lead and collaborate with diverse teams

But it's not just these skills that make you valuable. It's the years of education, rigorous training, and most importantly, your professional license that set you apart. Just like an attorney would never allow anyone to jeopardize their bar card, you should view your nursing license as a powerful asset – one that many corporations profit from but don't truly understand or respect.

As a licensed healthcare professional, you bring a level of expertise and accountability that no MBA can replicate. You're not just a cog in the healthcare machine – you're the engine that makes it run. It's time to embrace this professional mindset and recognize the true value you bring to the table.

In the pages ahead, we'll clear up the biggest myths about nurse entrepreneurship, uncover your hidden strengths, and start imagining how your nursing skills can open new doors for you.

We'll discuss how to leverage your license and expertise to create opportunities that respect your professional value, unlike some corporate environments that may take it for granted.

But don't worry – this isn't about abandoning your identity as a nurse. It's about expanding it, about finding new ways to make a difference and create the career you've always dreamed of.

So, are you ready to discover your nursing superpowers? Let's dive in and explore the exciting world of opportunities that await you beyond the bedside.

Common Misconceptions about Nurse Entrepreneurship

As nurses, we often hold beliefs about entrepreneurship that can prevent us from taking that first step. Let's address some of these misconceptions head-on:

1. "I don't have any business skills."

Reality: As a nurse, you already possess many of the skills needed to run a successful business. Your ability to manage time, prioritize tasks, communicate effectively, and solve problems are all valuable business skills.

For the specific skills you might not have, like accounting or marketing there are two things that can shift your mindset from "I can't do this" to "I can figure this out":

a) These things can be learned, just as you learned complex medical procedures. There are many resources available to help you develop these skills if you're interested.

b) You don't have to do everything yourself. Just as you work with a team in healthcare, you can build a team for your business. You can hire professionals or partners with small local businesses to handle specialized tasks like accounting, bookkeeping, or marketing.

Part of being a successful entrepreneur is knowing when to delegate and how to leverage your network. Your connections in the healthcare community might lead you to other professionals who can support your business ventures. This approach allows you to focus on what you do best – applying your nursing expertise to your business – while ensuring all aspects of your venture are handled professionally.

2. "I'll lose my nursing identity."

Reality: Becoming an entrepreneur doesn't mean you stop being a nurse. In fact, your nursing identity is your greatest asset in Nurse Entrepreneurship. You're not leaving nursing behind; you're finding new ways to apply your nursing expertise and values.

3. "It's too risky."

Reality: While all businesses involve some level of risk, so does relying on a single employer in today's healthcare landscape. Entrepreneurship allows you to diversify your income streams and take control of your career path. With proper planning and execution, it can actually provide more stability than traditional employment.

4. "I don't have any ideas."

Reality: As a nurse, you encounter problems and inefficiencies in healthcare every day. Each of these is a potential business opportunity. Your unique perspective as a healthcare insider gives you insights that non-healthcare entrepreneurs simply don't have.

Moreover, you're not alone on this journey:

a) This book is designed to help spark ideas and guide you through the process of identifying opportunities. By reading it, you've already taken a crucial first step towards entrepreneurship.

b) As the author and an experienced Nurse entrepreneur, I'm here to help inspire ideas and help you hone in on your unique experiences and strengths. Throughout this book, you'll find exercises and prompts to help you brainstorm and refine your business ideas.

c) The nursing community is vast and supportive. Engaging with other nurses, attending conferences, or participating in online forums can all be sources of inspiration for business ideas.

The best business ideas often come from solving problems you've personally experienced or observed. Your years of nursing experience are a goldmine of potential business opportunities – it's just a matter of looking at them through an entrepreneurial lens.

5. "I need a lot of money to start a business."

Reality: While some businesses require significant startup capital, many nursing-related ventures can be started with minimal investment. Consulting, coaching, or creating digital products are just a few low-cost startup options.

6. "I don't have enough experience."

Reality: Every nurse, regardless of their years of experience, has valuable knowledge and skills. New graduates might have fresh perspectives on emerging technologies, while experienced nurses have a wealth of practical knowledge. There's no "right" amount of experience – only the courage to start.

These misconceptions are often rooted in fear of the unknown. By challenging these beliefs and embracing your potential, you're taking the first step towards a fulfilling entrepreneurial journey.

Identifying Your Nursing Superpowers

As a nurse, you've already chosen a path that requires dedication, intelligence, and compassion. You've invested years in your education, from rigorous nursing programs to ongoing professional development. Every day, you make sacrifices to care for others, often putting your patients' needs before your own. This commitment hasn't just made you a great nurse – it's equipped you with an incredible set of skills that are highly valuable and marketable in the world of entrepreneurship.

Many nurses don't realize just how transferable and valuable their skills are outside of traditional healthcare settings. For instance, if you excel in wound care, did you know you could build a thriving business around this specialty? You could potentially work on your own terms, control your schedule, enjoy your PTO, and still match or exceed your current salary. This is just one example of how your nursing expertise can translate into entrepreneurial success.

Your nursing superpowers are the culmination of your education, experience, and the countless challenges you've overcome in your career. These aren't just skills – they're your competitive advantage in the business world. Let's explore these superpowers and how they translate to business success:

1. Critical Thinking and Problem-Solving In nursing: You assess complex patient situations and make quick, informed decisions. In business: You can analyze market trends, identify opportunities, and develop innovative solutions.
2. Empathy and Communication In nursing: You connect with patients and families, explaining complex information clearly. In business: You can understand client needs, provide excellent customer service, and negotiate effectively.
3. Adaptability and Resilience In nursing: You thrive in fast-paced environments and handle unexpected situations calmly. In business: You can pivot your strategy when needed and persevere through challenges.
4. Attention to Detail and Organization In nursing: You manage multiple patients,

medications, and tasks with precision. In business: You can create efficient systems, manage projects, and ensure quality control.

5. Leadership and Teamwork In nursing: You collaborate with diverse healthcare teams and often take charge in critical situations. In business: You can build and lead effective teams, delegate tasks, and foster a positive work culture.

6. Continuous Learning In nursing: You stay updated with the latest medical knowledge and techniques. In business: You can adapt to new technologies, market changes, and business strategies.

7. Ethical Decision-Making In nursing: You navigate complex ethical situations while prioritizing patient well-being. In business: You can build a reputation for integrity and make responsible business decisions.

These are just a few of the many skills you've honed as a nurse. Each of these "superpowers" can be leveraged in countless ways as you embark on your entrepreneurial journey.

Conclusion:

In this chapter, we've explored the incredible potential that lies within your nursing skills and experience. We've debunked common myths that might have held you back and revealed how your daily nursing activities have been preparing you for entrepreneurship all along.

Your nursing license isn't just a piece of paper – it's a testament to your expertise, dedication, and ability to make a difference in people's lives. As you move forward in your entrepreneurial journey, carry with you the confidence that comes from knowing you possess a unique set of superpowers.

In the next chapter, we'll dive deeper into how you can apply these superpowers in various entrepreneurial contexts. We'll explore specific business ideas that align with different nursing specialties and show you how to start transforming your skills into a thriving business.

Your journey from scrubs to startup begins now. Embrace your nursing superpowers and get ready to soar into the exciting world of Nurse Entrepreneurship!

Scan to Access Tools for Chapter Two

Chapter 3: A Nurse Entrepreneur's Self-Assessment Guide - Taking Stock of Your Value

As we embark on this journey, I want you to take a moment in this chapter and really see yourself. Not just as a nurse, but as the invaluable, highly educated, and skilled professional you are. You've been in the trenches so long that you might have forgotten a crucial truth: You are the very foundation of healthcare.

Think about it. Without your license, without the license of any nurse on the planet, corporations, hospitals, and home care agencies wouldn't be able to exist. YOU are the commodity here. It's time not only to recognize that but to capitalize on it.

This chapter is all about "taking stock" - understanding your true worth and potential. We're going to dive deep into self-assessment, but not in the way you might expect. This isn't about critiquing yourself or finding faults. It's about recognizing the incredible value you bring to the table and exploring how you can leverage that in new and exciting ways.

Why is this so important? Because you deserve to see yourself as clearly as those who depend on your skills do. You deserve to understand the full spectrum of possibilities open to you. And most importantly, you deserve to shape your career in a way that brings you fulfilment and joy.

In the pages ahead, we'll explore your current situation, your desires, your skills, and your potential. We'll look at whether entrepreneurship is the right path for you, or if you simply need a new perspective on your current role. We'll examine what truly makes you happy in your work and life.

There are no right or wrong answers here. This is about honest self-reflection and exploration. It's about understanding where you are now, where you want to go, and what you need to get there.

I'm right here with you every step of the way. Let's embark on this journey of self-discovery together. I promise you this: Your happiness is the only thing that matters here.

Are you ready to take stock of your true value and explore the incredible possibilities ahead? Let's begin!

This chapter is all about "taking stock" - understanding your true worth and potential. But what does "taking stock" really mean for a nurse considering entrepreneurship?

Think of this process as creating the perfect schedule - not just for a nursing role, but for your life and career. We're assessing your skills, passions, and potential to find where you'll thrive, whether that's in direct patient care, a nursing-adjacent field, or even in an entirely new arena that leverages your nursing background in unexpected ways.

We're asking: What are your strengths? Where do you shine brightest? What kind of "shifts" would best fit your skills and passions? This could be traditional nursing, but it could also be healthcare education, tech innovation, wellness coaching, or even something we haven't thought of yet. How can we optimize your talents to meet the needs of your ideal clients or audience? And importantly, how can we ensure this venture supports your personal well-being and financial goals?

This isn't about fitting you into a predetermined nursing role. It's about creating a custom career path that maximizes your potential, aligns with your values, and leads to both professional fulfillment and personal happiness. Whether you end up working directly as a nurse, in a nursing-adjacent field, or in an entirely new arena, the goal is to find where your skills and passions intersect with opportunity and personal satisfaction.

This self-assessment is your chance to explore all possibilities. It's about discovering what you're truly good at and figuring out how to incorporate that into a life that makes you happy. After all, your nursing skills and experience are valuable in countless settings - let's find the one that's perfect for you.

As we embark on this journey of self-exploration, I want you to hold on to one crucial thing: there are no right or wrong answers here. This process is about discovering what's right for YOU.

You might find yourself considering paths you've never thought of before - and that's okay. In fact, it's more than okay - it's exciting! Just because something hasn't been done before doesn't mean it can't be done. Every groundbreaking idea started with someone daring to think differently.

The world of entrepreneurship is all about innovation and new ideas. Your unique combination of nursing expertise, personal experiences, and individual passions might lead you to a completely novel business concept. Embrace that possibility!

Consider these entrepreneurs who dared to think differently:

- Sara Blakely, the founder of Spanx, saw a need for comfortable, seamless undergarments and turned it into a billion-dollar company.
- Blake Mycoskie of TOMS Shoes created a new business model of "One for One," giving a pair of shoes to a child in need for every pair sold.
- Our own Florence Nightingale revolutionized nursing and healthcare with her innovative approaches to sanitation and patient care.

These individuals didn't just follow an existing path - they created their own. And you can too.

As you go through this self-assessment, give yourself permission to dream big and think outside the box. Your next big idea could be the one that transforms not just your career, but an entire aspect of healthcare or beyond.

The goal here isn't to fit into someone else's definition of success. It's to discover your own path to fulfillment and impact. So be honest with yourself, be open to unexpected possibilities, and most importantly, be excited about the journey ahead. You never know where it might lead you!

Identifying Pain Points: Seeds of Innovation

As we take stock of your current situation, it's important to pay attention to the aspects of your work that frustrate you. These pain points aren't just sources of stress - they're potential goldmines of innovation.

Think about your typical day. What bothers you the most? Is it wrestling with clunky EMR software? Dealing with rude family members? Coping with lazy co-workers? A constant lack of supplies? The soul-crushing commute to work? Or perhaps it's supervisors or corporate bigwigs with unrealistic expectations?

Now, here's where it gets interesting. For each of these annoyances, ask yourself:

1. Is this a common problem for other nurses or healthcare workers?

2. Have I thought of ways this could be improved?
3. Could solving this problem be the basis for a business idea?

Some of the most successful businesses started because someone got fed up with a problem and decided to fix it themselves. Your frustration could be the seed of your next great idea.

For example, if you're constantly annoyed by the lack of comfortable, professional nursing shoes, could you design a better alternative? If you're frustrated by the lack of easy-to-use patient education materials, could you create a service to fill that gap?

Don't dismiss your daily irritations. They're not just things to complain about in the breakroom - they're opportunities waiting to be seized. Your unique perspective as a nurse means you understand these problems intimately. That understanding is the first step to creating innovative solutions.

As you identify pain points in your current role, consider how these could be catalysts for innovation. For example, nurse entrepreneur Lindsey Roddy turned her frustration with PPE shortages into an opportunity to design the Together Mask™, a new type of protective gear.

Lindsey's story shows us that innovations don't always have to be high-tech or complex. Sometimes, the most effective solutions come from nurses who are willing to look at everyday challenges with fresh eyes and the courage to try something new.

As a nurse, you're not just a cog in the healthcare machine. You're an educated, skilled professional with unique insights into the challenges facing healthcare today. This self-assessment isn't just about finding a new job or starting a business - it's about recognizing your power to create positive change. It's about understanding the ripple effect your innovations could have - on your own life, your family, the healthcare system, and potentially the world at large.

Imagine the impact of reclaiming control over your schedule, allowing you to be present for your family's important moments. Picture the satisfaction of solving a problem that's frustrated you and your colleagues for years. Envision yourself pioneering a solution that improves patient care across the country or even globally. And the best part? You'll be doing it on your own terms, with the autonomy to shape your career and your impact in a way that aligns with your values and goals.

This is about more than just changing jobs - it's about changing lives, starting with your own. It's about leveraging your skills and experience to make a difference, all while creating the work-life balance you've always dreamed of. You don't have to abandon your career or the skills you've worked so hard to develop. Instead, you can use them as a launchpad to become an active force for improvement in healthcare

31

and beyond, all while designing a life that brings you fulfillment and joy.

Current Lifestyle Assessment

Let's begin by taking a closer look at where you are right now. Be honest with yourself as you answer these questions, this is about understanding your current reality, not judging it. And no one else will see this but You, so go for it

4. Work-Life Balance:
- On a scale of 1-10, how satisfied are you with your current work-life balance
- How many hours per week do you typically work?
- Do you often miss important personal or family events due to work?
- How often do you feel mentally present when you're not at work?

5. Job Satisfaction:
- What aspects of your current job do you enjoy the most?

- What's your favorite part of nursing?

- What parts of your job do you find most frustrating?

• On a scale of 1-10, how fulfilled do you feel in your current role?

6. Financial Situation:
    - Are you satisfied with your current income?
    - Do you feel financially secure?
    - What are your major financial goals for the next 5 years?

7. Health and Wellbeing:
    • How would you rate your overall health and energy levels?

    • Do you have time for self-care and activities you enjoy?

    • How often do you feel stressed or burnt out?

8. Career Growth:
    • Do you see opportunities for growth in your current position?

    • Are you learning and developing new skills in your current role?

    • Where do you see your nursing career in 5 years if you continue on your current path?

Reflection: After answering these questions, take a moment to reflect. What surprises you about your answers? What patterns do you notice? Are there any areas where you feel particularly satisfied or dissatisfied?

This assessment isn't about making judgments. It's about gaining clarity on your current situation so you can make informed decisions about your future.

Now, ask yourself this crucial question: *When was the last time you left work smiling?*

Your answer to this question can be very telling. If you can't recall the last time, or if it's been a while, that's valuable information as you consider your future path.

This assessment isn't about making judgments. It's about gaining clarity on your current situation so you can make informed decisions about your future. Your happiness and fulfillment are crucial factors in your career journey.

Expanding Your Vision

Now that you've taken a good, honest look at your current situation, let's shift gears a bit. I want you to take a deep breath and let your imagination soar. We talked about seeing yourself as the foundation of healthcare, right? Well, now it's time to explore the possibilities and see yourself as an innovator and changemaker.

You might be thinking, "Me? An innovator?" Here's what you're not seeing from the trenches of traditional nursing – some of the most impactful healthcare innovations have come from nurses just like you. Nurses who saw a problem decided to do something about it. Nurses who dared to think beyond their traditional roles.

Let me share a couple of inspiring examples:

Rachel Walker was an addiction nurse who faced safety concerns in her daily work. Instead of just accepting it as "part of the job," she created "Safe Hands, Healing Hearts" – a specialized self-defense course for healthcare workers. She took her nursing experience, combined it with a new skill, and addressed a critical need in healthcare.

Then there's the Society of Nurse Scientists, Innovators, Entrepreneurs & Leaders (SONSIEL). When faced with PPE shortages during the COVID pandemic, they didn't just complain about the problem. They created the SHARE program, leveraging their networks to collect and distribute over 100,000 pieces of PPE to frontline workers.

These nurses saw beyond their immediate roles. They identified problems, yes, but more importantly, they saw opportunities to make a difference.

As you continue this self-assessment journey, I want you to keep these examples in mind. They're not meant to intimidate you, but to inspire you. To show you that your nursing experience – every frustration, every challenge, every moment of care – is fertile ground for innovation.

What problem have you encountered that you wish *someone* would solve? What if that *someone* is you?

Breanna Lathrop co-founded HelplineSOS, a telemedicine solution that connects vulnerable populations with healthcare resources. This demonstrates how nurses can use technology to bridge gaps in healthcare access and delivery. How many patients have you not been able to reach or obtained service for because they were simply out of your "area"? How many times does a problem like this have a simple answer, but your ideas were never validated by the corporation you worked for, so you worked with your hands tied and your spirit broken?

These examples illustrate the diverse ways nurses *can* apply their skills and insights beyond traditional roles. I'm just asking you to open your heart and mind to the possibilities. You don't have to be Marie Curie, but this book is license to give yourself permission to pull yourself out of the trench, breathe the fresh air and explore the possibility of being happy about the career you've chosen.
As you consider these examples and your own experiences, take a moment to revisit your self-assessment.

Think about:

- What unique challenges have you observed in healthcare that you're passionate about solving?
- How might your nursing skills translate to areas like product development, education, or healthcare technology?
- What innovative solutions can you envision that blend your nursing expertise with other interests or skills you possess?
- Have you ever thought that your nursing skills could transfer easily to another career?
- Have you seen another field and thought, 'Get a few nurses in there, and we'd get things straightened out quickly'?
- Also, simply consider what it is about your job that you just love. It could be as simple as that.

Your responses to the self-assessment questions, combined with these new insights, paint a picture of your potential. Your nursing background provides you with invaluable insights into healthcare needs and challenges. Combined with your unique experiences and perspectives, this knowledge can be the foundation for truly innovative and impactful ventures.

Now that you've taken stock of your current situation, explored your potential, and started to envision new possibilities, you might be wondering, "What's next?"

Before we move on, I want to remind you about the self-assessment checklist at the end of this chapter. Take some time to complete it thoroughly. It's not just a tool for this book - it's a resource you can return to again and again as you progress on your nurse entrepreneur's journey.

This self-assessment is just the first step in a larger adventure. This book is designed to be your inspiration, your gut check, and your permission slip, as well as your guide, but it's also part of the baseline of what I do every day. You can join me anytime on social media or in a live session in the No More ScrubsTM community where I can answer questions specific to Your journey. I also have group sessions where I work with like-minded Nurse entrepreneurs, and we share our successes and failures so you can learn from them. These additional resources and community connections will guide you deeper into the world of nurse entrepreneurship, providing real-time support and insights as you progress on your journey. The exercises and insights you've gained here are the baseline and will be invaluable as we move forward.

In the next chapter, we're going to dive into the exciting world of entrepreneurial opportunities as a nurse. We'll explore specific niches where nurses are making waves, from telehealth and health tech to wellness coaching and beyond.

You'll discover how nurses are leveraging their expertise in unexpected ways, and we'll help you identify areas where your unique skills and passions could fill a gap in the market. Whether you're drawn to patient education, product innovation, or healthcare consulting, there's a world of opportunities waiting for you.

So, complete your self-assessment checklist, jot down any ideas or "what ifs" that come to mind, no matter how wild they might seem. Because in our next chapter, we're going to show you how those "what ifs" could become "why nots?"

Ready to explore the entrepreneurial landscape? Let's go!

Scan to Access Tools for Chapter Three

Chapter 4: The Nurse Entrepreneur Mindset: Overcoming Fears and Recognizing Your Potential

Alright, my fellow nurses, it's time for some real talk.

You've put in the hours, you've weathered the storms, and you've probably got student loans to prove it. But here's the thing – all that hard work, all of those sleepless nights and all of those grueling shifts, are not just part of your past. They're the building blocks of your future. A future that you get to shape.

I'll bet you're thinking, "Ha! Laurie, I'm *just* a nurse." Let me stop you right there. You're not "just" anything. You're a healthcare professional with a unique set of skills that are in high demand far beyond the hospital walls. Every day, whether you're in a hospital, a clinic, a school, or someone's home, you're solving complex problems, communicating with people from all walks of life, and making decisions that profoundly impact people's wellbeing. That's not "just" anything – that's a superpower.

In this chapter, we're going to explore what it really means to be a nurse entrepreneur. We'll dive into the motivations driving nurses to take this exciting leap, examine the various paths you can take, and look at some inspiring success stories. We'll also tackle some of the fears and doubts you might be feeling and equip you with the basic principles you'll need to get started.

Some of you might be saying, "I need a steady paycheck. I can't just quit my job and start a business."

I hear you. You've endured the job you're doing for so long because they keep dangling that Overtime in your face. Where has that gotten you? How's that working for you? Would you be reading this book if you were truly happy?

Let's talk about risk and reward for a moment. You've missed months, maybe even years, in the blink of an eye because of that overtime, that paycheck, that complacency you've come to both complain about and find comfort in. But here's the question, when is it time to be brave for YOU?

What am I asking? Think about it, you're brave every time you step into a shift, not knowing what you'll be faced with. But you do know one thing for certain - your administration isn't going to back you up if something goes wrong or if you get hurt. Let's be honest, they'll do one of two things: 1) ask you what you could've done better, or 2) be mad that they need to find someone else for the shift you were scheduled to do. I dare you to tell me I'm wrong.

It's time to channel that bravery you show every day on the job into something for yourself. Yes, entrepreneurship has inherent risks - that's true. But you know what else is true? You've got knowledge, strong skills, and the ability to build a supportive network and find mentorship so you always have someone in your corner. These are your tools now.

Your happiness is worth the risk. I promise. When you step into entrepreneurship, you're not just risking failure - you're opening yourself up to the possibility of a fulfilling career where you're in control, where your expertise is valued, and where you can make a difference on your own terms.

Staying where you are, enduring the stress, the unpredictable schedules, the physical and emotional toll, that's a risk too. It's a risk to your wellbeing, your happiness, and your future.

Your happiness is worth the risk. I promise. When you step into entrepreneurship, you're not just risking failure, you're opening yourself up to the possibility of a fulfilling career where you're in control. And here's the beautiful thing about being in control: you get to define what success looks like for you. For some, that's having a beach house and a Mercedes. For others, it's being able to whisk away to the islands for a quick weekend retreat. And for many, it's simply being able to say, "Yes, I can be my child's class mom," or "Yes, I can be with my aging Mom when she needs me."

Success and risk are subjective. Some of these things are priceless. Some of these things you will never be able to get back. That's what I see as the real "risk."

As a nurse, it's never been about money for me. Someone will always pay you for doing the job. But they couldn't give me the time I needed to spend with my Mom when she was dying of cancer. So, I took it. I left my job after my FMLA ran out. I've never regretted it even for one second. That's when I realized my definition of risk and success are very different.

The risk isn't in trying something new. The risk is in staying put and missing out on the moments and experiences that truly matter to you. Whether that's time with family, pursuing a passion project, or simply having the freedom to breathe without the weight of constant stress – that's the success that entrepreneurship can offer.

So, are you ready to be as brave for yourself as you've always been for your patients? The rewards of taking this leap might just surprise you – and they might be far more valuable than any paycheck.

The truth of the matter is – you don't have to make any drastic decisions right now. The beautiful thing about nurse entrepreneurship is that many of the opportunities we'll discuss can start as side hustle, growing at a pace that feels comfortable for you. And some of you might realize that your current role is exactly where you *want* to be – and that's perfectly okay too. The point is; after reading this book, it'll be *your choice*. An informed, empowered *choice*.

Let's dive in and discover how you can turn your nursing experience into your next exciting venture. Trust me, you've got this, and I'll be here cheering you on every step of the way.

The Why: What's Pushing Nurses to Think Outside the Box?

You might be wondering, 'Why are nurses even considering this entrepreneur's thing?' Great question! Coming up we're going to explore what's motivating your fellow nurses to take this leap.

Reclaiming Your Power and Dignity

Let's talk about control for a minute. Not just the surface-level stuff, but the deep, meaningful control that affects every aspect of your life as a nurse

When nursing was a revered career? When people admired you for your caregiving, patience, and kindness in tough situations? Somewhere along the line, that admiration got twisted into something that feels a lot like exploitation.

These days, control for a nurse means saying, "Hey, without nursing licenses, you couldn't run your business." It's about standing up and demanding what you deserve:

- The right to use your PTO without guilt or fear
- Benefits that actually benefit you
- A work environment free from physical abuse and psychological manipulation
- Fair pay that reflects your skills and dedication (without watching travel nurses earn double for the same work)

- Staffing ratios that prioritize patient care and nurse wellbeing

As a nurse entrepreneur, you're not just gaining control - you're reclaiming your power and dignity. You're saying:

- I choose my schedule. No more missed family events or denied vacation requests. No more begging for time off.
- I design my own benefits package. One that actually meets my needs and values my health.
- I select my clients. No more feeling helpless in the face of abusive situations.
- I decide what, where, and how I do my job.

Your expertise, your rules.

It's about creating a career where you're respected, valued, and in charge of your own destiny. Where your license is recognized as the valuable asset it is, not just a tool for corporate profit.

Entrepreneurship isn't just about being your own boss - it's about being your own advocate. It's about building a nursing career that honors your skills, protects your wellbeing, and allows you to thrive both professionally and personally.

Solving Problems, Your Way

How many times have you thought, "There's got to be a better way to do this"? As nurses, we're natural-born problem solvers. But in traditional settings, our hands are often tied.

Entrepreneurship gives you the freedom to tackle those healthcare problems head-on. Got an idea for a better wound care product? You can make it happen. See a need for more accessible health education? You can create it.

Show Me the Money (and the Life Balance)

Let's be real for a second. Nursing is rewarding, but the pay doesn't always match the blood, sweat, and tears we put in. And don't even get me started on the work-life balance. We get paid for our time, but we don't get paid for the toll it takes on our lives.

While entrepreneurship isn't a get-rich-quick scheme, it does open up possibilities for increased earning potential. Plus, you get to design a schedule that works for you. Imagine being able to attend a party or your kids' soccer game without begging for a shift swap!

Personal Growth (Without the Growing Pains)

How exciting was it when you first started nursing, learning new things every day? Entrepreneurship brings back that excitement. You'll stretch yourself in new ways, learning about business, marketing, maybe even tech. It's like continuing education, but you're the one calling the shots.

Making Waves in Healthcare

As traditional healthcare nurses, we impact lives every day. But as entrepreneurs, we have the potential to create ripples that turn into waves. Your innovative product could improve patient outcomes across the country. Your health tech app could revolutionize how people manage chronic conditions.

Turning "If Only" into "I Did It"

How many times have you said, "If only they would listen to us nurses. The ones in the trenches doing the work." Well, here's your chance to be the one making the decisions. To take all those "if onlys" and turn them into your new reality.

Does any of this strike a chord? Maybe you're nodding along to all of this, or perhaps one point really hits home. Whatever your motivation, know this: your nursing experience has equipped you with a unique perspective and valuable skills that can translate into entrepreneurial success.

The Nurse's Superpower: A Skill Set Like No Other

Have you ever been in a situation where you're with a nurse friend, and you're watching something, and you just have to look at your friend and there's this nod? A knowing that's incomparable. What I'm saying is, whether you recognize it or not, there is a language, there is knowledge, there is psychology in a Nurse's experience that is unique in the world. These skills are easily transferrable to non-traditional healthcare careers. The world needs your skills. It needs the way you think. It needs your fortitude. It needs your calm, clear, intuitiveness, decisiveness.

Tell me, how many people walk toward trouble? How many people do you know in the "civilian" world who act clearly and decisively when the shit hits the fan? How many see it before it happens?

Let me share a personal story that illustrates this point:

I was simply driving to the grocery store with my family; my husband had just turned the corner onto a 4-lane road when an elderly couple veered off and entered the oncoming lane of travel. They hit a car head-on. My husband looked at me and immediately pulled over. I got out and of course ran straight to the oncoming car and held a child's head up with my hand through a "vent window" until the ambulance got there. Had I not done that, the child would have certainly died. I could hear the gurgling.

Yeah... I'm just saying, you are not just anybody. You come prepared for anything, even when you're out grocery shopping. That type of problem-solving, that clear decision-making isn't easily found, and it translates to an invaluable resource you can offer to the world.

This is what sets nurses apart. It's not just about medical knowledge, though that's certainly important. It's about:

1. Quick, decisive action in crisis situations
2. The ability to remain calm under pressure
3. A natural instinct to help and protect others
4. Clear communication in high-stress scenarios
5. The capacity to make critical decisions with limited information

These skills are not just valuable in healthcare settings. They're highly prized in:

- Business management
- Crisis consultation
- Safety and risk assessment
- Training and education
- Product development and innovation

As you consider your entrepreneurial journey, your nursing experience isn't just a background, it's your superpower. It's a unique set of skills and instincts that can set you apart in any field you choose to enter.

So, the next time someone asks what makes you qualified to start a business or venture into a new field, you say that "*You're a nurse*". You're trained to save lives, solve problems, and make critical decisions under pressure. Challenges in the business world are a walk in the park. You just have to know the rules. You passed a national exam for your license; you take classes every year to keep current. What classes do you think Jeff Bezos takes to keep current? Right. Now you get it. You are more than qualified.

In this next section, we'll look at how nurses are turning these motivations into action. Get ready to be inspired by amazing nurse entrepreneurs who've blazed the trail before us!

The How: Pathways to Nurse Entrepreneurship

Alright, so you're feeling that entrepreneurial itch. Maybe you're ready to scratch it, or maybe you're just curious about what it might look like. Here's the thing: there's no one-size-fits-all approach to becoming a nurse entrepreneur. It's not about following a strict set of steps; it's about finding the path that works for you, your lifestyle, and your goals.

Let's break down some of the ways nurses are making this transition. These aren't the only ways, but they're common paths that have worked for many of your fellow nurses.

The Side Hustle: Dipping Your Toes In

Picture this: You're still working your regular nursing job, but you're also building something on the side. Maybe you're doing some health coaching on the weekends, or you're developing a product idea in your spare time.

Meet Judy: With 37 years of experience as an RN, Judy created a unique side hustle as a "school field trip nurse." She contracts with schools to be on-site during field trips, ensuring children get their medications and handling any emergencies that arise. It's a perfect blend of her nursing skills and the flexibility she craved.

Pros:

Maintain financial stability of your nursing job

Test your idea without full commitment

Build your business gradually

Utilize your skills in creative ways

Cons:

Juggling two roles can be challenging

Slower growth due to time constraints

The Gradual Transition: One Foot In, One Foot Out

This is for those who want to ease into entrepreneurship. You might start by reducing your nursing hours as your business grows.

Take Lisa: She is a Nurse who started writing children's books after having her first child. It quickly became a very important part of her life. A creative outlet she found to be her niche. The demand for her attention grew so much that she dropped to part-time nursing and eventually transitioned fully into writing and appearances.

Pros:

- Allows for a smoother financial transition
- Provides time to build your business while maintaining some income stability
- Keeps you connected to the nursing world

Cons:

- It can be challenging to balance both roles
- It might take longer to fully establish your business

The Full Leap: All In, All at Once

This is for the bold and the brave. You've got an idea, you've done your research, and you're ready to dive in headfirst.

Meet Jackson: After 15 years as an ICU nurse, he quit his job to start a healthcare staffing agency. It was scary, but his deep understanding of staffing needs, and nurse preferences helped him succeed boldly.

Pros:

- Full focus on your business
- Potential for faster growth
- Complete autonomy from day one

Cons:

- Higher financial risk
- Can be stressful without a safety net

The Intrapreneur: Innovating from Within

Who says you have to leave your organization to be an entrepreneur? Some nurses are finding ways to innovate and create new programs within their current healthcare systems.

Consider Riannah's path: As a nurse manager, she developed a new patient education program that was so successful, her hospital turned it into a "patient education department" with Riannah at the helm.

Pros:

- Utilize existing resources and connections
- Potentially easier to implement ideas
- Maintain job security while innovating

Cons:

- Less autonomy than starting your own business
- Success may be dependent on organizational support

These aren't mutually exclusive. You might start with a side hustle that grows into a gradual transition and eventually a full leap. Or you might try intrapreneurship and decide you want to take your ideas and run with them independently.

The key is to choose a path that aligns with your goals, your risk tolerance, and your life circumstances. Maybe you've got kids in college and can't afford to lose your steady paycheck right now. Or maybe you're at a point where you're ready to bet on yourself fully.

Whatever path you choose, know that it's okay to start small. You don't have to have it all figured out from day one. The beauty of nurse entrepreneurship is that you can grow and evolve at your own pace.

You might be wondering: Is this really a viable path? Are other nurses actually doing this? The answer is a resounding yes, and the numbers prove it. In the next section, we'll dive into some eye-opening statistics and trends in nurse entrepreneurship. These aren't just dry facts and figures – they're evidence of a growing movement, a testament to the innovative spirit of nurses just like you who've decided to chart their own course.

Let's explore the data that shows not only is nurse entrepreneurship possible, but it's becoming an increasingly popular and successful career choice for nurses across the country. These trends might just inspire you to take that first step, whatever it might be for you.

Statistics and Trends: The Rising Tide of Nurse Entrepreneurship

You might be surprised to learn just how many nurses are venturing into entrepreneurship. Let's look at some numbers that paint a picture of this growing trend:

The Scale of Nurse Entrepreneurship

According to a 2019 survey by the National Nurses in Business Association (NNBA), approximately 0.5% to 1% of all registered nurses in the United States are nurse entrepreneurs. That might not sound like much, but with over 6 million Nurses in the country, we're talking about 30,000 to 60,000 nurse-owned businesses!

Growth in Nurse-Owned Businesses

The same NNBA survey found that the number of nurse entrepreneurs has been growing by about 5% each year over the past decade. That's faster than the overall growth rate of all small businesses in the U.S.

Areas of Opportunity

Nurse entrepreneurs are making their mark across various sectors:

- 35% in consulting and education
- 25% in direct patient care services
- 20% in products and innovation
- 15% in health tech and digital health
- 5% in other healthcare-related businesses

Income Potential

Here's an eye-opener: The average income for nurse entrepreneurs, according to a 2023 study by Nurse.org, was $101,000 - and that's just an average. Many nurse entrepreneurs reported earning well into six figures, especially those in consulting and health tech.

Job Satisfaction

Perhaps the most compelling statistic: 92% of nurse entrepreneurs reported higher job satisfaction compared to their previous traditional nursing roles. They cited increased autonomy, a better work-life balance, and the ability to make a broader impact as key factors.

Future Outlook

According to the Bureau of Labor Statistics, healthcare occupations are projected to grow faster than the average for all occupations from 2022-2032, with an average of 1.8 million openings per year. This growth, combined with ongoing changes in healthcare delivery models, suggests that opportunities for nurse entrepreneurs will continue to expand exponentially.

What do these numbers tell us? They show that nurse entrepreneurship isn't just a pipe dream - it's a viable and growing career path. Nurses are increasingly recognizing their value beyond traditional roles and are successfully leveraging their skills in the business world.

But behind each of these statistics is a nurse just like you who decided to take that first step. They faced the same doubts, the same fears, and the same challenges you might be feeling right now. The difference? They chose to push forward despite those obstacles.

In the next section, we'll explore some of the common fears and obstacles that nurse entrepreneurs face, and how to overcome them. Because while these statistics are encouraging, we know that taking the leap into entrepreneurship isn't that easy. But don't worry - we've here with you.

Now that we've seen the encouraging trends in nurse entrepreneurship, you might be feeling a mix of excitement and apprehension. That's completely normal. Let's address some of the common fears and obstacles that might be holding you back, and how to overcome them.

"I don't have any business skills."

Okay, let's chat about this one for a minute. What specific business skills do you think you don't have? An MBA is probably running the corporation that owns your hospital. They have no healthcare experience at all, and yet they're running a hospital. How? They have people who work for them who know the things they don't. People like you!

So, let's break this down a bit. Depending on what kind of business you're looking at, the "business skills" you need could all be different. It might be accounting, billing and coding, or maybe it's about managing supplies and inventory, or perhaps it's product development. But here's the thing – you don't need to know it all from day one.

Think about it this way: you're already running a small business called Your Household, Inc. You manage a budget, you make sure the bills get paid, you keep the lights on, and you might even be doing some payroll if you've got kids with allowances! Those are all basic business skills.

And for the stuff you don't know? There are thousands of resources out there. We're talking apps, software, local bookkeepers, accountants, and attorneys who can help with contracts, budgets, and licensing. Trust me, whatever arena you choose, there are experts ready to support you.

Plus, don't forget – we'll be providing you with tutorials on how to draft a business plan and start your marketing efforts. And between you and me? This is much easier than taking the NCLEX. You've already conquered that mountain, so this? This is just a new challenge you're more than equipped to handle.

You don't have to be a master of all trades. You just need to know enough to get started and know where to find help when you need it. And guess what? Knowing when to ask for help is a business skill in itself – one that you've been honing throughout your nursing career.

- Take online courses if you want to in business basics, marketing, or finance
- Seek mentorship from experienced entrepreneurs
- Consider partnering with someone who has complementary business skills

You don't have to know everything from day one. Many successful nurse entrepreneurs learn as they go.

"What if I fail?"

But, what if you don't? Fear of failure is natural, but don't let it paralyze you into not pursuing a career that could give you the life you've been dreaming about while you make other people rich.

Let's redefine "failure". I don't know about you, but I've never given up on anything ever. It's just not in me. I was the person who continued with something because of the time, energy, and money that had been invested.

Let me share a bit of my journey. I left nursing for the first time after 10 years. I was tired. I had been in Long Term Care and Hospice for a decade, and my emotional equity was spent. I ventured into Digital Marketing and Website building. It was fun learning something new, and it made good money. Then Covid hit, and Nursing called me back.

This time, I was ready. I knew I wasn't going to do the same thing again. I decided to be on the business side of things - Director of Operations, Administrator, Healthcare Consultant, Startup Consultant, Compliance Specialist. The learning experiences were phenomenal! I wouldn't change a thing. They have become the impetus for this book.

Here's what I've learned: Failure is inevitable. We won't get it right every time. But as long as we don't give up and keep consistently showing up, the journey is going to be a blast. Each "failure" is just a steppingstone to your next success.

So, instead of fearing failure:

- Reframe failure as a learning opportunity. Every misstep teaches you something valuable.
- Start small to minimize risk. You don't have to quit your job and invest your life savings on day one.
- Have a fallback plan (like keeping your nursing job part-time initially). This gives you a safety net while you build your business.

Even if a venture doesn't succeed, the skills and experience you gain are invaluable. They're yours to keep and use in your next endeavor.

In the world of entrepreneurship, the only real failure is not trying at all. So, are you ready to take that first step?

"I can't afford to start a business."

What can't you really afford? Is it the cost of starting a business, or is it the price of staying where you are?

Think about it. What's the expense of remaining stagnant and unhappy? It's astronomical, both physically and psychologically. The stress of a job that doesn't fulfill you, the frustration of having your PTO requests denied, the constant worry about jeopardizing

61

the license you've worked so hard for – these costs add up, and they're not just financial.

That vacation account you never use because you can never get the time off. Or that rainy day fund you've been saving. Well, my friend, it's pouring. Stress causes physical illness; we know this all too well as nurses. So, I guess you need to redefine what "afford" really means to you.

Now, I'm not saying entrepreneurship is for everyone. It's not. But staying where you're miserable or risking your license every day is a cost no one should have to pay.

If you're still concerned about the financial aspect, consider this:

- Many nursing ventures can be started with minimal investment. Think consulting, online education, or health coaching.
- Start as a side hustle while maintaining your current job. This allows you to build your business without losing your steady income.
- Explore low-cost business models. In today's digital age, you can start a business with just a laptop and a good idea.
- Look into small business loans or grants for healthcare innovations. There are resources out there specifically for healthcare professionals like you.

Investing in yourself and your happiness is never a waste. The returns – in terms of job satisfaction, work-life balance, and yes, even financial rewards – can be immense.

"I'm worried about legal and regulatory issues."

I hear you. Healthcare is indeed a highly regulated field, but guess what? This is where your nursing background gives you a leg up. You've been navigating complex regulations and protocols your entire career. Now, you'll just be applying that knowledge in a new way.

Here's how to tackle this:

- Consult with a healthcare attorney to ensure compliance. They can help you understand the specific regulations that apply to your business idea.
- Stay updated on regulations in your area of practice. This is something you're already doing as a nurse, so you're ahead of the game.
- Consider joining professional associations for nurse entrepreneurs. These groups offer ongoing support, information, and a network of peers who've walked this path before you.

Now, here's something you might not realize: that nursing license you worked so hard for? It's not just a piece of paper. It's the foundation for many healthcare and healthcare-adjacent businesses. You've already got the crucial credential that many entrepreneurs in this field lack.

In the coming chapters, I'll provide you with resources tailored to different areas of nurse entrepreneurship. Whatever direction you choose, the right resources and mentorship can steer you towards success. You don't have to figure it all out on your own.

The key is to approach regulations the same way you approach patient care: with attention to detail, a commitment to best practices, and a willingness to consult experts when needed. You've got this!

"I'm afraid of losing the stability of my nursing job."

Let's talk about what you really can't afford. Is it the cost of starting a business, or is it the price of staying where you are?

How many nursing positions have you held in your career?

How many open positions are on Indeed right now?

How many hospitals have closed their doors without notice?

Have you ever been let go because you stood up for safe staffing ratios or butted heads with administration?

The truth is, what we often think of as "stability" in nursing is more of an illusion. It's the carrot they dangle so you don't leave. Like the 1% pay raise every year, when the new hires are making 25% more on day one. You might have a steady paycheck, sure, but at what cost? The constant stress, the unpredictable schedules, the physical and emotional toll - these aren't exactly hallmarks of stability.

Now, I'm not saying we should all quit our jobs tomorrow and dive headfirst into entrepreneurship. But I am saying we need to reframe how we think about stability.

Here's how you can approach this transition in a smart way:

- Start your business part-time while keeping your nursing job. This gives you the best of both worlds - a steady income while you build your dream.
- Build up savings before making the full transition. Having a financial cushion can ease a lot of stress as you grow your business. Make that OT work for you for a change!

Entrepreneurship can potentially offer greater long-term stability and income. When you're in control, you're not at the mercy of hospital budgets or administrative whims.

Stability isn't about clinging to a job that drains you. It's about creating a career that fulfills you, challenges you, and yes, rewards you financially. We're not talking about jumping off a roof here. We're talking about jumping into a new, happier life - one where you're in control.

So, are you ready to create your own version of stability?

"I don't have any innovative ideas."

You don't need to invent the next big thing to be a successful entrepreneur. Often, the best businesses come from:

- Solving a problem, you've encountered in your nursing career
- Improving an existing product or service
- Bringing a nursing perspective to a non-healthcare field

Your years of experience give you insights that non-nurses simply don't have. Think about how many times you've thought "there has to be a better way". There is. It's You!

Every successful nurse entrepreneur once stood where you are now, facing these same fears and obstacles. The difference is, they decided to take that first step despite their fears.

In the next section, we'll equip you with some practical tools to help you get started on your entrepreneurial journey. Because while it's normal to have fears, it's also possible to overcome them and create the nursing career you've always dreamed of.

The Nurse Entrepreneur's Toolkit

Recognizing Your Business Superpowers

As we wrap up this chapter, let's talk about something exciting – the business tools you already have but might not recognize. That's right, your nursing career has equipped you with more entrepreneurial skills than you might realize.

Networking:

Think about how effortlessly you build relationships with patients, families, and colleagues. That's networking gold in the business world.

Budgeting:

Ever managed unit supplies or staffing schedules or overtime? Congratulations, you've been budgeting and resource allocation.

Continuous Learning:

Keeping up with the latest medical advancements? That's the same skill entrepreneurs use to stay ahead in their markets.

Time Management and Productivity:

Juggling multiple patients, tasks, and emergencies? You're a productivity pro.

Compliance and Attention to Detail:

Your ability to follow protocols and maintain accurate records is crucial in business operations.

Digital Literacy:

If you're using Electronic Health Records and digital charting, you're already tech-savvy.

Problem-Solving:

Every shift, you're solving complex problems under pressure. That's the essence of entrepreneurship.

Communication:

Explaining complex medical information to patients? That's top-notch communication and customer service.

See? You're better prepared for entrepreneurship than you thought!

Now, as you step into the business world, you'll need to level up some of these skills:

- *Protecting Your Business.* You'll need to think beyond protecting just your license. It's about safeguarding your entire business entity. You might have people working for you, that depend on their salary. We'll guide you in expanding your focus from individual patient care to a holistic business vision. This means learning to apply your compassion and expertise not just to patients, but to every aspect of your enterprise - from your services and team to your overall business strategy. It's about seeing the bigger picture while still honoring your nursing roots.

- Financial Management: While you understand budgets, you'll need to learn about business finances, taxes, and investment.
- Marketing and Branding: You'll need to understand and learn how to promote your services and build a brand.
- Legal and Regulatory Knowledge: Yes, compliance is black and white. No grey areas. Understanding healthcare regulations from a business perspective will be crucial. You'll need to learn the why and how's of running the business rather than just working for one.

Don't worry – we'll dive deeper into these advanced topics in later chapters. For now, take a moment to appreciate the valuable skills you already possess. You're not starting from scratch – you're building on a solid foundation of nursing expertise.

Conclusion: Your Journey Begins Here

We've covered a lot of ground in this chapter, haven't we? From exploring the motivations behind nurse entrepreneurship to addressing common fears and recognizing the business superpowers you already possess; you're now equipped with a solid foundation to begin your entrepreneurial journey.

Becoming a nurse entrepreneur isn't about abandoning your identity as a nurse. It's about expanding your impact, reclaiming control over your career, and applying your skills in new and exciting ways. We'll guide you in expanding your focus from individual patient care to a holistic business vision. This means learning to apply your compassion and expertise not just to patients, but to every aspect of your enterprise - from your services and team to your overall business strategy.

As we move forward, keep in mind that every successful nurse entrepreneur once stood where you are now, feeling a mix of excitement and apprehension. The difference is, they took that first step. And now, you're ready to do the same.

In the next chapter, we'll start exploring specific entrepreneurial opportunities in nursing. We'll dive into various business models, from direct patient care ventures to innovative health tech solutions. You'll discover the wide range of possibilities available to you and start to envision where your unique skills and passions might fit best.

So, take a deep breath, nurse entrepreneur. Your journey is just beginning, and the best is yet to come. Let go explore the exciting world of nurse entrepreneurship!

Scan to Access Tools for Chapter Four

Chapter 5: Transitioning to Autonomy: Work-from-Home Opportunities in Nursing

It's Monday morning, and instead of battling traffic or hunting for parking, you're sipping coffee from your favorite mug, settling into your home office. Your commute? A leisurely stroll from your bedroom. Your dress code? Whatever makes you comfortable. Welcome to the world of work-from-home nursing.

If you're reading this, chances are you're intrigued by the idea of more autonomy in your nursing career — but you're not quite ready to dive headfirst into full-blown entrepreneurship. Good news: the healthcare industry is evolving, and with it, a whole new world of remote work opportunities is opening up for nurses.

For many, the real dream isn't just leaving the bedside — it's reclaiming a sense of peace, fulfillment, and personal control after years of being stretched too thin. Autonomy isn't a luxury anymore. We keep waiting for healthcare leadership to fix it.
But here's the truth: most of them don't even know what we really need. They've never had to chart through tears, hold a dying hand, or miss meals because the call bell won't stop.
They don't know — because they've never had to.
And yet we hand over our schedules, our energy, and our careers to them like they're qualified to protect it.
Autonomy is a need for survival. After constantly being at the mercy of short staffing, unsafe assignments, or the emotional whiplash of a broken system, the idea of working on your own terms — in a

quiet space, without being physically or emotionally cornered — isn't just appealing. It's lifesaving.

This chapter is for those ready to reclaim that control, one grounded, powerful step at a time. We'll explore a variety of work-from-home roles that let you leverage your nursing expertise while gaining back time, space, and breathing room. These aren't just job listings — they're steppingstones toward greater career satisfaction and a version of nursing that finally includes you.

From case management to telemedicine, from quality assurance to legal nurse consulting, pharmaceuticals and technology the possibilities are more diverse than you might think. And the best part? Many of these roles offer set schedules (often those coveted 9-5, Monday to Friday hours), competitive pay, and benefits that include that holy grail of nursing – guaranteed PTO.

But before you start imagining yourself in your new home office, let's be clear: transitioning to remote work isn't without its challenges. We'll also be discussing how to maintain work-life balance when your living room becomes your workplace. And how to stay connected to the nursing community when you're no longer rubbing elbows with colleagues at the nurses' station.

By the end of this chapter, you'll have a comprehensive understanding of:

- The variety of work-from-home opportunities available to nurses
- The skills and qualifications needed for these roles
- How to transition from bedside nursing to remote work
- Strategies for finding and securing remote nursing positions
- The pros and cons of working from home in healthcare

So, if you're ready to explore how you can put your nursing skills to work... from home, Let's dive in and discover the world of remote nursing opportunities waiting for you.

Case Management and Care Coordination

There are always patients you wished you could follow up with after discharge, aren't there? As a remote case manager or care coordinator, that's exactly what you get to do – minus the hospital corridors and beeping monitors.

Case management and care coordination involve overseeing a patient's entire care journey — ensuring they receive the right services at the right time, and helping them navigate the often-complex healthcare system. In a remote role, you'll provide this support through phone calls, video conferencing, and electronic health record systems.

Who's it for? This role is perfect for nurses who:

- Love building relationships with patients
- Excel at coordinating care across multiple providers
- Enjoy problem-solving and advocating for patients
- Are looking for a role that combines clinical knowledge with administrative skills

LPN Alert: Don't skip this section! Many organizations are now offering care coordination roles specifically for LPNs. These positions often focus on non-clinical aspects of patient care, like appointment scheduling, transportation coordination, and connecting patients with community resources and follow-up on chronic health processes.

Skills You'll Need:

- Excellent communication skills (both verbal and written, effectively engaging with healthcare professionals, patients, and families alike.)
- Proficiency with electronic health records and other digital tools
- Strong organizational and time management abilities
- Knowledge of healthcare systems and insurance processes

A Day in the Life: Imagine starting your day by reviewing your caseload. You might have a video call with a patient who was recently discharged from the hospital, coordinating their follow-up appointments and ensuring they understand their new medication regimen. Later, you could be on the phone with a specialist's office, advocating for a quicker appointment for a patient with concerning symptoms. Between calls, you're updating care plans, documenting interactions, and collaborating with other healthcare providers via secure messaging systems.

How to Transition:

- Gauge your experience: Many remote case management roles require at least 2-3 years of clinical experience.
- Get certified: Consider obtaining certifications like the Certified Case Manager (CCM) or a certification in Care Coordination and Transition Management (CCCTM). (This will also help if you decide to go out on your own later with your own Care Manager agency.)
- Develop your tech skills: Familiarize yourself with common case management software, telehealth platforms and EHRs.

- Highlight transferable skills: When applying, emphasize your experience in patient education, care planning, and interdisciplinary collaboration.

- The Perks:

- Regular business hours (often 9-5, Monday to Friday)
- Competitive salaries, often with performance bonuses
- Comprehensive benefits, including reliable PTO
- Opportunity to impact patient care on a broader scale

Nurse Story: "I never thought I'd love nursing from behind a computer screen, but remote case management has given me the best of both worlds. I still get to use my clinical skills and build relationships with patients, but I also have the flexibility to be there for my kids' after-school activities. It's been a game-changer for my work-life balance." - Tiffany, RN, Remote Case Manager

Ready to explore case management opportunities? Check out the QR code at the end of this chapter for a curated list of companies currently hiring for remote case management and care coordination roles.

Quality Assurance and Performance Improvement (QAPI)

Ever found yourself thinking, "There's got to be a better way to do this"? Welcome to the world of QAPI, where your knack for spotting inefficiencies and your drive for better patient care can shine – all from the comfort of your very own home workspace.

What is it? QAPI is all about systematically improving the way healthcare is delivered. It's a data-driven, proactive approach to quality improvement and solving problems. In a remote QAPI role, you'll be analyzing data, identifying areas for improvement, and developing strategies to enhance patient care and outcomes.

Who's it for? This role is ideal for nurses who:

- Have a keen eye for detail and love working with data
- Enjoy problem-solving on a systemic level
- Are passionate about improving healthcare processes

- Have experience in various healthcare settings

- Skills You'll Need:

- Strong analytical and critical thinking skills
- Proficiency in data analysis and interpretation
- Excellent written and verbal communication
- Knowledge of healthcare regulations and standards
- Familiarity with quality improvement methodologies (like Six Sigma, Lean or Baldrige)

A Day in the Life: Picture yourself starting the day by reviewing the latest patient satisfaction scores. You notice a trend of complaints about discharge instructions & support. You dig deeper into the data, maybe run a few reports, and then brainstorm with your team (via video conference, of course) on how to improve the discharge process. Later, you might be drafting a new policy based on recent regulatory changes or creating a presentation on the success of a recent quality improvement initiative.

How to Transition:

- Gain diverse experience: QAPI roles often require a broad understanding of healthcare operations and regulatory standards
- Get certified: Consider certifications like Certified Professional in

Healthcare Quality (CPHQ), QAPI Certified Professional (QCP) or Six Sigma certifications.

- Develop your tech skills: Familiarize yourself with data analysis tools and quality improvement software.
- Highlight your problem-solving wins: When applying, emphasize times you've identified and solved problems in your nursing career.

The Perks:

- Regular business hours, often with flexibility
- Competitive salaries, sometimes with performance-based bonuses
- Opportunity to impact care on a system-wide level
- Continuous learning and professional development
- Ability to work with more than one employer at a time

Nurse Story: "I never thought my tendency to question everything would be an asset, but in QAPI, it's my superpower. I get to use my nursing knowledge to improve care for thousands of patients, all while working from home. Plus, no more night shifts!" - Dillon, RN, Remote QAPI Specialist

Ready to dive into the world of QAPI? Don't forget to check out the QR code at the end of this chapter for a list of organizations currently hiring for remote QAPI positions.

Pro Tips: Many healthcare organizations are now required to have robust QAPI programs, making this a growing field with plenty of opportunities. Keep an eye out for titles like "Quality Improvement Specialist," "Performance Improvement Coordinator," or "Clinical Quality Analyst." This is also a very good field of expertise to offer to multiple agencies / facilities. Check out the video module by using the QR code below to see how this could become a very successful business model for you.

Healthcare Effectiveness Data and Information Set (HEDIS) Review

Ever wonder how health plans and managed care plans measure their performance? Enter HEDIS, the healthcare world's report card. And guess what? They need nurses like you to help compile the information to either substantiate their success in meeting goals or to gain the knowledge needed to make improvements.

What is it? HEDIS (Healthcare Effectiveness Data and Information Set) is a tool used by more than 90% of America's health plans to measure performance on important dimensions of care and service. As a HEDIS reviewer, you'll be diving into patient records to extract and validate data that helps assess the quality of care provided.

Who's it for? This role is perfect for nurses who:

- Have a meticulous eye for detail
- Enjoy working with data and analyzing information
- Are comfortable with technology and electronic health records
- Like the idea of contributing to large-scale quality improvement

Skills You'll Need:

- Strong analytical and critical thinking skills (those detective skills are a blessing)
- Excellent attention to detail
- Proficiency in navigating electronic health records
- Understanding of medical terminology and coding
- Ability to work independently and meet deadlines

A Day in the Life: You will be starting your day by logging into a secure health plan database. You'll review patient records, looking for specific information related to the HEDIS measures. For example, you might be checking if diabetic patients received their annual eye exams or if children got their immunizations on schedule. You'll extract this data, validate its accuracy, and input it into the HEDIS software. Throughout the day, you might consult with team members via chat or video call to clarify any ambiguous findings.

How to Transition:

- Familiarize yourself with HEDIS measures: The National Committee for Quality Assurance (NCQA) website is a great resource.
- Gain experience with electronic health records: Many HEDIS positions require proficiency in navigating various EHR systems.
- Develop your data analysis skills: Consider taking an online course in healthcare data analytics. (It can give you a jump start on the mindset you need and it's great for the resume)
- Highlight your attention to detail: When applying, emphasize times in your nursing career where accuracy and thoroughness were crucial. Give a brief summary of the outcomes.

The Perks:

- Seasonal opportunities (HEDIS reviews often happen annually) which can be great for nurses wanting flexibility
- Competitive pay, often with opportunities for overtime during busy seasons
- Work-from-home setup, sometimes with equipment provided
- Regular business hours, though deadlines may occasionally require extra hours

Nurse Story: "HEDIS review combines my love for nursing with my secret passion for detective work. I get to dig into records, piece together patient stories, and contribute to improving healthcare quality — all while working from my home office. Plus, the seasonal nature of the work allows me to travel during off-seasons!" - Heidi, RN, Remote HEDIS Reviewer

Pro Tip: HEDIS review seasons typically run from January to May each year. Many health plans and healthcare consulting firms hire additional staff during these months, making it a great opportunity to "test drive" this type of work.

Ready to explore HEDIS review opportunities? Don't forget to check the QR code at the end of this chapter for a list of companies currently hiring for remote HEDIS positions.

Clinical Documentation Improvement (CDI)

Was there ever a time that you wished you could clarify a doctor's notes or ensure a patient's chart truly reflected their condition? Welcome to the world of Clinical Documentation Improvement, where your clinical knowledge meets your inner detective.

What is it? CDI specialists work behind the scenes to ensure that patient records are accurate, complete, and properly reflect the complexity of patient care. In a remote CDI role, you'll review clinical documentation, work with healthcare providers to clarify information, and help ensure that documentation supports appropriate reimbursement and quality reporting.

Who's it for? This role is ideal for nurses who:

- Have a strong clinical background and understanding of medical terminology
- Enjoy the challenge of solving puzzles and connecting the dots
- Are detail-oriented and have excellent analytical skills
- Can communicate effectively with physicians and other healthcare providers

Skills You'll Need:

- In-depth knowledge of clinical conditions and treatments
- Familiarity with ICD-10 coding and MS-DRG systems
- Strong written and verbal communication skills
- Ability to tactfully question and clarify physician documentation
- Proficiency with electronic health records and CDI software

A Day in the Life: Your day might start by logging into the hospital's EHR system. You review patient records, looking for opportunities to improve documentation. You might notice that a patient's chart mentions "sepsis" but doesn't include all the clinical indicators to support this diagnosis. You would then draft a query to the physician, asking for clarification or additional information. Throughout the day, you might participate in virtual team meetings, provide education to clinical staff on documentation best practices, or analyze CDI program metrics.

How to Transition:

- Gain diverse clinical experience: Most CDI positions require at least 3-5 years of acute care experience.
- Get certified: Consider certifications like the Certified Clinical Documentation Specialist (CCDS) or the Certified Clinical Documentation Improvement Practitioner (CCDIP).
- Develop your coding knowledge: While you won't be coding, understanding the basics of ICD-10 and MS-DRG systems is crucial.
- Highlight your communication skills: When applying, emphasize times you've effectively communicated complex clinical information.

The Perks:

- Regular business hours, often with some flexibility
- Competitive salaries, sometimes with performance-based bonuses
- Opportunity to use your clinical knowledge in a new way

- Continuous learning as medical knowledge and coding rules evolve
- Flexibility to make this a stand-alone business of your own

Nurse Story: "As a CDI specialist, I feel like I'm the bridge between the clinical and administrative sides of healthcare. I get to use my nursing knowledge every day, but in a way that impacts not just individual patient care, but also hospital quality metrics and reimbursement. Plus, I love that I can do this without leaving my home!" - Rodney, RN, Remote CDI Specialist

Pro Tip: Many healthcare systems are expanding their CDI programs to outpatient settings, creating even more opportunities in this field. Keep an eye out for titles like "Outpatient CDI Specialist" or "Ambulatory CDI Coordinator."

For those who are in Home Health, Hospice, Long Term Care and Assisted Living, don't feel left out of this opportunity. This can be a stand-alone business offer. We'll explore this in an upcoming chapter.

Ready to explore CDI opportunities? Check out the QR code at the end of this chapter for a list of healthcare systems and consulting firms currently hiring for remote CDI positions.

Telephone Triage and Telemedicine

Does telemedicine seem like a futuristic concept? Well since covid, the future is now, and it's bringing exciting opportunities for nurses to provide care to patients without ever having to commute anywhere.

What is it? Telephone triage nurses assess patient symptoms over the phone, provide care advice, and determine the appropriate level of care needed. Telemedicine nurses, however, use video technology to conduct virtual patient visits, monitor chronic conditions, and provide patient education.

Who's it for? These roles are perfect for nurses who:

- Have strong assessment skills and can think critically without a hands-on exam.
- Are excellent communicators and active listeners
- Can build rapport quickly, even in a virtual setting
- Are comfortable with technology and can troubleshoot basic tech issues

Skills You'll Need:

- Strong clinical knowledge across a wide range of conditions
- Excellent verbal communication and phone etiquette
- Ability to quickly build trust and rapport with patients

- Proficiency with telemedicine platforms and electronic health records
- Good decision-making skills under pressure

A Day in the Life: As a telephone triage nurse, you might start your shift by logging into the call system. Throughout your day, you'll answer calls from patients describing various symptoms and issues. You'll use your nursing knowledge and standardized protocols to assess their condition, provide appropriate advice, and determine if they need to seek in-person care.

In a telemedicine role, you could be conducting video visits with patients managing chronic conditions like diabetes or hypertension. You might review their home monitoring data, adjust care plans, provide education, and coordinate with their primary care providers.

How to Transition:

- Gain diverse clinical experience: Most triage and telemedicine positions require at least 2-3 years of hands-on nursing experience.
- Get certified: Consider certifications like the Ambulatory Care Nursing Certification (RN-BC) or Telehealth Certification (CTNS).
- Familiarize yourself with telemedicine platforms: Many companies offer free trials or demos of their software.

- Hone your 'webside manner': Practice building rapport and conducting assessments without physical touch.

The Perks:

- Flexible scheduling, often with options for part-time or per-dem work
- Elimination of commute and exposure to hospital short staffing and drama
- Opportunity to work with diverse patient populations
- Continuous learning as telemedicine technology evolves

Nurse Story: "I never thought I'd say this, but I love nursing again. Working from home has given me the opportunity to connect with my patients again. As a telemedicine nurse, I still get to use all my assessment skills and build relationships. The best part? I can provide care to people who might otherwise struggle to access it, all while having more time for my own family." - Darya, RN, Telemedicine Nurse

Pro Tip: With the rapid growth of telemedicine, many specialties are moving into the virtual nursing space. Keep an eye out for niche opportunities in areas like telepsychiatry, behavioral health and addiction health, telemetry and tele-ICU, or even telemedicine case management.

Ready to explore triage and telemedicine opportunities? Don't forget to check the QR code at

the end of this chapter for a list of companies
currently hiring for remote nursing positions in these
fields including some federal government entities.

Virtual Nursing: Continuous Care from Home

While telemedicine and triage often operate during
business hours, Virtual Patient Monitoring takes
virtual care to the next level, offering 24/7 support
and opening opportunities for nurses who need more
flexible schedules.

What is Virtual Nursing? It's where Nurses use
technology to monitor patients' vital signs, symptoms,
and other health data from a distance. This can include
monitoring patients with chronic, acute and behavioral
conditions, providing bedside attention and follow-up,
but can also be a position where you are responsible
for clinical support to the onsite-bedside staff in
various healthcare settings. You become the eyes and
ears at the bedside while the on-site staff take on the
clinical work at hand.

Who is this for? This role is ideal for nurses who:

- Need flexibility due to family
  commitments or other life circumstances
- Are comfortable with technology and can
  troubleshoot basic tech issues
- Have strong clinical assessment and
  decision-making skills
- Can adapt to varying shift patterns,
  including nights and weekends

The Perks:

- Flexibility to work various shifts, including nights and weekends
- Opportunity to maintain and enhance clinical skills while working from home
- Elimination of commute and childcare expenses
- Ability to work for healthcare systems across the country

Nurse Story: "As a single mom, Virtual Nursing has been a game-changer for me. I can be there for my kids while still using my nursing skills to impact patient care. The remote, work from home scheduling, means I can work and take care of my family's needs. I'm saving a fortune on childcare and commuting costs." - Ava, RN, NursiConnect-Virtual Nurse Staffing

Pro Tip: Many Virtual Nurse positions offer training in specialized areas like cardiac monitoring or virtual ICU care. This can be a great way to expand your skill set while working from home.

Ready to explore Virtual Patient Monitoring opportunities? Don't forget to check the QR code at the end of this chapter for a list of companies currently hiring for remote nursing positions in these fields.

Compliance Consulting: Keeping Healthcare on the Straight and Narrow

Ever found yourself explaining to a colleague why a certain procedure needs to be done a specific way? Congratulations, you've already dipped your toes into the world of compliance!

What is a compliance role? Nurses ensure that healthcare organizations adhere to federal and state regulations, accreditation standards, and internal policies. As a remote compliance consultant, you'll help healthcare providers navigate the complex web of healthcare laws and regulations, develop policies and procedures, and implement compliance programs.

Who is this for? This role is perfect for nurses who:

- Have a keen eye for detail and a passion for doing things "by the book"
- Enjoy interpreting and applying complex regulations
- Are good at explaining rules and procedures to others
- Have experience in multiple healthcare settings

Skills You'll Need:

- In-depth knowledge of healthcare regulations (e.g., HIPAA, OSHA, CMS guidelines)

- Strong analytical and problem-solving skills
- Excellent written and verbal communication
- Ability to develop and deliver training programs
- Proficiency in creating and updating policies and procedures
- Experience with Day-to-Day facility / agency operations

A Day in the Life: Your day could start by reviewing recent changes to CMS guidelines. You might then hop on a video call with a client to discuss how these changes impact their agency operations. Later, you could be drafting a new policy for a hospital's infection control procedures or creating a training module on HIPAA compliance for a medical practice. Your day might end with a risk assessment for a home health agency, identifying potential compliance issues in their documentation practices. Compliance specialists also assist agencies with survey prep, post survey they could assist with plans of correction and for others it may be assisting with start-up processes for licensure and /or accreditation.

How to Transition:

- Gain diverse experience: Familiarity with various healthcare settings is valuable in compliance consulting.
- Get certified: Consider certifications like Certified in Healthcare Compliance

(CHC) or Certified HIPAA Professional (CHP).

- Get Certified with the accrediting bodies, CHAP, ACHC and JCAHO
- Stay updated: Subscribe to regulatory newsletters and attend webinars on healthcare compliance topics.
- Develop your teaching skills: Much of compliance work involves educating others.

The Perks:

- Lucrative consulting fees or 1099 positions, often higher than traditional nursing salaries
- Flexibility to work with multiple clients or focus on specific areas of compliance for one employer
- Opportunity to positively impact patient care on a systemic level
- Continuous learning as healthcare regulations evolve

Nurse Story: "I never thought my perfectionist tendencies would be an asset, but in compliance consulting, they're my superpower. I get to use my nursing knowledge to help organizations provide better, safer care and flex my regulation and accreditation knowledge. I love the variety – one day I'm working with a small rural clinic, the next I'm consulting for a major hospital system." - Shavaonna, RN, Remote Compliance Consultant

Pro Tip: Compliance consulting can be a great steppingstone to higher-level healthcare administration roles if that's something you aspire to. Many Chief Compliance Officers started their careers as compliance consultants.

Heads up, LPNs – this isn't an RN-exclusive position. Someone with a variety of experience and regulatory knowledge can excel in this area. In fact, as a 30-year LPN, I can attest that compliance consulting has been my absolute favorite and most lucrative position to date. There's something incredibly rewarding about helping Home Health and Hospice Agencies get their initial licenses, prepare for surveys, or work towards accreditation. It's exciting to be on this side of the table, where your years of hands-on experience are truly valued and appreciated.

For LPNs who've felt undervalued in clinical settings, compliance consulting can be a breath of fresh air. Your practical knowledge of day-to-day operations, combined with an understanding of regulatory requirements, makes you an invaluable asset to healthcare organizations. Whether you're crafting policies that work on the front lines or explaining regulations in a way that makes sense to clinical staff, your LPN perspective brings a unique and necessary viewpoint to the compliance field.

In compliance consulting, it's not about your nursing license level – it's about your actual knowledge, experience, and ability to interpret and apply regulations effectively. This field offers a chance for

LPNs to leverage their years of experience into a rewarding career that respects and values their expertise.

Ready to explore compliance consulting opportunities? Check out the QR code at the end of this chapter for resources on getting started in this field, including training programs and professional associations. There are also a few positions available at consultancy agencies around the country if you want to get your feet wet and try it out before setting out on your own.

Insurance Industry Opportunities: Where Clinical Expertise Meets Corporate Healthcare

Ever wondered who reviews all those insurance claims or decides what treatments get covered? Turns out, the insurance industry needs nurses like you to make these crucial decisions.

What is it? Nurses in the insurance industry can work in various roles, including Utilization Review, Pre-Authorization, Case Management, and handling Appeals and Grievances. These positions involve applying clinical knowledge to insurance processes, ensuring appropriate use of healthcare resources, and advocating for patient needs within the constraints of insurance policies.

Who would a position like this be for? These roles are ideal for nurses who:

- Have a strong clinical background and enjoy applying it in a non-traditional setting
- Are analytical and enjoy working with data and policies
- Have good decision-making skills and attention to detail
- Can balance patient advocacy with business considerations

Key Roles:

- Utilization Review Nurse:
  - Reviews and approves insurance claims based on medical necessity
  - Ensure treatments align with evidence-based guidelines
- Pre-Authorization Specialist:
  - Reviews and processes requests for medical procedures, treatments, or medications before they are provided
  - Evaluates medical necessity based on the patient's condition, plan benefits, and clinical guidelines
- Case Manager:
  - Coordinates care for complex or high-cost cases

- o Develops care plans to optimize patient outcomes and manage costs
- Appeals and Grievances Specialist:
  - o Reviews and responds to patient appeals for denied claims
  - o Investigates complaints about insurance coverage or service

Skills You'll Need:

- Strong clinical knowledge across various specialties
- Familiarity with insurance terminology and processes
- Excellent written and verbal communication skills
- Ability to interpret and apply complex policies and guidelines
- Strong computer skills, including proficiency with databases and EMRs

A Day in the Life: In these roles, your day might start by reviewing a list of cases - whether they're pre-authorization requests, claims for review, or appeals. You'll examine patients' medical histories, proposed treatment plans, and your company's clinical guidelines.

Throughout the day, you might find yourself:

- Evaluating medical necessity for various procedures or treatments
- Communicating with healthcare providers to gather additional information
- Coordinating care plans for complex cases
- Drafting detailed explanations for claim decisions or care recommendations
- Consulting with medical directors on particularly challenging cases
- Investigating and responding to patient complaints or appeals

The specific balance of these tasks will depend on your specific role, but all will involve applying your clinical knowledge to make informed decisions that balance patient needs with insurance policies.

How to Transition:

- Gain diverse clinical experience: Most insurance roles require at least 3-5 years of hands-on nursing experience.
- Familiarize yourself with insurance processes: Consider taking courses in basic health insurance or medical billing and coding.
- Develop your computer skills: Proficiency with various software programs is crucial in these roles.

- Highlight your analytical skills: When applying, emphasize times you've had to make complex clinical decisions or interpret guidelines.

The Perks:

- Regular business hours (often 9-5, Monday to Friday - No weekends No holidays)
- Competitive salaries with potential for bonuses
- Comprehensive benefits packages
- Opportunity to impact healthcare on a broader scale

Nurse Story: " I always wondered how these decisions were made. I've found working for an insurance company to be incredibly interesting and a great learning experience. I get to use my nursing knowledge every day to ensure patients get the care they need while also helping to manage healthcare costs. Plus, the work-life balance is fantastic – no more night shifts or weekends!" - Mark, RN, Utilization Review Nurse

Pro Tip: Many insurance companies offer extensive training programs for nurses new to the industry. Don't be afraid to apply even if you don't have specific insurance experience – your clinical background is invaluable in these roles.

Ready to explore insurance industry opportunities? Check out the QR code at the end of this chapter for a list of insurance companies currently hiring nurses for remote positions

Long-Term Care MDS Coordination: The Nexus of Resident Care, Reimbursement, and Strategic Planning

All those assessments and care plans you've created while working in long-term care are coming into play for this role. In the world of MDS Coordination, these have become the cornerstone of quality care, proper reimbursement, and strategic facility management. As an MDS Coordinator, you're not just documenting resident care - you're the linchpin connecting resident needs, facility finances, and regulatory compliance.

What is MDS?

MDS (Minimum Data Set) Coordinators are responsible for completing comprehensive assessments of long-term care residents and developing strategic care plans. These assessments and plans not only guide resident care but also determine facility reimbursement. As a remote MDS Coordinator, you'll be analyzing data, ensuring its accuracy, developing care plans, and identifying reimbursable services - all while ensuring compliance with regulations.

Key Responsibilities:

- Conducting comprehensive resident assessments
- Developing strategic care plans that align resident needs with reimbursable services
- Identifying care plan goals that can be reimbursed and tracking facility efforts to meet those goals
- Ensuring accuracy of MDS coding for proper reimbursement
- Collaborating with interdisciplinary teams to implement and adjust care plans
- Monitoring and reporting on facility performance metrics

Skills You'll Need:

- In-depth knowledge of MDS 3.0 and care area assessments
- Familiarity with Medicare and Medicaid reimbursement systems
- Strong computer skills, especially with MDS software
- Excellent written and verbal communication
- Ability to interpret and apply regulatory guidelines
- Strategic thinking to align care plans with reimbursement opportunities
- Keen eye for detail to identify reimbursable services within care plans

- Ability to translate clinical observations into accurate MDS coding

A Day in the Life:

An MDS Coordinator starts their day by logging into their facility's electronic health record system. They might begin by reviewing new admissions and scheduling their initial assessments. Throughout the day, they could be analyzing assessment data, identifying care areas that need addressing, and collaborating virtually with the care team to develop personalized care plans. An MDS Coordinator might also find themself conducting training sessions for staff on proper assessment techniques, documentation or preparing reports for Medicare audits. A significant part of their day might involve reviewing care plans, identifying reimbursable goals, and ensuring that the facility's efforts towards these goals are well-documented. They will be part detective, part accountant, and part coder, piecing together the puzzle of resident needs, facility capabilities, and reimbursement opportunities.

How to Transition:

- Gain experience in long-term care: Most MDS Coordinator positions require at least 2-3 years of LTC experience.
- Get certified: Consider becoming a Resident Assessment Coordinator-Certified (RAC-CT) through the American Association of Nurse Assessment Coordination.

- Familiarize yourself with MDS software: Many facilities offer training, but prior experience is a plus.
- Brush up on Medicare regulations: Understanding PPS and case-mix systems is crucial in this role.

The Perks:

- Regular business hours, often with some flexibility
- Competitive salaries, sometimes with performance-based bonuses
- Opportunity to impact resident care on a facility-wide level
- Continuous learning as regulations and best practices evolve

Nurse Story: "I always thought being an MDS Coordinator was an RN only position. I was wrong. After looking into it, I took a brief course and became certified in less than a month. It has been an incredible experience ever since. I get to use my clinical skills to ensure residents receive appropriate care, and the facility is reimbursed for every aspect of care they provide, all while working from home. Plus, I love that I'm constantly learning and problem-solving." - Dana, LPN, Remote MDS Coordinator

Pro Tip: Many facilities are now open to remote MDS Coordinators, especially if you have experience with their specific software systems. Don't be afraid to approach facilities about remote work possibilities, even if they haven't advertised for it.

Ready to explore MDS Coordination opportunities? Check out the QR code at the end of this chapter for resources on MDS certification and job listings for remote MDS Coordinators.

Your Path to Work-From-Home Nursing

We've explored a wide range of work-from-home opportunities for nurses in this chapter, from Case Management and Clinical Documentation Improvement to MDS Coordination and Compliance Consulting. Each of these roles offers a unique way to leverage your nursing skills and experience while enjoying the benefits of working from home.

The key to success in any of these roles is to find the one that aligns with your skills, interests, and lifestyle needs. As we've seen, whether you're an RN or LPN, there are opportunities out there that can provide you with the work-life balance and job satisfaction you're seeking.

But don't just take my word for it. Let me introduce you to Jennifer Myers, a nurse who has successfully navigated the transition to work-from-home nursing. Jennifer currently balances working two days a week in the hospital with a work-from-home position for the rest of the week. Her journey exemplifies what's possible when you explore these opportunities.

Jennifer emphasizes, as I do, the importance of finding happiness in whatever you choose to do. Her TikTok content is a treasure trove of work-from-home resources and job opportunities for nurses.

And while this chapter focuses on popular remote roles, don't forget to look beyond traditional nursing spaces.
Pharmaceutical companies need clinical insight for compliance, side effect tracking, and education.
Tech firms — from EMR platforms to medical device startups — are looking for nurse voices in design, development, and product education.
Your expertise is more portable than you think.

As we wrap up this chapter, it's noteworthy to remember that the world of work-from-home nursing is constantly evolving. New opportunities emerge all the time — and with your clinical skills, your judgment, and your insight, you are already more qualified than you've been led to believe.

Nursing isn't just what you *do*. It's what you *know*.
And that knowledge has value far beyond the bedside.

Companies pay top dollar for experts, and that includes nurses who understand workflows, safety, compliance, education, and outcomes. You are more than your stellar attendance record. You are a licensed, experienced professional. Don't let a time clock define your worth. You are well-positioned to take advantage of these newly emerging positions.

In the next chapter, we'll explore how you can take these work-from-home opportunities a step further and start your own nurse-based business. But for now, take some time to reflect on the options we've discussed. Which ones resonate with you? What steps can you take to start exploring these opportunities?

Your journey to a more flexible, fulfilling nursing career starts here. For some of you, the roles in this chapter will be the destination. For others, they're just the beginning. Whether you're looking for a side gig or a complete career change, the world of work-from-home nursing is waiting for you to make your mark.

If this chapter gave you hope, you're going to love what comes next...

Scan to Access Tools for Chapter Five

Chapter 6: Direct Healthcare Ownership Opportunities - From Nurse to Entrepreneur

What would it feel like to set your own schedule, to make decisions about patient care without corporate constraints, to build a team that shares your vision for healthcare? How would it feel to create a workplace where nurses are happy, respected, supported, and empowered to provide the best possible care? Sounds like a great place to work!

The idea of owning your own healthcare business probably seems like a distant dream. I'm here to say, it's time to wake up to the possibilities. In this chapter, we're going to explore how you can take your nursing skills and experience and transform them into your very own healthcare business.

The leap from employee to owner is more than just a career change – it's a mindset shift. As an owner, you're upping the ante on responsibility. Every decision, from patient care protocols to staff management, rests on your shoulders. But with this increased responsibility comes an unprecedented level of control over your career trajectory and the ability to shape patient outcomes on a broader scale.

Imagine being able to create the kind of healthcare environment you've always envisioned – one where nursing staff are truly valued, where their expertise is recognized and rewarded. As an owner, you have the power to change the landscape of healthcare from the inside out, starting with how you treat and empower your own team.

In the pages ahead, we'll dive into various direct healthcare ownership opportunities, including:

- Home Health Agencies
- Personal assistance services
- Specialized Clinics
- Staffing
- Outpatient Surgery
- Other Direct Patient Care Businesses

For each of these, we'll explore the nuts and bolts of getting started, the challenges you might face, and the immense rewards that come with being your own boss in healthcare.

We'll also tackle the practical aspects of business ownership, from financial considerations and legal compliance, to building your team and marketing your services. Most importantly, we'll discuss how you can create a culture that values nurses and other healthcare professionals, setting a new standard in the industry.

Are you ready to trade your scrubs for a startup?

Let's begin this exciting journey!

Home Health Agencies: Riding the wave of the Silver Tsunami (And Loving Every Minute of It!)

Let's talk about a golden opportunity that's staring us right in the face - Home Health Agencies. And when I say golden, I mean it both figuratively and literally!

You've probably heard whispers about the "Silver Tsunami" - that massive wave of Baby Boomers entering their golden years. But here's the kicker: these aren't your grandma's seniors (no offense, Grandma). These folks are living longer, they're more active, and - here's the exciting part - they've got a more disposable income than any generation before them.

Now, put on your nurse entrepreneur's hat for a second. What do you get when you combine an aging population with a strong desire to stay in their own homes? Ding ding ding! You've got yourself a booming market for home health services.

"But Laurie," I hear you say, "starting a home health agency sounds complicated!" I get it. The idea of jumping from nurse to business owner can feel like trying to start an IV on a rollercoaster. But here's the thing - you've already got the hard part down. You know healthcare inside and out. The business side? That's just a new skill to master, and I know you're up for the challenge.

Let's break it down:

- **Medicare-Certified Home Health** agencies: Think of these as the Swiss

Army knives of home health. They provide skilled nursing, therapy services, and more, all covered by Medicare, Insurance and/or Medicaid. It's like bringing a mini hospital right to the patient's living room! (Don't get me started on the New *"Hospital at Home"* opportunities, because they are coming!) We all know hospital stays are getting shorter and shorter. Patients are getting sent home on IV antibiotics and Peritoneal dialysis, wound vacs and so much more. Post-Ops are immediate discharges now and the patients are going home with orders that were acute care exclusive 5 years ago. A Medicare certified Agency can and will meet them at their house and provide everything they need. You can be on the front line, with your own agency and the best team behind you, because they know you value them. Home Health can be challenging but it gives all the rushes of excitement without giving you nightmares when you lay your head down at night.

- **Home** *Care* **agencies** (or Personal Assistance Agencies): This is where you can really flex your entrepreneurial muscles. From medication management to companionship, you're offering a smorgasbord of services tailored to each client's needs. These Boomers want to age

111

in place. They're not "going to a home" is their mantra. So, we can support them. A person should be able to stay in their home for as long as they can safely do so. This generation is very service oriented, and they value that service. A Home Care agency can have a dozen clients and pull a 7-figure year. When you think about the numbers it's staggering. I've personally been a part of an agency owned by a CNA turned Administrator who made his first million in his first year. He never turned back.

- **Specialty agencies:** Got a passion for wound care? Obsessed with pediatric health? Have a passion for End-of-Life Care? This is your chance to become the go-to expert in your field. Look at your landscape. Explore your market. It will tell you what's needed. And to be completely transparent, if you have a specialty, you absolutely love, business will gravitate to you because it will be your soft spot. Network in your community. Stop by that Adult day care nearby, play a round of bingo, get to know your neighbors at the farmer's market. You'll find the gap to fill.

Now, I won't sugarcoat it - starting a home health agency isn't all sunshine and rainbows. There are

112

regulations to navigate, staff to hire, and marketing to do. But just think, when you first started nursing and everything seemed overwhelming but you did it anyway, right? This is different. You make the rules (well, except for the regulations) so you can hire someone to do the things you are weak in or simply don't like or want to do. You can also hire a consultant to mentor you along the way. Creating a strong team is part of the best leadership. I promise, I have seen hundreds of people who had zero experience, literally *zero* and they create very successful home health businesses simply because they were great leaders. Look at you. You've got this!

Here's a quick guide to get started:

- Dream big, plan smart: Develop a killer business plan. Think of it as a care plan, but for your business. We're going to help you with the basics in a later chapter.
- Show me the money: Secure that startup funding. Time to sweet-talk the bank, grab a partner, or cash in that 401K! This is your investment in *yourself*. Your happiness is worth every dime.
- Dot your I's and cross your T's: Get all your licenses and certifications in order. It's like charting, but for your business.
- Build your dream team: Hire staff who share your vision. You're not just building a business; you're creating a healthcare business. You'll value these people so much more than any other employer ever

has because you know exactly what they're feeling. That will have people lining up with you for the long haul. Spread the
- word: Market your agency like your business depends on it (because it does!). Your network is gold. Don't have one, get out there, join associations, show up at local groups and community events. I know it sounds hokey but stopping by the local wills and estate attorney's office with a snack basket and some business cards will make an impression for referrals every single time.

- Join the No More Scrubs™ Community, we can help with marketing ideas and support. With hundreds of people who have been there and have success stories or have failures you'll want to avoid, we have answers, plans and mentorship for days. Your network is your power.

Still feeling overwhelmed? Let me tell you about Jessica, a nurse who took the plunge five years ago. "I was terrified at first," she said, "but now? I'm providing the kind of personalized, quality care I always dreamed of. And let's just say, my bank account is a lot healthier too!" She partnered with her Mother-In-Law. Jessica is the DON, and her Mother-In-Law is the Administrator. They are an unstoppable team. Her MIL is always marketing and networking and Jess has all the regs and CMS tasks on point. They are the Dynamic Duo.

So, are you ready to catch this silver tsunami wave? The tide is rising, and it's bringing a sea of opportunities with it. It's time to grab your surfboard (or your stethoscope) and ride it all the way to success. You've got the skills, you've got the passion, and now you've got the know-how. All that's left is to take that first step. Your home health empire awaits!

Overview:

Types of Home Health Agencies:

- **Medicare-certified Home Health agencies**: Provide skilled nursing care, therapy, social services and nutrition services covered by Medicare and Medicaid.
- **Personal Assistance / Home** *Care* agencies: Offer a wider range of services, often including non-medical care at a longer period of time, paid out-of-pocket or through long-term care insurance.
- **Hospice Agencies:** Provide Medicare-certified, end-of-life care focused on comfort and quality of life rather than curative treatment. Services include skilled nursing, home health aides (CNAs), medical social workers, spiritual counselors, and trained volunteers. Hospice care also supports the patient's family through bereavement counseling and education, with care delivered in the

home, a facility, or inpatient setting when
needed.
- **Specialty agencies**: Focus on specific
conditions or types of care, such as
wound care, IV services hospital at home
and pediatric home health.

Steps to Starting a Home Health Agency:

Getting started requires a few clear steps — from
planning and licensure to team-building. Starting a
home health agency doesn't require a business degree,
just clarity and direction. We've included a full step-
by-step checklist in the companion workbook to walk
you through the basics — so you don't have to guess
what comes next.

Regulatory Requirements: Home health is heavily
regulated — but that doesn't mean it has to be
confusing. Whether you're Medicare-certified or state-
licensed, your team and paperwork need to reflect that
standard. To help you keep it clear, we've included a
regulatory and staffing overview in the companion
workbook with role definitions and prep notes.

Technology and Equipment: Investing in the right
technology can streamline your operations and
improve patient care. Don't let tech hold you back but
do set yourself up with the essentials.
We've listed key software, documentation tools, and
scheduling systems in the workbook so you can see
what's needed at a glance.

116

Marketing and Building Referral Relationships: Success in home health often depends on strong relationships. Marketing is one of the most powerful levers in this business. No business survives on passion alone, you'll need a referral map.
In the companion workbook, we've created a worksheet to help you map out referral sources, outreach scripts, and leave-behind ideas that don't feel awkward or pushy.

Common Challenges and Solutions:

- Regulatory compliance: Stay informed and consider hiring a compliance officer.
- Staff retention: Create a positive work culture and offer competitive benefits.
- Cash flow management: Implement efficient billing practices and consider a line of credit.
- Competition: Differentiate your agency through specialized services or exceptional quality of care.

Overview of Personal Assistance Services:

Personal Assistance Services, also known as non-medical home care, provide assistance with activities of daily living (ADLs) and instrumental activities of daily living (IADLs). These services are crucial for individuals, particularly seniors, who wish to maintain their independence and age in place.

Unlike Home Health Agencies, Personal Assistance Agencies in many states can be started without RN oversight, making them an attractive option for entrepreneurs with various backgrounds in healthcare.

Services typically include:

- Assistance with bathing, dressing, and grooming
- Meal planning, shopping, preparation and feeding assistance
- Light housekeeping and laundry
- Medication reminders (not administration)
- Transportation and errands
- Companionship

If you're leaning toward personal care or private duty services, the workbook outlines your steps for licensure, non-clinical staffing, and onboarding workflows.

The Concierge Care Opportunity:

It's important to note that Personal Assistance Agencies are highly sought after in the concierge care world. Baby Boomers, a generation with significant wealth, are determined to age in place and are willing to pay premium prices for high-quality, personalized care that allows them to do so.

While Personal Assistance Agencies can't offer medical services like in-home IV hydration, they can partner with or refer to companies that do, creating a comprehensive care network for client demand.

The Regulatory Landscape:

While Personal Assistance Agencies generally face fewer regulations than skilled nursing services, it's crucial to understand that regulations vary significantly by state.

Some key considerations:

- Licensing requirements: Most states require licenses for Personal Assistance Agencies, while others do not. Educate yourself on your local state regulations or contact a Consultation agency who can help you through the "start-up" process.
- Caregiver training: Requirements for caregiver training and certification vary by state, but if you've worked in healthcare at all the process of hiring a "home health aide" and the training required is a process easily learned.
- Insurance: Liability insurance is typically necessary, regardless of state requirements.

Tip: Always check with your specific state's Department of Health or Aging Services for exact requirements.

Starting Your Personal Assistance Agency:

- Market research: Understand the demographics and needs of your target area.
- Business planning: Develop a comprehensive business plan.

** *Be sure of your local state requirements*

- Funding: Secure necessary capital for startup costs.
- Legal structure: Establish your business entity (LLC, Corporation, etc.).
- Licensing: Obtain any required state licenses or registrations.
- Policies and procedures: Develop comprehensive operational guidelines.
- Staffing: Recruit, screen, and train caregivers.
- Marketing: Develop strategies to reach potential clients and referral sources.

Success Factors:

- Quality of care:
  - Prioritize training and oversight to ensure high-quality service.
  - Be consistent. Always provide the service promised to your client. The ability to show up when you say you're going to go a very long way with clients and will set you apart in the landscape.

- Client-centered approach: Tailor services to meet individual needs and preferences. Listen to your clients. In providing "Personal assistance services" this isn't a Medicare/Medicaid outlined service. All services are tailored to the clients' wishes if they are within the scope described in your state's regulations. Be attentive and listen to the client and their caregiver to be sure you're providing everything they need.

- Technology integration:
  - Use scheduling and communication tools to improve efficiency.
  - Emergency technology is also a consideration when starting your business. Be sure to have a plan that includes a way to communicate with staff and clients in the event of an emergency.

- Strong relationships:
  - Build partnerships with healthcare providers, senior communities, and other referral sources.
- Referring sources can quite literally be anyone. Your neighbor, your local deli counter guy, your dentist. This is a personalized service.

Watch for clues of caregiver fatigue, while at your local barber or hairdresser. Those conversations can be a goldmine.

The Personal Assistance Services sector offers a unique opportunity for nurse entrepreneurs to leverage their healthcare knowledge in a business with lower barriers to entry compared to skilled nursing services. By focusing on high-quality, personalized care, you can tap into a growing market of seniors determined to age in place, potentially creating a thriving and rewarding business that can average in the 7-figure range easily.

Concierge Nursing Agencies: Personalized Care for Discerning Clients

As we continue to explore entrepreneurial opportunities in nursing, let's dive into a growing niche that combines high-quality skilled care with premium service: Concierge Nursing Agencies. This category includes specialized services such as post-op care and post-partum support.

Overview: Concierge nursing agencies offer personalized, skilled nursing services to clients who desire or require more intensive, one-on-one care that traditional home health agencies would typically provide but are bound by Medicare/Medicaid guidelines as to the amount of time spent and the covered services provided. These agencies cater to clients who are willing to pay out-of-pocket for premium services and individualized attention.

Types of Concierge Nursing Services:

- General Concierge Nursing: Providing comprehensive, personalized care for clients with various health needs.
- Post-Op Care: Offering specialized care for patients recovering from surgery, ensuring smooth transitions from hospital to home and proper follow-up care.
- Post-Partum Support: Providing new mothers with expert care, lactation support, and newborn care education in the comfort of their homes.
- Wellness and Prevention: Offering health coaching, preventive care, and lifestyle management for health-conscious clients.
- Travel Nursing Companion: Providing nursing care for clients while they travel, ensuring continuity of care and peace of mind.

Key Advantages:

- Higher profit margins due to premium pricing
- More control over scheduling and caseload
- Opportunity to provide truly personalized, high-quality care
- Less reliance on insurance reimbursements
- Potential for building long-term relationships with clients

Starting a Concierge Nursing Agency:

- Define Your Niche: Decide which specialized services you'll offer based on your expertise and local market needs.
- Develop a Business Plan: Outline your services, target market, pricing strategy, and financial projections.
- Legal Structure: Set up your business entity and obtain necessary licenses and insurance.
- Staffing: Recruit highly skilled nurses who excel in customer service and clinical care.
- Marketing: Develop strategies to reach high-net-worth individuals, partner with luxury hotels, high-end obstetricians, or plastic surgeons depending on your niche.
- Technology: Invest in scheduling software and secure communication

platforms to ensure smooth operations and client privacy.

- Quality Assurance: Implement rigorous quality control measures to maintain the premium nature of your services.

Nurse Story: Lisa, an experienced RN, started "Elite Post-Op Care," a concierge nursing agency specializing in post-operative care. "I saw a gap in the market for patients who wanted more personalized care after complex surgeries," she explains. "We provide 24/7 care in the client's home or a hotel suite near the surgery center, coordinate with their surgical team, and offer a level of attention that surpasses what's typically available. It's demanding work but incredibly rewarding both professionally and financially."

Regulatory Considerations: While concierge nursing agencies often face fewer regulatory hurdles than Medicare-certified home health agencies, it's crucial to:

- Ensure all nurses are properly licensed and credentialed
- Maintain proper insurance coverage, including professional liability insurance
- Develop clear service agreements outlining the scope of care provided
- Stay informed about any state-specific regulations governing private duty nursing

Concierge and post-op nursing are rising fast, and they require a different kind of planning. This model, including specialized post-op and post-partum care, offers a unique opportunity for nurses to provide high-quality, personalized care while building a profitable business. By focusing on premium services and exceptional customer care, nurse entrepreneurs can create successful agencies that cater to clients seeking a higher level of attention and service in their healthcare experience.

If this kind of hands-on, patient-centered model excites you — you're not alone. We've outlined the core planning prompts in the companion workbook, including service menu tips, pricing notes, and ways to market yourself confidently.

Specialized Clinics: Advanced Practice Opportunities

As we delve deeper into direct healthcare ownership opportunities, it's important to highlight a category that's particularly suited for Advanced Practice Registered Nurses (APRNs), especially Nurse Practitioners (NPs): specialized clinics. While this option may not be accessible to all nurses, it represents a significant opportunity for those with advanced degrees and certifications.

Before we begin, it's crucial to understand that regulatory requirements for these clinics vary significantly from state to state. Some states grant NPs full practice authority, allowing them to operate independently, while others require physician collaboration or supervision. Always check your state's specific regulations before embarking on this path.

Types of Specialized Clinics:

- Primary Care Clinics: Offering general health services to a specific population (e.g., pediatrics, women's health, geriatrics).
- Condition-Specific Clinics: Focusing on managing health issues like diabetes, hypertension, behavioral, addiction or mental health.
- Aesthetic Clinics: Providing services such as Botox injections, dermal fillers, and other cosmetic procedures. These clinics have seen a surge in popularity and can be a lucrative option for NPs with appropriate training.
- Hydration Clinics: Offering IV hydration therapy for various purposes, from hangover relief to athletic recovery. This is a growing trend in the wellness sector.
- Wellness and Prevention Clinics: Concentrating on holistic health, nutrition counseling, and preventive care.

Getting Started:

- Assess Your Qualifications: Ensure you have the necessary certifications and experience for your chosen specialty.

- Market Research: Identify gaps in your local healthcare market that align with your expertise.
- Business Planning: Develop a comprehensive business plan, including financial projections and marketing strategies.
- Legal Structure: Decide on your business structure (LLC, S-Corp etc.) and register your business.
- Licensing and Certifications: Obtain all necessary state and local licenses and certifications.
- Location and Equipment: Secure a suitable location and invest in necessary medical equipment.
- Insurance: Obtain malpractice insurance and other relevant coverage.
- Staffing: Hire additional staff as needed, including administrative support.

Medical Director Oversight:

It's worth noting that obtaining a Medical Director (a licensed physician to provide oversight) is often not as challenging as it might seem. Many physicians find this role attractive as it can provide additional revenue with a relatively small, time investment. This can be particularly important in states where NPs don't have full practice authority.

Key Considerations:

- Scope of Practice: Understand and adhere to your state's regulations regarding NP practice.
- Collaboration Agreements: If required, establish clear agreements with collaborating physicians.
- Insurance and Billing: Set up systems for insurance billing and consider options for cash-pay services.
- Technology: Invest in electronic health records and practice management software.
- Marketing: Develop strategies to attract patients and build referral networks.
- Continuing Education: Stay updated with the latest developments in your specialty.

Nurse Story:

Meet Somer, an NP who opened a women's health clinic in a suburban area. "I saw a need for comprehensive women's health services that went beyond what was offered in traditional OB/GYN offices," she says. "We offer everything from annual exams and contraception counseling to menopause management and sexual health services. It was challenging to start but being able to provide the kind of patient-centered care I've always envisioned is incredibly rewarding."

Specialized clinics offer APRNs an exciting opportunity to leverage their expertise, provide focused care, and enjoy the benefits of business ownership. While the regulatory landscape can be complex, the potential for professional autonomy and financial reward makes this an attractive option for many advanced practice nurses.

Residential Assisted Living: Redefining Senior Care on Your Terms

As nurses, we've all seen the gaps in senior care - the understaffing, the cookie-cutter approaches, the lack of dignity. But what if you could change that? Residential Assisted Living (RAL) offers an opportunity to revolutionize senior care while building a fulfilling business that values your expertise.

RAL facilities provide a middle ground between independent living and traditional nursing homes. They're smaller, more personalized environments where seniors receive the support they need while maintaining their autonomy. And who better to create and run these facilities than nurses who understand the nuances of quality care?

This isn't just about opening a business; it's about leveraging your hard-earned skills and knowledge to create a care model that you can be proud of. One where you set the standards, where your staff is valued, and where residents receive the individualized attention, they deserve.

The RAL market is growing rapidly, driven by an aging population that's looking for better options. This presents a unique opportunity for nurses to step into entrepreneurship and make a significant impact.

Key considerations for starting an RAL facility include:

- Understanding state-specific regulations
- Selecting and adapting appropriate properties
- Developing comprehensive care protocols
- Building a team that shares your vision for quality care
- Creating marketing strategies to reach potential residents and their families

Yes, it's challenging. But as a nurse, you're no stranger to challenges. You've navigated complex healthcare systems, managed difficult situations, and advocated for your patients. Those same skills will serve you well as an RAL owner.

This is your chance to create the kind of care environment you've always envisioned - one that respects both the residents and the staff. It's an opportunity to build a business that aligns with your values and allows you to shape the future of senior care.

Are you ready to take your expertise to the next level and create a senior care facility that sets new standards in the industry? Your experience, your vision, and your dedication to quality care could be the foundation of a successful RAL business. It's time to turn your frustrations with the current system into action and build something that truly makes a difference.

The changing dynamics of family caregiving are also driving the demand for RAL facilities. Unlike previous generations, many adult children of Baby Boomers are less inclined to become full-time caregivers for their aging parents. Life has changed. We no longer have a stay-at-home spouse who can adjust her daily schedule to take care of Mom or Dad. Both partners are working full-time jobs and if they have kids that stretches them even further. This shift is partly due to changing family structures, increased geographic dispersion, and evolving perspectives on familial obligations. Many Gen Xers, feel they received less support during their own upbringing, are seeking alternative care options for their parents that don't require them to sacrifice their careers or personal lives. This trend is creating a growing market for professional, home-like care environments such as RAL facilities.

This brings me to Tonia. Tonia is a passionate RAL owner I've had the pleasure of getting to know via TikTok. Tonia owns five RAL facilities in the Tampa area. She has only been in the business for 4 years. She also has just bought land to build a 6th. Her journey is a testament to what's possible when you combine passion for quality care with entrepreneurial spirit.

Tonia built her RAL empire from the ground up, handling everything herself in the beginning. Even now, with five thriving facilities under her belt, she hasn't lost touch with the day-to-day operations. Every weekend, she personally conducts rounds at her facilities, ensuring everything is running smoothly and taking the time to check in on her residents. For Tonia, this isn't just a business - it's a calling.

Of course, the path hasn't always been smooth. Tonia has faced her share of challenges, particularly with Homeowners Associations (HOAs) that were initially resistant to having RAL facilities in their neighborhoods. But her perseverance and commitment to providing exceptional care have won over even the toughest critics. Tonia is no shrinking violet. She'll tell you what it is and how to get it done.

What sets Tonia apart is her unwavering dedication to her vision of what senior care should be. She's created environments where residents truly feel at home, where staff feel valued and empowered, and where families have peace of mind knowing their loved ones are receiving top-notch care. Her facilities are absolutely Beautiful and top of the line. Her residents are comfortable and well taken care of. Please have a look at my interview with Tonia by scanning the QR code below.

Tonia's story shows us that success in the RAL business isn't just about the bottom line - it's about passion, perseverance, and a genuine desire to improve the lives of seniors. Her journey from nurse to successful RAL owner is an inspiring example of how you can leverage your nursing skills and experience to create something truly meaningful and financially rewarding.

Conclusion: Charting Your Course in Direct Patient Care Entrepreneurship

We've explored a range of direct patient care opportunities - from home health agencies and personal assistance services to specialized clinics and residential assisted living facilities. Each of these paths offers a unique way to leverage your nursing skills and experience to create a business that aligns with your values and vision for healthcare.

These opportunities aren't just about becoming your own boss or increasing your income (although those are certainly appealing benefits). They're about reshaping healthcare from the ground up, creating environments where both patients and healthcare professionals are truly valued. It's where you create your own happiness. You can finally have a career, you're happy to be a part of day in and day out. By the way you'll never have to fight for a PTO day again.

As you consider these options, your years of nursing experience have equipped you with more than just clinical skills. You've developed problem-solving abilities, emotional intelligence, and a deep understanding of patient needs - all invaluable assets in the world of healthcare entrepreneurship.

Whether you're drawn to the personalized care of a home health agency, the specialized focus of a boutique clinic, or the community-building aspect of a residential assisted living facility, there's a path that can align with your passions and strengths.

The journey from being a nurse to being a healthcare entrepreneur isn't always easy, but it can be incredibly rewarding. You have the power to create the kind of healthcare environment you've always envisioned - one that prioritizes quality care, respects healthcare professionals, and makes a real difference in people's lives. You control the narrative.

As we move forward, we'll shift our focus from direct patient care to new ventures in healthcare-adjacent services. These are opportunities that leverage your nursing knowledge and skills in non-traditional ways, opening up even more possibilities for your entrepreneurial journey.

The next chapter will delve into areas such as healthcare consulting, health tech and innovation, and medical device development. These fields offer exciting ways to impact healthcare on a broader scale, influencing systems and technologies that can improve patient care and healthcare delivery across the board. So, let's continue our exploration of the vast landscape of nursing entrepreneurship. The skills you've honed at the bedside may be the key to revolutionizing healthcare in ways you've never imagined. Are you ready to discover how your nursing expertise can shape the future of healthcare beyond direct patient care? Let's dive in!

Scan to Access Tools for Chapter Six

Chapter 7: The Consulting Path: Turning Expertise into Income

Okay, that was alot of information. Right?

Let's take a moment to catch our breath. We've covered a lot of ground so far, haven't we? We've talked about the challenges of bedside nursing, discovered our hidden superpowers, and even explored some exciting work-from-home opportunities. But here's the thing – there's even more.

When you decided to go to Nursing School, you thought nursing was all about hospitals and clinics, right? Well, buckle up, because we're about to blow that idea wide open.

You've been consulting for free your whole career — giving guidance, fixing broken processes, writing policies, training new hires, calming survey chaos — and never once realizing those were billable services. Let's change that.

In this chapter, we're shifting the lens. You're not "just a nurse." You're someone with expert insight into how healthcare actually works. And there are companies, startups, long-term care chains, even solo agency owners that are desperate for your kind of brain.

Whether it's helping an agency survive survey prep, launching QAPI processes, building staff education, or simply rewriting broken systems, consulting is how you reclaim the value of what you already know.

You're about to learn how to stop giving away your brilliance for free — and start building income, impact, and independence one insight at a time.

Think about it for a second. You're a problem-solver, a communicator, an educator, a strong decision maker and let's face it, probably a mind-reader some days. These skills? They're gold in the business world my friend.

So, grab your coffee (or wine, or heck, that green smoothie you've been meaning to try), and let's dive into some exciting ways you can put your nursing superpowers to work outside the traditional healthcare setting. We're talking about consulting.

And don't worry, I promise we'll look at real examples of nurses who've ventured into these fields. Because sometimes we need to see it to believe it, right?

You're now ready to explore the wild and wonderful world of healthcare-consulting opportunities. Let's do this.

Healthcare Consulting: From Following Orders to Calling the Shots

Let's start with Healthcare Consulting. Up until 5 years ago, I didn't even know this existed, or what its purpose was. Now, I know what you're thinking. "Consulting? Isn't that for suits with MBAs?" Maybe for some, but from what I've experienced, it's for everyone from Billion-dollar corporations to small 2-person home health start-ups.

Think about all those times you looked at a process in your unit, in your agency, on your floor and thought, "This is ridiculous. There's got to be a better way to do this"? Or when you rolled your eyes at yet another policy that clearly wasn't written by someone who'd ever set foot on a floor? Guess what? That right there, is the foundation of a consulting career.

As nurses, we're on the front lines. We see what works, what doesn't, and most importantly, why. That insider knowledge is gold. And it's time we started treating it that way.

Take Chrys, for example. After 10 years as a nurse, she was fed up with the constant stress of nursing and short staffing. So, she decided to be the solution. Now, she runs a successful consulting business, helping hospitals, long-term care facilities and healthcare corporations with all aspects of their businesses. "I'm still using my nursing skills," she says, "but now I'm calling the shots and making three times what I did in my previous nursing positions."

The best part? You're not just clock-punching anymore. You're leveraging your expertise to improve healthcare quality on a broader scale. Chrys says in her meetings she is usually the only clinical person in the room, so her expertise is always valued. And let's be honest, it feels pretty good to be the expert that administrators turn to finally.

Let's break down some areas where your nursing know-how can translate into a lucrative consulting career:

Survey Preparation and Compliance

The feeling of panic that sets in when you hear "The Joint Commission is here". Well, what if I told you that you could be the calm in that storm and get paid handsomely for it?

Survey Preparation Consulting is a field where your experience can shine. You know the standards inside and out because you've lived them. But here's the kicker - you also know where the skeletons are buried. Your time in the trenches means you've seen firsthand where facilities tend to fall short, where the vulnerabilities lie, and what surveyors are likely to zero in on. This insider knowledge makes you uniquely qualified to help healthcare organizations prepare for surveys, whether it's from The Joint Commission, state health departments, or CMS. You're not just familiar with the rules; you understand the real-world challenges of implementing them and where things are most likely to go wrong. That's the kind of insight that administrators desperately need but rarely have access to.

Here's what this might look like:

- Conducting mock surveys to identify areas of improvement
- Helping facilities develop and implement Plans of Correction
- Setting up QAPI (Quality Assurance Performance Improvement) programs
- Preparing organizations for accreditation processes

So, next time you're grumbling about another policy that doesn't make sense, you're not just a nurse following orders. You're a consultant with the power to shape how healthcare organizations operate. And trust me, that power feels pretty darn good.

Quality Improvement Consulting: Turning Frustrations into Solutions

Picture this: You're trudging through a 20-step infection reporting process for the 10th time this year that hasn't been updated since the Clinton administration. You know it's inefficient and this is a trend, you know it caused issues in your last survey, and you know exactly how to fix it. But every time you bring it up, you're met with shrugs and "that's just how we do it." Sound familiar?

Welcome to the world of Quality Improvement Consulting, where your frustration with outdated processes isn't just valid – it's essential.

As nurses, we're on the front lines. We see firsthand what works, what doesn't, and most importantly, why. That insider knowledge? It's everything in the world of quality improvement consulting.

So, what exactly does a Quality Improvement Consultant do? Glad you asked!

As a QAPI consultant, you might:

- Analyze healthcare processes to identify inefficiencies and areas for improvement.
- Develop and implement strategies to enhance patient safety and outcomes.
- Help organizations meet quality benchmarks and improve their quality scores.
- Train staff in quality improvement methodologies.
- Facilitate process improvement projects.
- Update outdated policies and procedures to meet current state and federal regs.

Now, I know what you're thinking. "But Laurie, I'm not a quality expert!" Here's the thing: as a nurse, you're more of an expert than you realize. What about all those times you've made a point of reporting the same issues over and over to get things changed? That's quality improvement in action!

After 12 years as a Home Health Nurse, Kellie was fed up with the constant "band-aid" solutions to recurring problems and the halfhearted measures on creating new, more efficient and compliant processes. "I kept thinking, if only administration would listen to us nurses, we could fix these issues once and for all," she says.

That frustration led Kellie to get her QCP certification, with the American Association of Post-Acute Care Nursing (AAPACN). Now, she runs her own consulting business, helping Home Health agencies and Assisted Living facilities streamline their processes and improve patient outcomes.

Kellie says, her eyes lighting up, "I'm finally doing work that truly excites me. Every day brings a new challenge, a new puzzle to solve. I'm not just treating symptoms anymore – I'm curing systemic issues. And when I see processes improve, knowing it's going to make life better for both patients and staff? That feeling is absolutely priceless.

And let's talk about lifestyle changes. Kellie sets her own schedule, works with a variety of healthcare organizations, and is happier now that her work-life balance is exactly what she wants it to be. "Don't get me wrong, it's still hard work," she admits. "But now, when I solve a problem, it doesn't just help one person – it can impact patient care across an entire healthcare system."

So, the next time you're rolling your eyes at an inefficient process or a quality metric that doesn't reflect reality, you're not just a nurse dealing with a broken system. You could be a quality improvement consultant with the power to fix that system. And trust me, there are plenty of healthcare organizations out there willing to pay good money for your insights.

Healthcare Policy and Regulatory Compliance Consulting: Shaping the Future of Healthcare
Imagine waking up every morning excited, eager to dive into your day's work? Sound too good to be true? Well, welcome to my world, the world of Healthcare Policy and Regulatory Compliance Consulting. This is my specialty now. I have worked in Policy and Regulatory compliance for a while now. It's not something I ever thought about but like many others in this book, it fell into my lap. Later in this section I'll explain how I got into it and how I learned it's a very big area of need in the Healthcare community.

In this role, you're not just following the rules – you're helping shape them. You're taking your years of frontline experience and using it to influence policies that affect patient care on a broad scale while staying in line with compliance regulations. It's about reclaiming your voice in healthcare and using it to drive positive changes.

Let me tell you how I stumbled into the world of Healthcare Policy and Regulatory Compliance Consulting. It's a classic case of "right place, right time" with a dash of "be careful what you're good at, you might just make a career out of it!"

It all started when I was hired as an Administrator for a Home Health Agency. The owners, bless their hearts, decided I needed to join them at a "Boot Camp" for startups run by a company called Healthcare Consulting Company. Little did I know, this *boot camp* would be the launchpad for my consulting career.

Now, I had been in home health for years, and let's just say I had a few questions. Okay, more than a few. By the end of the boot camp, I think the presenters were a bit shell-shocked by my knowledge of Florida home health regulations. But here's the kicker – a few weeks later, the main presenter called me and offered me a job!

Before I knew it, I was diving deep into state home health regulations across the country. I became the go-to person for regulatory questions. Even the other nurse consultants started calling me to double-check state-specific regulations. Talk about a plot twist in my career!

These days, I do it all – licensing application consultations, policy revisions, continuing education, onboarding in-services, ADRs (Additional Development Requests), and my personal favorite: Plans of Correction.

Let me tell you about my first Plan of Correction for a client. I spent 16 hours on it, submitted my invoice, and nearly fell off my chair when I saw the payment $2,500! That's when it hit me: not only was there a huge need for this kind of expertise, but it was also a fantastic opportunity for nurses to leverage their knowledge in a whole new way.

The best part? I wake up every morning excited about my work. I'm not just following regulations – I'm helping healthcare organizations understand and implement them effectively. It's challenging, it's *always* changing, and it allows me to use my nursing experience in ways I never imagined.

So, if you're a nurse with a knack for details and a passion for doing things right, let me tell you, there's a whole world of opportunity waiting for you in Healthcare Policy and Regulatory Compliance Consulting. And trust me, it's a world where your nursing expertise isn't just valued, it's something truly sought after.

Since that eye-opening start, I've taken my expertise to the next level. I've earned consultant certifications from CHAP, ACHC, and JCAHO. These certifications aren't just fancy acronyms – they're keys that have unlocked doors to helping hundreds of brand-new home health agencies get their licenses.

And let me tell you, there's nothing quite like the thrill of helping someone start their own healthcare business. It's like being a midwife for entrepreneurs –

you're there for the labor pains of paperwork and the joy of seeing their dream come to life. It's exhilarating, and it never gets old.

Want to know the best part? It's waking up on a Saturday morning and knowing – really knowing – that work isn't going to intrude. No on-call shifts. No worries about a caregiver not showing up or a patient's condition worsening. Just me, my coffee, and the freedom to enjoy my weekend. And when I do work, I can do it from anywhere with Wi-Fi. No office politics, no stress – just the satisfaction of doing work I love, on my own terms.

Here's something that might surprise you: there are million-dollar companies out there charging thousands to help existing agencies navigate the murky waters of compliance. But here's the secret, a nurse with experience in home health, long-term care, or assisted living is worth their weight in gold to any owner needing compliance help. Your hands-on experience gives you insights that no textbook can teach. You know the regs. You've been there, done that, argued with the surveyors and won!

So, if you're intrigued by this path, here's my advice: start by taking a few classes with accrediting bodies. Learn your local state regulations inside and out. Use your network – those connections you've made over the years are invaluable. Join local healthcare business groups. Trust me, compliance consultants are rare and in high demand these days.

In the world of healthcare policy and compliance consulting, your nursing experience isn't just valuable — it's your superpower. You understand the real-world implications of policies and regulations in a way that non-clinical consultants simply can't. And that understanding? It's what can set you apart in this field.

So, if you're looking for a way to use your nursing skills that offers flexibility, intellectual challenge, and the chance to shape healthcare from a whole new angle — well, welcome to my world. The world of healthcare policy and compliance consulting just might be your next exciting chapter.

Scan to Access Tools for Chapter Seven

Chapter 8: Education & Systems — Teaching What You Know

You've been a nurse-educator longer than you realize. Every time you trained a new hire, built an orientation binder, or translated a clunky EHR workflow into something usable — you were doing billable work.

In this chapter, we're going to flip the script on how you see your own expertise.
Whether it's onboarding new teams, customizing EHR rollouts, or teaching OASIS with clarity — you already have the skills. Now it's time to turn that know-how into income.

Because if you've ever said, "This whole process would fall apart if I didn't keep explaining it," congratulations — you're already a systems consultant. Let's show you how to make it official.

EHR Consulting

Alright, my fellow nurse managers, what is something we all love (or love to hate): training and electronic health records.
Now, before you roll your eyes and reach for that second cup of coffee, hear me out.

When you first started using your EHR system were you a whiz?
Or when you had to onboard a new nurse and show them the ropes?
I'll bet you wished there was someone who could

make that whole process smoother, right?
Well, guess what? That someone could be you.

Educational Development and EHR Consulting is a field that's practically begging for nurses to step in. Why? Because we're the ones who actually use these systems day in and day out.
We know what works, what doesn't, and most importantly, how to explain it in a way that doesn't make people want to throw their computers out the window.
Here's what this kind of consulting might look like:

Remote Onboarding and Training

Instead of healthcare organizations hiring a full-time staff development person (who, more often than not gets pulled into staffing anyway) they could hire you - a remote consultant, to handle all their onboarding and ongoing training needs. Some agencies would jump at the chance to have someone contracted, rather than pay a full-time staff person, to save them start-up money.
You could develop orientation programs, create training materials, and even conduct virtual training sessions. And the best part? You could do this for multiple organizations, all from the comfort of your home office (or your couch, we don't judge).

EHR Implementation and Training

Let's talk about EHRs. We all know that the training provided by EHR developers often leaves a lot to be desired. It's usually too generic, too rushed, and too tech based. It doesn't account for the specific needs of different departments, specialties or patients. That's because the people who are doing those trainings built the software. They're tech people. They're not healthcare people. They don't have your hands-on experience. They know the *tools* and how they're *suppose* to work but they can't apply them to the nurse's real-life process. This is where you come in. As a nurse, you understand the workflow. You know the questions and concerns your colleagues are likely to have. You can bridge the gap between the technical aspects of the EHR and the practical needs of healthcare providers.

You could offer:

- Customized EHR training for different specialties or departments

- Ongoing support and education as EHR systems are updated
-Consultation with the EHR software company for optimization and ways to improve workflow and patient care documentation

Take Stephen, for example. After 14 years as an ICU manager, and part-time tech guru, he was known as the go-to person for anything EHR-related. "I felt like I was spending more time teaching people how to use the system than I was caring for patients," he says. "So I thought, why not make this my full-time gig?"

Today, Stephen runs a thriving consulting business, helping healthcare businesses implement and optimize their EHR systems. Working mostly from home, he enjoys the flexibility of setting his own schedule while earning more than he ever did at the bedside. "The best part," he says with a smile, "is being home every night for dinner with my family. By turning what came naturally to me into a career, I've found a way to love nursing in a whole new way."

So, the next time you're explaining to a colleague for the hundredth time how to document something in the EHR, you're not just a nurse. You're a potential educator, trainer, and EHR guru. And trust me, there are plenty of organizations out there willing to pay good money for your expertise.

OASIS and Reimbursement Consultation for Home Health Agencies

Now, for those of you with home health experience, let's talk about everyone's favorite topic: OASIS and reimbursement. (I can almost hear the collective groan!) We all know that accurate OASIS documentation is crucial for home health agencies. It's not just about compliance. It directly impacts reimbursement and, ultimately, the agency's bottom line. But truthfully, it's also complex, time-consuming, and often a major headache for agencies trying to maximize their reimbursement while staying compliant. Nurses are interested in the business part of patient care. They just want to provide care. So how do you train a Nurse to see it from both sides?

This is where you, as a consultant, can really make a difference. Think about it. How many times have you seen OASIS assessments that were incomplete or inaccurate? Or agencies struggling to understand why their reimbursement doesn't match the care they're providing and payroll? As an OASIS and Reimbursement Consultant, you can offer:

-OASIS accuracy audits to identify areas of improvement
-Strategies to optimize OASIS documentation for appropriate reimbursement
-Analysis of an agency's case mix to ensure they're capturing all billable services
-Guidance on navigating the complex world of Medicare reimbursement for home health
-Training on how OASIS impacts the agency's quality measures and star ratings.

Take Barbara, for instance. After 15 years as a home health nurse and then administrator, she had a wealth of knowledge for OASIS. So much so that at every networking event someone would ask her an OASIS question. "When I realized this was a thing and agencies were leaving money on the table because of poor OASIS understanding or just plain inaccurate documentation compliance, it was an easy side gig. It quickly evolved and replaced the everyday responsibilities of my Administrator position. I could make my own schedule. Work with whomever I wanted to and enjoy my new freedom." she says.

"I saw an opportunity and grabbed it." Now, Barbara works remotely, analyzing agencies' documentation and providing targeted recommendations. "The best part," Barbara says "is seeing the impact. When an agency implements my recommendations, they often see a significant increase in their reimbursement sometimes as much as 20%. And it's not about gaming the system it's about accurately capturing the care they're already providing." So, the next time you're puzzling over a denial or an ADR and finally figure out why your agency's reimbursement is lower than what you expected, know that your OASIS expertise is incredibly valuable and can afford you the work life balance you've been craving.

There's a whole world of home health agencies out there who would love to have your knowledge. Working with them as a consultant can help them navigate the complex world of OASIS and reimbursement and give you the feeling of being valued for what you know instead of what you do. That's what this is all about, right? Consulting isn't just about sharing your expertise. It's about being recognized and compensated for the incredible value you bring. It's about taking those skills you've honed over years of hands-on experience and using them to make a broader impact. And if you're honest with yourself it's probably been a while since you've felt good to be the expert in the room.

Now, agencies can turn to you when they're in a bind. How would that feel?

So, are you ready to turn your OASIS headaches into a thriving consulting career? Trust me, there are plenty of home health agencies out there who would see you as their OASIS superhero!

Scan to Access Tools for Chapter Eight

Chapter 9 Legal & Policy
The Nurse is the Expert Witness

You've already been reading between the lines of medical records for years. Now, you can get paid for it **Legal Nurse Consulting**: Where Medicine Meets the Law

Let's talk about a field that might make you feel like you're starring in your own episode of "Law & Order: Nursing Unit". Legal Nurse Consulting. This is where your clinical expertise becomes a secret weapon in the legal world.

What is Legal Nurse Consulting? As a Legal Nurse Consultant (LNC), you'll use your medical knowledge to assist attorneys in cases involving health, illness, or injury. You're essentially the translator between the medical and legal worlds, helping lawyers understand the nuances of healthcare that can make or break a case.

I could tell you all day what legal nurse consultants do but it's better to show you what it looks like in real life. Meet Abigail. Her story might just feel a little familiar. Abigail is a former Acute Care nurse who now runs a successful Legal Nurse Consulting business. "One afternoon a friend of mine who was a Lawyer asked me how much I made. I looked at him kind of funny and asked why? He then said, I'll pay you more!". I turned him down, but went into business for myself and that same friend has been paying me $150 an hour for my services. The rest is history. Now, I use my Nursing skills to help attorneys understand the medical aspects of their cases. Last year my business cleared 7 figures. I would never have done that at the bedside."

Abigail's favorite part? The intellectual challenge. *"Every case is like a puzzle. I get to dive deep into medical records, research best practices, and then explain my findings in a way that non-medical professionals can understand."*

Best Perk of all? The pay is great, and I work on *my* terms! I work with clients I choose, and I work when I want. I'm making more than I ever would have and this is *MY* business. I couldn't be happier"

Feeling that little spark of curiosity? Let's fan the flame — because now that you've seen what's possible, it's time to talk about what legal nurse consultants actually *do*. This is where your clinical brain, attention to detail, and years of real-world experience become billable assets. Here's how it works.

What do Legal Nurse Consultants Do?

- Review and analyze medical records for attorneys
- Identify and explain the significance of medical facts in legal cases
- Educate attorneys about medical terminology and procedures

155

- Assist in preparing for depositions of healthcare providers
- Serve as expert witnesses in trials
- Help attorneys understand standards of care and potential deviations

Why Nurses Excel at This:

- You understand medical terminology, procedures, and standards of care
- You have experience reading and interpreting medical records
- Your critical thinking skills help you spot inconsistencies or red flags in cases
- You can explain complex medical concepts in understandable terms

Getting Started:

- Consider getting certified as a Legal Nurse Consultant (LNCC)
- Familiarize yourself with legal terminology and processes
- Network with local law firms specializing in medical malpractice or personal injury
- Develop a portfolio showcasing your medical expertise and analytical skills

The Perks:

- High earning potential (LNCs can charge significant hourly rates)

- Intellectually stimulating work that combines medicine and law
- Flexibility to work independently or with law firms
- Opportunity to make a difference in ensuring justice in healthcare-related cases

The Challenges:

- Need to stay updated on both medical advancements and legal precedents
- Potentially emotionally challenging cases
- Building a client base in a competitive field

So, what do you think? You're still solving problems. Only now, you're not charting vitals, you're charting the course of a legal case. Every time you've pieced together a patient's story from their medical record or explained a complex procedure to a family member; you've been honing skills that are incredibly valuable in the legal world. It's time to take those skills to the courtroom (or at least to a law office near you) and turn them into a thriving Legal Nurse Consulting business!

Scan to Access Tools for Chapter Nine

Chapter 10 Health Tech and Innovation:

Your Experience Is the Blueprint for Better Tools

So, it's 7:30 PM, your 12-hour shift ended half an hour ago, but here you are, still clicking through screens in the EHR, trying to finish your charting. Sound familiar? Or maybe you're a home health nurse, finally home after a long day of patient visits, only to face another few hours of documentation before you can truly call it a day.

Can we talk about how many times we've complained saying, "There's got to be a better way to do this"? Well, you're absolutely right. And here's the kicker — you, yes YOU, could be the one to create that better way.

Welcome to the world of Health Tech and Innovation, where nurses are turning their daily frustrations into groundbreaking solutions.

Have you heard of the Beata Clasp we talked about earlier? That nifty device that keeps IV lines organized and out of the way. It wasn't invented by some tech guru who's never set foot in a hospital. Nope, it was created by Lenore Henning, a nurse who got fed up with tangled IV lines and decided to do something about it.

And that's just the tip of the iceberg. From streamlining EHR workflows to developing apps that make patient education a breeze, nurses across the country are leveraging their frontline experience to revolutionize healthcare technology.

In this section, we're going to explore how you can join this wave of nurse innovators. We'll look at areas like:

- Medical device development (spoiler alert: it's not just for engineers!)
- Health apps and software (because who better to design them than the people who'll use them?)
- Telemedicine and digital health platforms (bringing healthcare into the 21st century, finally!)
- Wearable technology in healthcare (making "I've fallen, and I can't get up" a thing of the past)
- AI and machine learning in nursing (no, the robots aren't coming for your job — they're here to make it easier)

So, the next time you're grumbling about staying late to finish charting or wrestling with a piece of equipment that seems designed by someone who's never actually used it, you're not just dealing with a problem. You're looking at an opportunity. An opportunity to innovate, to create, and to shape the future of healthcare technology.

Ready to turn your "there's got to be a better way" into "I've got a better way"? Let's dive in!

Medical Device Development and Healthcare Innovation: You're Already an Innovator!

Okay, nurses, pop quiz time: Have you ever designed a more comfortable fluid drainage bag for a patient to wear? Or maybe you've given a confused patient a soft booty to hug like a stuffed animal to keep them from pulling out their IV lines?

If you've done anything like this - and I bet you have - then congratulations! You're already an innovator.

That's right. All those times you've thought, "There's got to be a better way," and then found that better way? That's innovation, my friends. And it's high time we recognized it for what it is.

You see, innovation isn't always about inventing the next big gadget or writing complex software. Sometimes, it's as simple as figuring out a more efficient way to organize your supply cart or coming up with a clever trick to help a patient remember their medication schedule.

As one nurse put it, "Nurses are naturally gifted problem solvers. Whether it be designing and improving new products, like more comfortable fluid drainage bags for people to wear or giving a confused patient a soft booty to hug like a stuffed animal so they quit pulling their IV lines out, nurses are constantly innovating. As nurses, we do it because we see a need, so we take action to make things better."

That last part is key: we see a need, so we act. That's the essence of innovation, and it's baked into our DNA as nurses.

Have you heard of "Cluster Nursing"? That brilliant idea of grouping tasks together to reduce trips in and out of a patient's room? That wasn't dreamed up in a boardroom or a tech lab. That came from nurses like you and me, looking at our workflow and thinking, "How can we do this better?"

Every day, in hospitals, clinics, and homes across the country, nurses are innovating. We're problem-solving on the fly, improvising solutions, and finding ways to provide better care with the resources we have. That's the spirit of innovation.

So, the next time you jury-rig a solution to a problem or come up with a clever workaround, don't just brush it off as "part of the job." Take a moment to recognize it for what it is: innovation in action.

And here's the exciting part: once you start seeing yourself as an innovator, you open up a world of possibilities. Maybe that clever trick you use to keep IV lines organized could be developed into a product that helps nurses everywhere, like Lenore did with the "Beata Clasp". Or perhaps your method for explaining complex medical information to patients could become an app that improves health literacy.

Here's something really exciting: More and more healthcare institutions are recognizing the value of nurse-led innovation and are creating opportunities for nurses to flex their creative muscles.

For instance, did you know that places like the University of Pennsylvania School of Nursing, University of Connecticut, Kaiser Permanente, and Brigham and Women's Hospital have initiatives specifically designed to promote innovation? One strategy that's becoming increasingly popular is the "hackathon."

Now, before you start thinking this has something to do with computer hacking, let me explain. A hackathon is an event where people from diverse backgrounds - nurses, engineers, educators, entrepreneurs, you name it - come together to "hack" (or devise a solution to) a specific problem within a short period of time.

Imagine this: You're in a room full of creative minds, all focused on solving a healthcare challenge you've faced countless times. The energy is electric, ideas are flying, and suddenly, that problem that seemed insurmountable starts to look a whole lot more solvable.

These events are not just about coming up with ideas - they're about turning those ideas into reality. Many hackathons offer prizes or even funding opportunities for the best solutions. It's like "Shark Tank" for healthcare innovation!

So, keep an eye out for hackathons or innovation challenges in your area. Your hospital or local nursing school might be hosting one. And if they're not? Well, who says you can't suggest it or even organize one yourself?

Some of the best innovations come from collaboration. Your nursing insight combined with an engineer's technical know-how or an entrepreneur's business acumen could be the perfect recipe for the next big healthcare breakthrough.

The point is, you're already an innovator. You've been doing it all along. Now, it's just a matter of recognizing your ideas, refining them, and maybe - if you're so inclined - taking them to the next level.

So, keep solving problems. Keep improvising. Keep saying, "There's got to be a better way." Because in those moments, you're not just being a great nurse - you're being an innovator. And who knows? Your next on-the-fly solution might just be the next big breakthrough in healthcare.

Every great innovation started with someone like you thinking, "What if...?" So, what's your "What if...?" going to be?

Now that we've established that you're already an innovator, let's look at some inspiring examples of nurse-led innovations that have made a real difference in healthcare:

- Community Pop-Up Clinics: KaSheta Johnson-Jackson, ARNP, in North Carolina, started "Community Pop-Up" clinics. A series of non-permanent healthcare settings in fields, farms, and baseball fields. These clinics provide healthcare services to people who struggle to access traditional healthcare settings. What started as simple health screenings grew to offer COVID-19 testing, vaccinations, mental health resources, access to fresh produce, and even employment opportunities.
- Redi-Stik Wearable Simulation Devices: A group of multidisciplinary frontline nurses at Texas Children's Hospital created RediStik®, wearable simulation devices that allow nursing students to practice inserting and maintaining various types of catheters. This innovation provides a more realistic and flexible way for nursing students to learn crucial skills, even allowing for virtual feedback via Zoom.
- Virtual Nursing: Jean Putnam, DNP, MS, RN, CPHQ, NEA-BC, and her team at Community Health Network in Indiana pioneered a virtual nurse program in 2022, showcasing how nurses can lead the way in leveraging technology to improve patient care and nursing workflows.

These innovations didn't just happen by chance. They were born out of the unique perspective that nurses bring to healthcare.

So, what makes nurses such great innovators?

- Extensive time with patients: We spend more time with patients than any other healthcare professional, giving us unparalleled insights into their needs and challenges.
- Hands-on problem-solving: We're constantly troubleshooting patient needs directly at the bedside.
- Pattern recognition: We encounter the same issues repeatedly, allowing us to identify systemic problems and potential solutions.

When considering your own innovative ideas, ask yourself:

- What inspired this idea? Was it a recurring problem you've noticed, or a sudden "aha" moment?
- Why would a healthcare organization adopt this innovation? Does it offer easier workflow, enhanced efficiency, or lower operational costs?
- What are the potential long-term effects of using this innovation?

Ready to take your innovative idea to the next level? Here's a simple guide to get started:

- Document your idea: Write down the problem and your solution in detail.
- Research: Check if similar solutions already exist and how your idea is different.
- Prototype: Create a simple version of your idea, even if it's just a sketch or a mock-up.
- Seek feedback: Share your idea with colleagues to get their input.
- Explore resources: Look into nurse innovation programs at hospitals or universities.
- Consider protection: If your idea is unique, consider speaking with a patent attorney.

You don't have to go it alone. Organizations like the American Nurses Association's Innovation Advisory Committee offer support, grants and resources for nurse innovators. Many hospitals and universities also have innovation programs that can help you develop your ideas. You can also start a "hackathon" to get a cooperative effort in your workplace started.

Just look at Rebecca Love — the first nurse ever featured on a TED stage talking about nurse innovation. She helped launch the first nurse hackathon and has made it her mission to ensure nurses are at the forefront of healthcare invention. "No one understands patient care more than nurses," she says, "so why aren't we the ones designing the future of care?" She's proof that your ideas don't need a title — just a voice.

So, the next time you find yourself thinking, "There's got to be a better way," Your mindset now will be to think, "I'm not just a nurse, I could be an innovator." And your next idea could be the one that transforms healthcare for the better. You don't need permission to innovate. You've already been doing it. Now, what will you bring to life?

Technology at Your Fingertips: Apps, Software, and AI in Nursing

We've talked about physical innovations, but let's not forget the digital world. In an age where everyone's got a smartphone in their pocket, the potential for nurse-led digital innovation is huge.

Think about it: How many times have you wished for an app that could make your job easier? Maybe something that could streamline your documentation process, or help you explain complex medical concepts to patients more effectively?

Marion Leary, the Director of Innovation at the University of Pennsylvania School of Nursing took her bedside experience and applied it to cutting-edge simulations, healthcare design thinking, and nurse-led innovation strategy. She calls nurses "natural systems thinkers" and her work proves it. When we see ourselves as inventors, not just end users, everything changes.

Here are a few areas where nurses are making waves in the digital space:

- Documentation Apps: Frustrated with staying late to finish charting? Why not create an app that allows for real-time, efficient documentation? Imagine being able to speak your notes as you work, with the app transcribing and organizing them for you.
- Patient Education Tools: How about an app that uses augmented reality to show patients exactly how their medication works inside their body? Or one that provides easy-to-understand, customizable discharge instructions?
- Workflow Optimization Software: Think about software that could intelligently manage nurse schedules, ensuring fair distribution of shifts and optimal staffing levels based on patient acuity.
- AI in Nursing: Here's an exciting idea - what if there was an AI listening device that could assist during patient assessments? It could gather information as you talk with the patient, then summarize it to help answer OASIS questions. This could revolutionize home health documentation!

Like Lenore Henning, who created the Beata Clasp, the digital world is waiting for its own Lenore. Nurses who understand the day-to-day challenges of the job and can envision digital solutions.

You don't need to be a coding expert to get started. Your nursing knowledge is the key ingredient. The tech part can be learned or collaborated on.

So, the next time you find yourself wishing for a better app or a smarter software solution: Don't just be the end-user. You could be the creator. Your frontline experience makes you uniquely qualified to design solutions that truly work for nurses and patients. What digital innovation will you bring to nursing?

Scan to Access Tools for Chapter Ten

Chapter 11: Wellness and Prevention: Nurturing Health Beyond the Traditional Role in Healthcare

Let's talk about a path that might raise a few eyebrows in the break room: the wellness space. Now, I can almost hear some of you thinking, "Isn't that just 'soft nursing'?" Well, my *doing hard stuff builds character* friends, we're about to challenge that notion head-on.

First things first: there's nothing soft about building your own dream instead of clocking hours for someone else's business. And there's definitely nothing soft about having the courage to step outside the traditional nursing role to explore new ways of promoting health and well-being.

The wellness industry is booming, and guess what? Nurses are uniquely positioned to make a massive impact in this space. Why? Because we understand health from the inside out. We've seen what happens when wellness takes a backseat, and we know how to guide people towards better health choices.

Now, I'm not here to tell you that wellness entrepreneurship is better or worse than traditional nursing roles. That's not my place, and frankly, it's different for everyone. What I am here to do is open your eyes to the possibilities and empower you to choose what's right for you – not what others think is best for you.

Let's take a moment to consider what the wellness space might look like for a nurse entrepreneur. We're talking about ventures like:

- Med-spas offering aesthetic treatments
- Wellness coaching practices
- Holistic health clinics
- Corporate wellness program development
- Nutrition and fitness consulting

And that's just scratching the surface.

To give you a real-world example, let me tell you about Alexis (Lexi) Holloway, RN-BSN. Lexi owns Touch Aesthetic Spa in Philadelphia, and let me tell you, there's nothing "soft" about what she does. She is a Wellness and Beauty Entrepreneurship rockstar! She's a Permanent Makeup Artist, a Nurse Injector, and a Licensed Lash Technician. And as if that wasn't enough, she's currently in school to become an APRN. Lexi is the real deal, combining her nursing expertise with advanced aesthetic skills to provide top-notch care to her clients.

Now, I know what some of you are thinking. "But Laurie, isn't this moving away from 'real' nursing?"

Here's my take: Nursing is about promoting health and well-being, whether that's in a hospital bed or an aesthetic spa. By moving into the wellness space, these nurse entrepreneurs are often reaching people before they become patients, potentially preventing the very health crises we deal with in traditional settings.

Is it different from bedside nursing? Absolutely. Is it any less valuable or impactful? Absolutely not.

Nursing Superpowers in the Wellness World

So, what makes nurses uniquely qualified to rock the wellness space? Let's break it down:

- **Clinical Knowledge**: Your understanding of anatomy, physiology, and pathology isn't just for hospital rounds. In the wellness world, it's your secret weapon for providing safe, effective treatments and advice. Knowing exactly what muscle innervation and what action makes an eyebrow move up or move down is paramount to the precise outcomes needed in this space.
- **Patient Education Skills**: All those times you explained complex medical concepts to patients and their families? That skill is the foundation of wellness coaching and educating clients about aesthetic procedures.
- **Holistic Approach**: Nurses are trained to see the whole person, not just symptoms. This holistic view is at the heart of many wellness practices.
- **Crisis Management:** Your ability to stay cool under pressure? It's just as valuable when running a business as it is in the ER.
- **Attention to Detail:** From medication doses to charting, nurses are sticklers for accuracy. This precision is crucial in areas like aesthetic treatments or developing wellness plans.

- **Empathy and Communication**: Your ability to connect with patients translates directly to building a loyal client base in the wellness industry.
- **Continuous Learning**: Nursing taught you to stay updated with the latest research and techniques. This adaptability is key in the ever-evolving wellness field.

Let's look at how Lexi applies these skills in her med-spa:

Her clinical knowledge ensures she can safely perform aesthetic procedures. Her patient education skills come into play when explaining treatments to clients. Her holistic approach helps her understand how aesthetic treatments fit into a client's overall well-being. Her crisis management skills? They're handy when running a business and handling any unexpected situations. Her attention to detail is crucial for achieving the best results in permanent makeup and lash treatments. Her empathy helps clients feel comfortable, understood and seen. And her commitment to continuous learning? It's evident in her pursuit of an APRN degree while running her business.

The beauty of these skills is that they're transferable to any wellness venture you might pursue. Whether you're drawn to aesthetic nursing, health coaching, corporate wellness programs, or holistic health practices, your nursing background gives you a robust foundation to build upon.

Stepping into the wellness space doesn't mean leaving nursing behind. It's about applying your nursing skills in new, innovative ways to promote health and well-being. You're not just a nurse entering the wellness industry - you're bringing the invaluable perspective of nursing to a field that desperately needs it.

So, the next time someone suggests that wellness ventures are "soft nursing," you can confidently explain how your nursing superpowers make you uniquely qualified to excel in this space. Because let's face it - there's nothing soft about leveraging years of healthcare experience to build a business that promotes health and changes lives.

Taking the Leap: Practical Steps for Your Healthcare-Adjacent Journey

So, you're intrigued by these healthcare-adjacent opportunities. Maybe you're picturing yourself running a med-spa like Lexi, or perhaps you've got an innovative idea brewing. But how do you get from here to there? Let's break it down into manageable steps.

- Assess Your Skills and Interests First things first: take stock of what you bring to the table. What are your strengths as a nurse? What aspects of healthcare fascinate you most? This self-reflection will help guide you towards the right opportunity. Dip Your Toes in. Here's a

- pro tip: you don't have to dive in headfirst. Many nurses start their entrepreneurial journey while keeping one foot in traditional nursing. For example, if you're interested in aesthetic nursing, why not try working one day a week at a med-spa while maintaining your regular nursing job? This approach allows you to:

    o Get a feel for the new field without giving up your financial stability
    o Build skills and connections in your area of interest
    o Confirm whether this new path truly aligns with your goals and lifestyle.

- Research Your Chosen Field Once you've identified an area of interest, dive deep. Read industry publications, attend conferences, and connect with nurses who've made similar transitions. Knowledge is power, especially when you're entering a new field.
- Build Your Network In the world of healthcare-adjacent ventures, who you know can be just as important as what you know. Attend industry events, join professional associations in your area of interest, and don't be shy about reaching out to potential mentors, you never know if they'd like a partner in their venture. It doesn't hurt to ask.

175

- Acquire Additional Skills or Certifications; Depending on your chosen path, you might need to expand your skill set. This could involve anything from taking a course in aesthetic procedures, to getting certified in health coaching. Your nursing background gives you a head start, but continuous learning is key.

- Create a Business Plan If you're planning to start your own venture, a solid business plan is crucial. This doesn't have to be a novel-length document, but it should outline your business idea, target market, financial projections, and marketing strategy.

- Seek Support. Those hackathons and innovation programs we talked about earlier, look for similar support systems in your area of interest. Many hospitals now have innovation incubators, and there are numerous programs designed to support nurse entrepreneurs. But don't limit yourself to acute care settings. Your ideas matter, regardless of your nursing specialty. Whether you're in Home Health, Long-Term Care, Hospice, Outpatient Surgery, or any other field, your day-to-day experience in meeting patient care goals is the spark for innovation across the healthcare spectrum. From wound care to tech to meal delivery, you have the insider knowledge that makes the system run every single day. Your unique perspective could be the key to groundbreaking improvements in any healthcare arena. So, seek out those innovation incubators and support programs – they're not just for hospital nurses, they're for all nurses with ideas to share.

- Start Small and Scale; You don't need to launch a full-fledged business overnight. Start with a side hustle, a small client base, or even just a blog sharing your expertise. As you gain confidence and clientele, you can gradually scale up.

- Embrace the Learning Curve; Every nurse entrepreneur started where you are now. There will be challenges and learning experiences along the way. Embrace them as part of the journey.

- Stay Connected to Your 'Why'; Throughout this process, keep reminding yourself why you're exploring these new opportunities. Whether it's to have more control over your schedule, to make a different kind of impact on health and wellness, or to challenge yourself professionally, staying connected to your motivation will help you persist through challenges.

There's no one-size-fits-all approach to transitioning into healthcare-adjacent ventures. Some nurses might choose to make a gradual transition, while others might decide to take the plunge all at once. The key is to find the path that feels right for you.

So, are you ready to take that first step? Whether it's signing up for a course, reaching out to a nurse entrepreneur you admire, or blocking out time to work on your business plan, the journey of a thousand miles begins with a single step. Your nursing career has prepared you for this moment. Now, it's time to expand your impact in ways you might never have imagined.

Charting Your Course: The Journey Ahead

As we wrap up our exploration of healthcare-adjacent ventures, I hope you're feeling inspired and empowered. We've journeyed through the realms of innovation, technology, and wellness, uncovering the myriad ways nurses can leverage their unique skills and experiences beyond traditional healthcare settings.

Whether you're dreaming up the next groundbreaking medical device, developing a health app, or considering opening your own wellness practice, your nursing background is your superpower. The skills you've honed at the bedside – problem-solving, empathy, attention to detail, and so much more – are the very qualities that can set you apart in these new ventures.

As we move forward, keep in mind that this journey is yours to shape. Whether you choose to dip your toes in slowly or dive in headfirst, the most important step is the first one. Your ideas, your experiences, and your passion for improving healthcare are valuable – don't let anyone tell you otherwise.

In our next chapter, we'll delve into the world of Education and Training Enterprises. We'll explore how nurses are revolutionizing healthcare education, from developing innovative training programs to creating online courses that reach learners around the globe. Get ready to discover how your expertise can shape the next generation of healthcare professionals and empower patients in whole new ways.

The future of healthcare needs nurses like you –

innovative, passionate, and ready to make a difference. So, are you ready for the next step? Let's continue this exciting journey together!

Scan to Access Tools for Chapter Eleven

Chapter 12: Education & Training Enterprises

Build a Business Around What You Know

Ever caught yourself explaining a medical concept to a friend and realizing how much you actually know? It's a funny thing, isn't it? In the day-to-day hustle of nursing, we often forget just how much knowledge we've accumulated. We're so busy applying our skills that we rarely stop to consider the wealth of information packed into our brains.

But here's the kicker: that knowledge you've gained through years of hands-on experience, continuing education, and probably more than a few nights of cramming for exams is valuable. And I'm not just talking about valuable to your patients or your healthcare facility. I'm talking about value in a "hey, I could build a business around this" kind of way.

Welcome to the world of Education and Training Enterprises, where your hard-earned nursing wisdom becomes your greatest asset. In this chapter, we're going to explore how you can take all that knowledge bouncing around in your head and transform it into a thriving business.

We're talking about opportunities like:

- Continuing Education for Healthcare Training
- Online Course Development and Digital Education

- Compliance Writing (Policies & Procedures)
- Article Writing for Journals and Nursing Blogs
- Educational Programs for Accreditation Bodies
- Writing Presentations for Conferences
- EHR Education and Training
- Professionals
- Patient and Community Health Education
- Corporate Health and Wellness

Now, I can almost hear some of you protesting, "But I've never taught before!" or "I'm not sure I have what it takes to be an educator." Here's a little secret: every time you've explained a procedure to a patient, oriented a new nurse, or broken down complex medical jargon for a family member, you've been teaching. You've been an educator all along, even if you didn't realize it.

So, grab your favorite caffeinated beverage (no judgment here - we all know nurses run on coffee), get comfortable, and let's dive into how you can turn your nursing know-how into an exciting and rewarding educational venture. By the end of this chapter, you'll be itching to dust off that PowerPoint and start spreading your nursing wisdom far and wide!

Ready to discover your inner educator and entrepreneur? Let's go!

Continuing Education for Healthcare Professionals: From Student to Teacher

You know those CEU courses you've sat through, year after year, fighting to keep your eyes open as someone drones on about the latest healthcare regulations? Or maybe you've taken some online courses, clicking through endless PowerPoint slides, thinking, "There's got to be a better way to do this."

Of course there's a better way, and you could be the one to make it happen.
Welcome to the world of Continuing Education for Healthcare Professionals, where your real-world nursing experience is worth its weight in annual CEUs. Think about it - who better to teach healthcare concepts than someone who's been there, done that, and has the scrapbook folder of certificates to prove it?

As a nurse, you've got a unique advantage in this field. You know what information healthcare professionals actually need, what challenges they face day-to-day, and most importantly, how to present information in a way that won't put your audience to sleep faster than a dose of Benadryl.

But here's the kicker - creating and delivering continuing education isn't just about sharing your knowledge. It's a business opportunity that can be both financially rewarding and professionally fulfilling. Whether you're looking to supplement your income or transition into a full-time education role, the continuing education market is ripe with opportunities for nurses willing to step up to the plate.

So, are you ready to transform those years of experience into engaging, practical continuing education programs? Let's dive in and explore how you can make the leap from CEU student to CEU superstar!

Continuing Education Opportunities: Pick Your Playground

Alright, let's break down the different ways you can share your nursing wisdom in the continuing education world. Think of these as different playgrounds where you can flex your teaching muscles:

1. **In-person Workshops and Seminars**: Those hands-on skills labs from nursing school are a great example. This is your chance to create your own. Picture yourself leading a group of nurses through a new procedure, watching those "aha!" moments light up their faces. It's like being a nursing instructor, minus the stress of final exams. Pro tip: These are great for teaching practical skills or complex concepts that benefit from face-to-face interaction.

2. **Online Courses and Webinars**: Welcome to the digital age of nursing education! With online courses, you can reach nurses across the country (or even

the world) without leaving your living room. Imagine sipping your morning coffee while your pre-recorded lecture on the latest wound care techniques is helping a night shift nurse in Alaska. Bonus: Once you create the content, it can keep earning a paycheck for you while you sleep. Have we talked about passive income?

3. **Conference Presentations:** Ever sat in a conference session thinking, "I could do better than this"? Well, here's your chance to prove it! Conferences are always looking for engaging speakers with real-world experience. Plus, you get to network with other healthcare pros and maybe even score a free trip to a cool city. The key here is to make your presentation as engaging as that Grey's Anatomy episode everyone's talking about. No snooze-fests allowed!

4. **Certification Programs**: This is the big league of continuing education. Creating a certification program means developing a comprehensive curriculum that can lead to a professional credential. It's a lot of work, but the payoff can be huge. Imagine being known as the go-to expert in your specialty area. Think about it: Your name could be on certificates hanging in nursing offices across the country!

5. **Lunch and Learns:** Don't underestimate the power of a good lunch break learning session. These short, focused presentations can be a great way to dip your toes into the CEU world. Plus, if you provide good food along with good info, you're guaranteed to have a captive audience!

The beauty of continuing education is that you're not limited to just one type. You can mix and match based on your strengths, interests, and target audience. Maybe you start with a lunch and learn, graduate to online courses, and eventually find yourself keynoting a major nursing conference.

The goal here isn't just to regurgitate information. It's about creating learning experiences that stick. So, whether you're designing an interactive online module or planning a hands-on workshop, think about how you can make the content come alive. After all, if you can make a 12-hour shift fly by, you can certainly

185

make a CEU course engaging!

Orientation and Onboarding Education: Be the Guide Every New Nurse Needs

Your first day on the job is always a mix of excitement and sheer terror as you try to navigate a new environment, learn new systems, and remembering everyone's names. Well, what if I told you that you could be the hero in that story for other nurses?

Enter the world of orientation and onboarding education. This is your chance to be the Yoda to a bunch of nursing Padawans, guiding them through their first steps in a new role or facility.

The best part about it: Many healthcare providers are now turning to contract educators for orientation and onboarding. Why? Because it's a win-win situation:

For the healthcare provider:
- They save money on full-time staff while still meeting education requirements
- They get an expert who specializes in creating engaging, effective orientations
- They can scale their education efforts up or down based on hiring needs

For You:

- You get to flex your teaching muscles without committing to a full-time education role
- You can work with multiple facilities, in multiple states, keeping things fresh and interesting
- You have the opportunity to continue with your finger on the pulse of what's going on in the healthcare arena.

Imagine designing an orientation program that actually gets new nurses excited instead of overwhelmed. Think about creating onboarding materials that don't just cover policies and procedures but really prepare nurses for success in their new roles.

You could be the one to:

- Develop interactive simulations for common scenarios in the facility
- Create engaging e-learning modules for policy and procedure training
- Design hands-on skills labs for equipment and procedures specific to the unit
- Craft 'survival guides' that new nurses will actually want to read

And here's a secret: Your real-world experience is your superpower here. You know the challenges new nurses face because you've been there. So, you'll be able to answer questions most HR specialists won't. You understand the culture shock of transitioning from nursing school to the floor, or from one facility to the other. You can anticipate the questions and concerns that new hires will raise. Let's face it, do nursing mentors ever have the time to actually go through material and answer questions? Not that I've ever encountered.

By offering orientation and onboarding education services, you're not just teaching – you're setting the tone for a nurse's entire experience at that facility. You're building confidence, instilling best practices, and maybe even keeping a few new nurses from running for the hills after their first week.

Bridging the Gap: Your Role in the Age of Online Onboarding

Now, I can hear some of you saying, "But wait, isn't most onboarding done online these days?" And you're not wrong. Many facilities have moved towards online modules for parts of their orientation process. But here's the thing – there's a huge difference between completing an online module and truly being prepared for the job.

This is where you, as a nurse educator, can truly shine. Think of yourself as the bridge between those online modules and real-world applications.

Here's how:

- **Hands-on Skills Training**: Sure, a nurse can watch a video on how to use a specific piece of equipment. But nothing beats having an experienced pro guides them through it in person.

You can provide that crucial hands-on experience that online modules just can't replicate.

- **Cultural Integration:** Online modules can explain policies, but they can't convey the culture of a unit or facility. As someone who's been in the trenches, you can help new nurses understand the unwritten rules and norms that make a unit tick.

- **Scenario-Based Learning**: You can create and facilitate real-world scenarios that apply the information from online modules. This helps new nurses connect the dots between theory and practice.

- **Personalized Support:** Every nurse learns differently. You can provide that personal touch, answering questions and offering additional support where online modules fall short.

- **Ongoing Mentorship**: Orientation doesn't end after the first week. You can be there to provide continued support and education as new nurses settle into their roles.

Now, here's where it gets really interesting for healthcare facilities. By bringing in a nurse educator contractor like yourself, they can optimize their Clinical Education and Development positions in other areas of the facility or eliminate the position altogether, saving money while fulfilling the need.

Online modules are a tool, not a complete solution. They're great for conveying information, but they can't replace the wisdom, experience, and personal touch that you bring to the table.

As a nurse educator, your role is to complement and enhance online training, not compete with it. You're not just teaching content – you're teaching context, nuance, and real-world application. And let's be honest, that's something no computer program can match.

So, don't let the rise of online onboarding deter you. Instead, see it as an opportunity to showcase the unique value that only an experienced nurse educator can provide. Trust me, healthcare facilities are starting to realize that a blended approach – combining online modules with expert nurse educators – is the secret sauce to successful onboarding.
So, whether you're creating engaging in-person orientations, designing blended learning experiences, or serving as the bridge between online modules and real-world applications. Your experience as a nurse is invaluable in shaping the next generation of healthcare professionals. You have the power to transform orientation from a dreaded chore into an inspiring start to a new chapter in a nurse's career.

Ready to put your nursing wisdom to work in new and exciting ways? Let's explore how you can leverage your unique skills and experiences to create impactful continuing education content.

From Bedside to Classroom: Why Nurses Make the Best CE Content Creators Got time for a little ego boost? You know all those years you've spent dealing with impossible patient loads, deciphering doctors' handwriting, and MacGyvering solutions with limited supplies? Well, those experiences have been secretly preparing you for a stellar career in continuing education.

Don't even start to say, "But I'm just a nurse, not some fancy educator." We've talked about this. You're a healthcare superhero with a unique set of skills that make you the perfect person to create continuing education content. Let me break it down for you:

- **Real-World Experience**: You've been in the trenches. You know what works and what doesn't in actual healthcare settings, not just in theory. This practical knowledge is key to creating relevant, applicable CEU content.

- **Problem-Solving Skills:** Every time you had to calm an anxious patient, handle a difficult family member, and fix a malfunctioning glucometer all before your first coffee break? That kind of creative problem-solving is exactly what's needed to design engaging, effective educational materials.

191

- **Adaptability:** Healthcare is always changing, and you've had to keep up. This adaptability is crucial in the ever-evolving world of continuing education.

- **Communication Skills:** You've explained complex medical concepts to scared patients and their families. If you can make "idiopathic thrombocytopenic purpura" understandable to a worried mother at 3 AM, you can certainly create clear, concise educational content.

- **Empathy and Understanding**: You know the challenges healthcare professionals face because you've faced them yourself. This empathy allows you to create content that truly resonates with your audience.

- **Critical Thinking:** Nursing has trained you to analyze situations quickly and make informed decisions. This skill is invaluable when developing comprehensive, thoughtful educational programs.

- **Attention to Detail:** From medication dosages to thorough documentation, nursing demands meticulous attention to detail. This precision is not only crucial in creating accurate, high-quality educational materials but it makes it an essential tool.

So, the next time you're wondering if you're qualified to create CEU content, know that your nursing experience isn't just relevant, it's your key to independence. You bring a perspective that no one else can offer. You're not just teaching facts; you're sharing hard-earned wisdom that can make a real difference in healthcare delivery.

Ready to transform your nursing know-how into dynamic educational content? Let's explore how you can leverage these unique qualities to create CEU materials that will have your fellow healthcare professionals saying, "Finally, someone who gets it!"

Turning Paperwork into Profit: The World of Compliance Writing

All those policies and procedures you've had to follow (or maybe grumbled about) throughout your nursing career, someone had to write those. Now, that someone could be you!

Compliance writing might sound about as exciting as watching paint dry but hear me out. This is a golden opportunity to put all your real-world nursing experience to use, potentially save your fellow nurses from confusing, impractical policies, and yes, make some serious money in the process. Especially in the State Specific policy and procedure world.

Think about it - how many times have you looked at a policy and thought, "This clearly wasn't written by someone who's actually worked a shift in their life"?

As a nurse-turned-compliance writer, you have the power to change that. It's my biggest contention when I'm writing policies. My thoughts always go to not hanging up my nurses at the bedside because they weren't doing something exactly as the policy was written, potentially causing the provider to vulnerable to potential survey tags. And all because the person who wrote the policy had never done the task and had no practical knowledge of how it was really done.

Having you at the keyboard can make all the difference. You can create policies and procedures that not only tick all the regulatory boxes but also make sense in practice. Your experience allows you to write guidelines that protect both the facility and the staff, ensuring compliance without compromising the reality of patient care. You're not just writing words on a page; you're crafting a blueprint for safe, efficient, and practical healthcare delivery.

If this is your thing, you'll be happy to know, there's always demand for this kind of work. Healthcare is one of the most regulated industries on the planet, and regulations are always changing. That means there's a constant need for clear, up-to-date policies and procedures. Ka$ching!

From Charting Chaos to EHR Mastery:
Becoming an EHR Educator

Yes, we've talked about this in a previous section, but it deserves reinforcement in a structured way. If you've trained staff on your EHR system more times than you can count, you've already built a curriculum you just haven't packaged it yet.

Nurses are now turning their internal training knowledge into *sellable educational assets*. See, I told you this section would have a new light. Instead of showing every new hire how to use a system one-on-one, they're recording tutorials, building onboarding libraries, and offering documentation cheat sheets for agencies, facilities, Dr.'s offices, Adult Day Cares, ALFs, Outpatient Surgery Centers and more, that don't have the time (or budget) to start from scratch.

Think of it this way: if you've ever said, "We need a more efficient and *nurse friendly* way to teach this," you might already have the bones of a course and there are plenty of healthcare businesses willing to pay for training that's been created by someone who's actually used the system in real life.

The world of EHR Education is a niche that's practically begging for nurses to step in and save the day. Why? Because we're the ones who actually use these systems day in and day out. We know the shortcuts, the workarounds, and yes, the pitfalls that can turn a simple task into a charting nightmare.

Most healthcare organizations are desperate for effective EHR training material with practical applications. HR folks can show you how to log in, sure, but they can't teach a new nurse how to efficiently document a complex patient assessment. And let's be honest, most DONs barely have time to login and document for themselves, let alone run comprehensive EHR training sessions.

195

That's where you come in. As an EHR educator, you can bridge the gap between the technical aspects of the system and the practical needs of healthcare providers. You're not just teaching people how to use software; you're empowering them to provide better patient care.

If I haven't said this loud enough, here it is again, the demand for this skill is huge. With healthcare organizations constantly updating their EHR systems or switching to new ones, there's always a need for trainers and training material that can speak both "nurse" and "tech."

Compliance Education: Your Next Big Opportunity in Home Health and Hospice

Hold onto your stethoscopes, because I've got some breaking news that could be your ticket to an exciting new career path. The federal government (CMS) and accrediting bodies have just dropped a bombshell in the world of Home Health and Hospice: they're now requiring a full-fledged Compliance Program. Not just a QAPI component. And guess what? This spells O-P-P-O-R-T-U-N-I-T-Y for nurses like you.

Now, you might be wondering, "Why the sudden push for compliance?" Well, let me hit you with some startling numbers. According to a recent OIG report:

CMS "Centers for Medicare & Medicaid Services' Comprehensive Error Rate Testing (CERT) program determined that the 2024 improper payment error rate for home health claims was 7.6 percent, or about

$31.7 billion. Recent OIG reports have similarly disclosed high error rates at individual HHAs."

You read that right home health claims had improper payments, totaling nearly $31.7 billion. With numbers like these, it's no wonder CMS is cracking down on compliance.

This isn't just a minor adjustment - it's a seismic shift in how Home Health and Hospice agencies need to operate. And here's where you come in: these agencies are going to need expert guidance to navigate these new waters.

Think about it - who better to teach healthcare concepts than someone who's been in the trenches, dealing with real patients, real emergencies, and real challenges? Your hands-on experience is exactly what makes you qualified to educate others. You're not just reciting textbook knowledge; you're sharing practical wisdom that only comes from years on the job.

Marketing Your Expertise:

Here's a pro tip for when you're ready to market your compliance education services: Use this eye-opening statistic to your advantage. Imagine opening your pitch with something like this:

"Did you know that many home health claims in 2024 had improper payments, totaling nearly $31.7 billion? As a compliance education expert, I can help your agency avoid being part of that statistic."

Boom! You've immediately captured their attention and demonstrated the critical need for your services. This statistic is your secret weapon - it clearly shows the risks of non-compliance and positions you as the solution. Whether you're creating marketing
materials, pitching to potential clients, or developing course content, this powerful data point can help you drive home the importance of comprehensive compliance education.

You're not just offering a service - you're offering peace of mind and protection against potentially costly errors. By leading with these statistics, you're showing agencies that you understand the challenges they're facing and that you have the expertise to help them navigate these turbulent compliance waters.

From Nurse to Compliance Education Expert: Owning Your Expertise

"How can I become a compliance education expert?" Glad you asked. You're a seasoned healthcare professional with a wealth of knowledge that's incredibly valuable in the world of compliance education. You just need to wrap your head around teaching people outside your circle of friends. As a professional, we do networking events all the time, and most times conversations happen around surveys, accreditation, reimbursement, etc. If you've been in healthcare for any amount of time, I'm sure you've had plenty to contribute to the conversation. Now is your chance to maximize those conversations and make it your business. Here's how to shift your mindset and prepare yourself for this exciting new role:

1. Recognize Your Unique Value: Those years of hands-on experience? They're gold. You've seen firsthand how policies and procedures play out in real-world scenarios. That practical knowledge is something no textbook can provide. Every single time you've had to implement a new policy and found all the hiccups that weren't accounted for? That's the kind of insight agencies are desperate for. You sometimes can't see the forest for the trees. Be their educational light.

2. Invest in Continuous Learning:

a. Stay updated on the latest CMS regulations and OIG reports.

Set up Google alerts for key terms like "home health compliance" or "CMS regulations" to stay in the loop.

b. Consider pursuing certifications in healthcare compliance or adult education. They're not terribly expensive and it takes away from your "imposter syndrome" mindset. Look into certifications like the Certified in Healthcare Compliance (CHC) or the Certified Professional in

Healthcare Quality (CPHQ).

c. Attend webinars and conferences focused on home health compliance. These networking opportunities can turn into consulting opportunities and educational opportunities. Accrediting bodies and Associations are always looking for "speakers" - this can give you an audience for marketing your expertise and it can snowball. Time to stop being a participant and get out in front. Make a goal to attend at least one major conference this year and introduce yourself to at least five *new* people.

3. Develop Your Teaching Skills:
   a. Take courses on adult learning principles and instructional design. There are so many easy-to-take short "public speaking" programs that can be a wealth of knowledge for your educational opportunities. Platforms like Coursera or edX offer courses on these topics.
   b. Practice explaining complex concepts in simple terms. Try explaining a complicated procedure to a non-medical

friend and see if they understand.

    c. Create sample training materials to build your portfolio. Start with a topic you know well, like proper documentation or infection control procedures and offer it at a local Home Health or DON luncheon. You'd be surprised how well it would be received!

4. Leverage Your Network:

    a. Reach out to former colleagues who've moved into leadership roles. They might need compliance training for their teams. Present specific current topical issues as easily digestible programs. It immediately makes you the "right now" expert to call on.

    b. Connect with vendors you've worked with. They often need nurses to train others on using their products compliantly. This is a network dream opportunity. Have you spoken to Lawyers and Ambulance people in your area? How about Assisted Livings? You could do an Advanced Directives, Patients' Rights or even Compliance Documentation

programs and they would be
happy to have you!

c. Join LinkedIn groups
focused on healthcare
compliance and start
engaging in discussions.

5. Start Small and Scale Up:
a. Offer to do lunch-
and-learn at your
current workplace
on a compliance
topic.

This will give you a chance to polish your delivery
and boost your confidence. The bottom line is you
know the material. You just need to feel confident
in teaching others what you know on a bigger
scale.

b. Write a blog post or create a
short video on a common
compliance issue you've
encountered. You can also
write an article for an
Association website,
Accreditation website or
educational source, nursing
journals. They always want
content. This is a wonderful
opportunity to validate your
expertise to the world and
increase your reach. It's a
win-win

c. Propose a compliance training program to your current employer It's a great way to test your materials and build your credibility.

6. Develop Your Business Acumen:

   a. Take a basic business course to understand pricing, marketing, and operations.

   b. Create a simple website showcasing your expertise and services.

   c. Draft a business plan for your compliance education services.

Every expert was once a beginner. The key is to start seeing your everyday nursing challenges through the lens of compliance education. That frustrating policy you had to follow. That's a teaching opportunity. The workaround you developed to make things run smoother. That's a valuable insight into your future clients.

You've been an educator all along - teaching patients, mentoring new nurses, explaining procedures to families. Now it's time to take those skills to a bigger stage and make a broader impact. And who knows? The freedom and fulfillment you find in this new role might just reignite your passion for healthcare in ways you never imagined.

Ready to take the plunge? Your expertise is needed, and there's a whole world of agencies out there waiting for someone just like you to show them the way.

CPR & AED Instruction: Your Ticket to a Flexible, Profitable Side Gig

Before we wrap up, let's talk about an educational opportunity that's often overlooked but can be a real game-changer: CPR & AED instruction. This isn't just a chance to share crucial, life-saving skills – it's also a potential goldmine for nurses looking for a flexible, profitable side gig.

Here's why CPR & AED instruction should be on your radar:

- High Demand: From healthcare workers to teachers, lifeguards to daycare providers, there's always a need for CPR certification. And let's not forget parents, community groups, and corporate teams looking to be prepared for emergencies.

- Low Startup Costs: Once you're certified as an instructor, your main investments are a manikin and an AED trainer. Compared to many other business ventures, the initial outlay is minimal.

- Flexibility: You can schedule classes around your existing commitments. Weekends, evenings, or whatever works for you – you're in control of your calendar.

- Impressive Income Potential: Let's break it down: At $65 per person with 10

204

people per class, you're looking at $650 per class. Run two classes a day, five days a week, and you're talking about $6,500 a week or around $26,000 a month. Even if you do this part-time, the numbers are attractive.

- Short Time Commitment: Most CPR classes run about 3-4 hours. This means you can make a significant income without having to dedicate full days to teaching.

- Utilizes Your Expertise: As a nurse, you bring real-world experience to these classes. You can enrich the standard curriculum with practical insights that make your classes stand out.

- Community Impact: Beyond the financial benefits, you're literally teaching people how to save lives. That's an amazing feeling.

Getting Started:

- Get certified as a CPR instructor through the American Heart Association or the Red Cross.
- Invest in your equipment (manikins, AED trainers).
- Set up a simple booking system and maybe a basic website.
- Start marketing to local businesses, community centers, and healthcare facilities.
- Consider partnering with local gyms or community colleges to host your classes.

You can start small. Maybe begin with one class a week and scale up as you get more comfortable and see the demand. This is a fantastic way to dip your toes into the world of nursing education while creating a profitable side business.

So, whether you're looking to supplement your income, transition into education full-time, or just want a flexible side gig, CPR & AED instruction could be your perfect next step. It's a prime example of how you can take your nursing knowledge and transform it into a rewarding educational venture.

Ready to turn your life-saving skills into a thriving side business? The world needs more CPR instructors, and who is better to teach than a nurse who's been there, done that, and knows exactly why these skills matter?

Embracing Your Role as a Nurse Educator: A World of Opportunities

As we wrap up this chapter, take a moment to reflect on the diverse educational paths we've explored. From continuing education and compliance training to orientation programs and even CPR & AED instruction, the world of nursing education is rich with possibilities.

Whether you're drawn to:
- Developing comprehensive continuing education courses
- Creating orientation and onboarding programs
- Offering specialized compliance training
- Writing for nursing publications
- Consulting on healthcare policies and procedures
- Teaching life-saving CPR & AED skills

Or any other educational opportunity we've discussed the core principles of success remain consistent:

- Recognize the unique value of your nursing experience.
- Invest in continuous learning to stay at the cutting edge of your field.
- Develop your teaching and communication skills.
- Leverage your professional network.
- Start small and scale up as you gain confidence.
- Cultivate business acumen to turn your knowledge into a thriving venture

As a nurse, you're already an educator. You've been teaching patients, mentoring colleagues, and navigating complex healthcare systems throughout your career. Now, it's time to take those skills and apply them on a larger scale.

The beauty of these educational opportunities lies in their versatility. Whether you're looking for a career overhaul, a profitable side gig or something in between, there's a path that can align with your goals and lifestyle.

The healthcare landscape is constantly evolving, and there's an ever-growing need for knowledgeable, experienced nurses to guide that evolution through education. Your experience, your insights, and your passion for nursing are valuable assets that the healthcare industry desperately needs.

So, as you consider your next career move, don't limit yourself. The strategies we've discussed can be your launchpad into any area of nursing education that excites you. Whether you choose to focus on high-level compliance training, practical skills like CPR, leadership development, or any other area, know this: your voice, your experience, and your expertise matter.

Are you ready to step into your power as a nurse educator? The opportunities are endless, and the impact you can make is profound. So go ahead, take that first step - whether it's signing up for an instructor certification, drafting your first CE course, or reaching out to your network about compliance training needs. The world of nursing education is waiting for you, and trust me, it's an exciting and rewarding place to be!

We've really explored the world of educational opportunities, I'm so excited for you. The number of opportunities for Nurses are tremendous. Sometimes we are so blinded by where we are that we don't see anything outside of what we're currently experiencing. My biggest hope for this book is that if for nothing else, you realize that if you're in a place you don't want to be there are many options.
Are you ready to take your entrepreneurial journey to the next level?

 In our next chapter, we'll dive into the realm of Healthcare Business Services. Get ready to discover how you can leverage your nursing expertise to provide crucial support services to healthcare organizations. From staffing agencies to practice management consulting, we'll explore a whole new set of opportunities that allow you to impact healthcare from a business perspective. So, get up, take a walk, shake your legs. Grab some fresh water, or a nice glass of wine (no judgment here) and let's continue our adventure into the world of nurse entrepreneurship!

Scan to Access Tools for Chapter Twelve

Chapter 13: Healthcare Business Services:
Your Skills, Their Solution: How to Sell What You
Know Without Leaving Nursing Behind

Alright my nursing friends, are you ready to put your
business hats on? In this chapter, we're not talking
about leaving nursing. We're talking about **leveraging
what you already know** to create in-demand business
services for healthcare organizations without going
back to school, changing your license, or abandoning
your roots.

If you've ever whispered under your breath, *"If they'd
just ask us how to fix this..."* — this is your moment.
We're about to walk through **actual business models**
built on skills you already have. Whether it's staffing,
consulting, marketing, or compliance — the
opportunities are endless when you stop seeing
yourself as just an employee and start thinking like a
service provider.

Let's dive in.

Think about this. For every single task a nurse does in
any arena of healthcare, there's a price tag attached by
the business leaders in the company. You may not see
it or feel it (that paycheck sure doesn't show the value
of what you do every day), so let's look at things from
a different perspective.

Let's create a business model from what you already
know and love to do.

I can almost hear you asking, "But Laurie, it's already a business. It's called a hospital, a nursing home, or a home health agency. What do you mean?"

Well, in this chapter, we're going to break it down. Instead of being a cog in the healthcare machine, you're going to learn how to be an engineer. We're talking about leveraging your nursing expertise to provide crucial services to healthcare organizations.

Think about all those times you've muttered under your breath, "If only they'd ask us how to run this place." It's time to be that person who gets asked - and paid - for your insights.

From staffing agencies to operations consulting, from marketing services to emergency management, we're about to uncover a treasure trove of opportunities that blend your clinical knowledge with business acumen. And the best part? Many of these services offer high returns for relatively low effort - music to any entrepreneur's ears!

So, grab your thinking caps, grab a notebook and jot down your thoughts as we move through these opportunities. I'm going to give you a creative push. A seasoned outline for how to create a business from something you already know, love and can do with very little effort. It's time to get into *"business mode"* by exploring how you can transform your nursing experience into a thriving business service. Trust me, by the end of this chapter, you'll be seeing dollar signs in all those inefficiencies you've been complaining about for years!

Let's turn your expertise into a business that healthcare organizations knew they needed help with but didn't know where to look. Let's get to it!

Staffing Agencies: From Shift Warrior to Staffing Guru

Nightmare shifts, short-staffed units, guilt trips over who's covering the weekend -you've lived it. But what if you flipped the script?

Nurses make exceptional staffing agency owners because we:

- Know what good staffing rr:alfy looks like
- Understand the nuances of facilities, units, and specialties
- Speak both "nurse" and "admin"

Whether you focus on traditional staffing (RNs, LPNs, CNAs) or specialize in high-demand niches (pediatric home health, outpatient clinics, hospice), **your insider knowledge becomes your superpower.**

Now, I know what you're thinking. "Staffing agencies? Aren't those the folks who send us those travel nurses who don't know where anything is?" Well, yes, but also no. Stick with me here, because this could be your ticket to solving staffing nightmares while building a successful business.

As a nurse, you've been on the frontlines of the *"short-staffing crisis"*. You've lived through the shortages, the mandatory overtime, and the juggling act of patient care when you're three nurses short. But here's the kicker - that experience is worth its weight in gold when it comes to running a staffing agency.

Why Nurses Make Great Staffing Agency Owners:

- You know what makes a good nurse. You've worked alongside the best (and maybe some of the worst).
- You understand the unique needs of different patients, facilities and specialties.
- You've got an insider's view of healthcare culture and what it takes to fit in.
- You speak both "nurse" and "administrator" - a rare and valuable skill.

Now, let's break down the two main types of staffing you could focus on:

- Traditional Nursing Staffing: This is your bread and butter. You'll be providing RNs, LPNs, and CNAs to hospitals, clinics, and long-term care facilities. You might cover short-term needs like sick calls or long-term contracts for travel nurses. Did you know there aren't many agencies who supply staff to Dr's offices, Outpatient Surgical and Walk-in/Urgent Care clinics? Wanna be the first one in your area?

213

- Specialized Staffing: Here's where you can really shine. Think about staffing for specific departments or specialties. Maybe you've got a knack for finding top-notch ER nurses or you know just what it takes to excel in the ICU. You could even focus on niche areas like pediatric home health or hospice care.

Getting started?

- Research market gaps (doctors' offices are
- often overlooked!)
- Build a small team and a system
  Vet nurses like your reputation depends on it. Because it *does*.

The Perks:

- High earning potential (think percentage of each placed nurse's salary)
- Flexibility to run the business from home
- Opportunity to improve healthcare by ensuring proper staffing
- Chance to help fellow nurses find flexible, well-paid positions

The Challenges:

- 24/7 availability (those 2 AM call-outs don't schedule themselves)
- Managing a large pool of nurses with different schedules and needs
- Keeping up with regulatory requirements and healthcare trends

Nurse Story: "I never thought I'd be on this side of staffing," says Martea, a former ER Department Manager who started her own specialized ER staffing agency. "But let me tell you, there's something incredibly satisfying about knowing I'm not just filling shifts - I'm matching the right nurses to the right shifts. And the flexibility? *"I haven't missed a single soccer game in two years."* Martea, former ER manager, became a staffing agency owner. She combined her nurse matchmaking skills with entrepreneurial drive — and now runs her agency with flexibility, purpose, and profit.

Martea learned that her sense of knowing who she worked with and what their strengths were really was her favorite part of her job. So, she capitalized on it for her own business and made money on the back end. She has the forethought to understand her employees, knowing where they'd fit best, and she enjoys seeing them happy because they can choose their own schedule and have the freedom to work when they want to. No more guilty feelings when you're scheduling your friends to work on the weekend. They sign up for whatever they're available for. They're calling her for shifts. What do you think? Ready to look at "staffing headaches" as potential for a thriving business? Every time you've thought "I could do this better," you were right. Now it's time to prove it!

Operations Management Consulting:
From Bedside MacGyver to Strategic Advisor

Let's talk about something that might sound fancy but

might be right up your alley: Operations Management Consulting. Think you need an MBA to improve healthcare operations? Think again.

If you've ever streamlined a discharge process,

improved handoffs, or solved a scheduling mess, Congratulations! You've already *done* operations consulting.

Healthcare systems need boots-on-the-ground

wisdom.

Your experience with:

- Workflow design
- Staffing patterns
- Compliance prep
- Quality improvement

can be translated into high-value consulting

engagements.

Let's look at it. How many times have you looked at a

workflow and thought, "This is ridiculous. If we just did X, Y, and Z, things would run so much smoother"? That's operations management in a nutshell, and healthcare organizations are willing to pay big bucks for that kind of insight. Here's your chance to finally bring those long-ignored ideas to life and make real changes in healthcare operations!

What is Operations Management Consulting and What Does it Entail?

Operations Management Consulting is all about optimizing the day-to-day functions of an organization to improve efficiency, quality, and overall performance. In healthcare, this can cover a wide range of activities:

- Analyzing and redesigning workflows to reduce bottlenecks and improve patient care
- Implementing new technologies or processes to streamline operations
- Developing strategies to improve resource allocation and reduce waste
- Creating and implementing quality improvement initiatives
- Assisting with regulatory compliance and accreditation preparation
- Designing and executing staff training programs to support operational changes

As an Operations Management Consultant, you might find yourself diving deep into data analysis one day, facilitating workshops with frontline staff the next, and presenting recommendations to C-suite executives the day after. It's a dynamic field that allows you to make a significant impact on how healthcare is delivered.

Why Nurses Make Fantastic Operations Management Consultants:

- You've seen firsthand what works and what doesn't on the frontlines.
- You understand the delicate balance between efficiency and quality patient care.
- You're used to juggling multiple priorities and making quick decisions.
- You speak the language of both clinical staff and administrators.

Here are some areas where your nursing expertise can really triumph in operations consulting:

- Process Improvement: Convoluted discharge processes that always cause delays, you could be the one to streamline it across an entire hospital system.
- Workflow Optimization: Think about how you organically developed your own system for managing your patient load. Now imagine applying that skill to redesign workflows for entire departments.
- Resource Allocation: You know better than anyone how critical proper staffing and resource management is. Use that knowledge to help facilities allocate their resources more effectively.

218

- Quality Management: Your experience with quality measures and patient outcomes is incomparable. Help organizations improve their quality scores and patient satisfaction.

This is just the tip of the iceberg. Hospital Systems, Nursing Education systems and Multi-Billion Dollar corporations in the healthcare arena are looking for someone to make the system better. Look at the Nurses who created Code Cards during COVID. Did they think they were creating a system that would be integrated throughout healthcare? I bet they didn't. What you see and work with every day. The processes you know and have manipulated to work efficiently when you're on the floor or in the field are just the thing a Boardroom full of MBAs cannot even imagine let alone implement. From something as form utilization to software tasks, to offset staffing... You have the knowledge those MBAs look for every single day. We simply need to add monetary value to it. That my friends is consulting. These corporations, facilities and business owners are paying you for your expertise. They pay you to solve their problems. You were Made for this. I promise!

Getting Started:

- Identify your niche. What area of operations did you excel at in your nursing career?
- Brush up on business concepts. Take some courses in process improvement methodologies if it will increase your confidence and reduce your "imposter syndrome".
- Start small. Offer to consult for your current employer or a local clinic.
- Build a portfolio. Document your successes and the improvements you've made.
- Network with healthcare administrators and decision-makers.
- Offer a masterclass on your area of expertise and how implementation of your method is beneficial to Nurse Managers and /or Accreditation Bodies.

The Perks:

- High earning potential (consultants can charge hefty hourly or project-based fees)
- Intellectual stimulation from solving complex problems
- Opportunity to impact healthcare on a system-wide level
- Flexibility to work with multiple organizations

The Challenges:

- Need to stay updated on latest healthcare regulations and trends
- Potential resistance to change from staff or management
- Balancing efficiency with quality patient care
- Proving your value in a field traditionally dominated by non-clinical consultants

Nurse Story: Heather, a former Long Term Care DON who now runs her own operations consulting firm says, "I used to get so frustrated with inefficiencies in my facility that the Administrator and Ownership refused to change but held me responsible for." she says. "Now, I get to show others how they can fix those issues across entire systems. Last month, I helped a rural long term care facility increase their unskilled bed rate by 40%. The best part? I'm making more money than I ever did as a DON, and I'm home for dinner with my family every night without worrying about an urgent call."

Heather's secret weapon? Her nursing experience. "When I walk into a facility, I can spot inefficiencies that non-clinical consultants might miss," she explains. "And because I've been in the nurses' shoes, I know how to implement changes in a way that staff will actually *embrace. I now teach others how to fix the problems I used to be blamed for.*"

So, what do you think? Ready to take your problem-solving skills to the next level? Make use of every single time you've thought, "There's got to be a better way to do this," because you were on to something. Heather was able to increase that rural facility's bed rate by 40% and she has never looked back.

Start small. Consult locally. Build a portfolio of wins. It's time to turn those insights into a thriving consulting business. Healthcare needs your frontline expertise more than ever!

Healthcare Marketing Services:

From Bedside Chats to Brand Strategy

Let's tackle something you might not have considered before: Healthcare Marketing Services. You've probably never thought about Marketing a Healthcare business. You've seen the ads or seen the Marketers on your floor looking for patients to admit to their Home Health agency, ALF or Rehab, but never stopped to think what it all entails. This might just be your ticket to combining your healthcare knowledge with your creative side.

How do you instinctively know how to *break it down*, make it relatable, maybe even throw in an analogy or two? Well, that knowledge is exactly what creating a marketing plan is. Simplicity, clear, concise and above all else relatable. Healthcare organizations are desperate for people who can do exactly that.

222

The ability to make a patient, doctor or case manager feel confident that the patient is in good hands is an art. Someone who knows exactly what the patient and family have been through knows exactly what to say to alleviate all the anxiety everyone is feeling as the discharge date gets closer. Healthcare Marketing is this and so much more.

What are Healthcare Marketing Services?

Healthcare Marketing Services cover a wide range of activities aimed at promoting healthcare services, educating patients, and building trust between healthcare providers and their communities. This can include:

- Creating engaging content for healthcare websites and social media
- Developing patient education materials that people might actually read
- Crafting email campaigns to promote wellness initiatives or new services
- Designing infographics that explain complex health concepts simply
- Writing blog posts or articles that translate the latest medical research for a general audience
- Helping healthcare providers build their personal brands and online presence

Why Nurses Make Exceptional Healthcare Marketers:
You understand medical terminology and
can translate it into plain English
You have firsthand experience of patient
concerns and questions
You know the healthcare system inside
out. It's strengths and its pain points.
You have a built-in ethical compass that
ensures marketing remains truthful and
patient-centered.
You bring credibility to health-related
content that a non-medical marketer
simply can't match.

Areas Where Your Nursing Expertise Can Stand Out
in a crowd:

Content Creation for Healthcare Providers:
Have you written a million discharge
instructions? Imagine creating clear, engaging
content for an entire hospital system's website.
Your knack for explaining things clearly could
revolutionize how a healthcare organization
communicates with its patients.

**Social Media Management for Medical
Practices:** Think about how you educate
patients one-on-one. Now picture doing that on
a larger scale, crafting social media posts that
inform, engage, and build trust with thousands
of potential patients.

Patient Education Materials Development: Those anatomy doodles you've sketched to explain procedures? They could become professional info graphics used across multiple healthcare facilities. your ability to make complex information digestible is a superpower in healthcare marketing.

Healthcare Influencer Collaborations: Your Clinical knowledge makes you the perfect liaison between healthcare providers and social media influencers, ensuring that health related content is both engaging and medically accurate.

Getting Started:

- Identify your niche. Are you passionate about women's health? Pediatrics? Chronic disease management? Hospice – End of Life?
- Start a blog.
- Offer patient education tools.
- Partner with providers or eldercare agencies who need *real healthcare voices* to communicate clearly.
- Consider collaborating with a graphic designer or web developer to offer more comprehensive services.

The Perks:

- Flexible work hours and often the ability to work remotely
- Opportunity to educate and impact health on a broader scale
- Chance to flex your creative muscles while using your medical knowledge
- Potential for diverse projects and continuous learning

The Challenges:

- Keeping up with rapidly changing social media trends and algorithms
- Balancing medical accuracy with marketing appeal
- Navigating healthcare regulations in marketing (like HIPAA compliance)
- Competing with traditional marketing agencies for healthcare clients

Nurse Story: "Now I help hospitals speak human."

Angela, a pediatric nurse turned healthcare marketing agency owner. Her vaccination campaign increased clinic turnout by 30% all rooted in her ability to speak both medical and emotional truth. The best part? I'm using my nursing knowledge every day, but I have the flexibility to pick up my kids from school and work from our family vacation spots!"

Angela's secret sauce? Her nursing background.
"When I create content, I'm not just thinking about what sounds good I'm thinking about what patients and families really need to know, what questions

they're afraid to ask, and how to present information in a way that promotes better outcomes," she explains. "Plus, healthcare providers trust me because I've shown that I understand the medical-business side of things as well."

What do you think? Ready to use your communication superpowers to revolutionize healthcare marketing? Every time you've successfully explained a complex medical concept to a patient, you were flexing your marketing muscles. Now it's time to turn those skills into a business that can educate and engage patients on a much larger scale. The healthcare industry needs your unique blend of medical knowledge and communication skills – are you ready to deliver?

High-Return, Low-Effort Services:
The Nursing Tasks You Forgot Were Valuable

Ready for a mind-bending exercise? I want you to take everything you think you know about the value of your nursing skills and throw it out the window. Why? Because we're about to enter a realm where those everyday nursing tasks you take for granted are about to be your key to entrepreneurial success.

Welcome to the world of High-Return/Low-Effort Business Services in healthcare. This is where real, tangible value is placed on your specific areas of expertise, skills, or even those routine tasks you do without a second thought.

It's hard to imagine that a single, everyday task, something you do automatically as part of your job, could form the foundation of an entire business. Well, it's not only true, but it's a trend that's almost on a revolutionary level. Buckle up, because we're about to go on a wild ride through a landscape where entire companies have been built around single aspects of what you do every day.

Think about it for a second. All the times you were called to help a colleague navigate the complex maze of coding or when you expertly prepared your unit for an upcoming survey? How about when you trained the entire staff on the latest HIPAA regulations in an email handout? Each of these tasks - tasks that you might consider "just part of the job" - represents a specialized skill set that organizations are willing to pay top dollar for.

In this section, we're going to explore a variety of high-return, low-effort business services that you, yes YOU, are uniquely qualified to offer. We're talking about things like:

- Compliance and Regulation Services
- Facility Setup and Support Services
- Administrative Services
- Technology Services

There's gold in the little things.

Things like:

- HIPAA education
- Policy and POC writing
- Survey prep
- Onboarding workflows
- EMR tips and fixes.

Sound like chores? Those are services. And organizations will gladly pay to have them done right.

Let's break these down into categories.

Compliance and Regulation Services

In the world of healthcare, compliance isn't just a buzzword – it's a critical component of daily operations. You know by now that this is my area of expertise, so I'm pretty passionate about it. Your experience navigating the complex web of healthcare regulations is exactly what will distinguish you from everyone else. This category includes:

- HIPAA compliance training and auditing
- Survey preparation and plans of correction
- Accreditation preparation

Let's zoom in on HIPAA compliance training and auditing, because if there's one thing that keeps healthcare administrators up at night, it's the fear of a HIPAA breach.

HIPAA Compliance Training and Auditing:
Turning Privacy Protection into Profit

Think about all those times you've had to explain to a new nurse why they can't discuss Mrs. Johnson's condition in the elevator. Or when you've had to gently remind Dr. Smith that, no, he can't access his ex-wife's medical records just because she's in the system. Guess what? You've been doing HIPAA compliance training all along!

As a HIPAA compliance consultant, you can:

- Develop and deliver training programs for healthcare organizations
- Conduct audits to identify potential HIPAA violations
- Create policies and procedures to ensure HIPAA compliance
- Assist with breach notifications and mitigation strategies

Why Nurses Excel at This:

- You understand the day-to-day realities of patient care and data handling
- You've seen firsthand how HIPAA applies in various clinical situations
- You can translate complex regulations into practical, actionable steps for staff

Getting Started:

- Brush up on the latest HIPAA regulations (they're always changing!)
- Consider getting certified as a HIPAA Security Professional
- Develop a training curriculum that's engaging and relevant to healthcare staff
- Start by offering your services to your current employer or local clinics

The Perks:

- High demand (HIPAA isn't going anywhere, folks)
- Ability to work with multiple organizations
- Potential for both on-site and remote work
- Satisfaction of helping protect patient privacy and preventing costly breaches

The Challenges:

- Staying updated on evolving regulations
- Dealing with resistance from staff who see HIPAA as a burden
- Balancing strict compliance with practical implementation

You've lived HIPAA. You've explained it a hundred times. Why not get paid to teach and audit it?

- Deliver engaging compliance training
- Conduct HIPAA audits
- Create staff-friendly policies
- Help with breach mitigation

"I make HIPAA memorable. They actually apply it."

— Mario, former OR nurse turned compliance consultant

Mario's secret? He uses real-world scenarios and interactive exercises to make HIPAA relatable. "Last month, I helped a huge multi location practice revamp their HIPAA program. Not only did they pass their audit with flying colors, but their staff reported feeling more confident in handling patient information. And let me tell you, my consulting fee for that project was more than I made in three months as a bedside nurse!"

HIPAA breaches have become a real threat in the healthcare landscape. Analyzing existing software that falls short or learning where new software and increased compliance training can make HIPAA breaches a much less common occurrence can be something that saves these healthcare companies millions of dollars in damages and federal fines. Your expertise could be a saving grace to those businesses.

So, what do you think now? Think you can turn your privacy-protecting superpowers into a profitable venture? Every time you've caught something that threatened patient confidentiality, you've been honing skills that organizations are willing to pay top dollar for. It's time to take those skills and turn them into a business that not only pays well but also contributes to better, more secure patient care in the entire ecosystem.

Facility Setup and Support Services

What about a field where your frontline nursing experience can quite literally shape the future of healthcare delivery?
Facility Setup and Support Services.
This category includes:

- Home Health agency setup and support
- Residential Assisted Living Facility (ALF) setup and support
- Telemedicine setup and support
- Memory Care Unit set-up and support

We're going to zoom in on Home Health agency setup and support, because if there's one thing the healthcare industry needs right now, it's more high-quality home health services. The Silver Tsunami isn't going to take care of itself.

Home Health Agency Setup and Support: Building Healthcare from the Ground Up

Have you ever thought "If I ran this agency things would be different"? Well, here's your chance to put your money where your mouth is. As a Home Health consultant, you're not just filling out paperwork you're crafting the blueprint for patient-centered care in the community.

As a Home Health Agency start up consultant, you can:

- Guide entrepreneurs or healthcare organizations through the licensing process
- Develop policies and procedures that align with regulations and best practices
- Create staffing models and recruitment strategies
- Set up quality assurance and performance improvement (QAPI) programs
- Establish billing and coding systems
- Train staff on home health-specific skills and documentation

Why Nurses Excel at This:

- You understand the day-to-day realities of home health care delivery
- You've seen what works (and what doesn't) in various healthcare settings
- You can anticipate potential challenges and proactively address them

- You know how to balance regulatory requirements with practical, patient-centered care

Getting Started:

- Brush up on your state's home health licensing requirements (they vary widely!)
- Consider getting certified in, Home Health nursing or administration
- Develop a comprehensive "agency setup" checklist, guide or even a course that you can teach online.
- Network with healthcare entrepreneurs and business consultants
- Start by offering your services to a local healthcare organization looking to expand into home health
- Get on social media and add value to small home health businesses. Let your expertise shine. Answer questions and offer assistance. It will get the ball rolling quickly.

The Perks:

- High demand (aging population = growing need for home health services)
- Potential for both short-term setup projects and ongoing support contracts
- Satisfaction of shaping healthcare delivery in your community

- Opportunity to create agencies that prioritize both patient care and staff well-being

The Challenges:

- Navigating complex and ever-changing regulations
- Balancing the clinical ideal with business realities
- Potential for long hours during the initial setup phase

Edwin, a former home health nurse who now runs a thriving Home Health Consultant company says: "I used to come home frustrated, thinking about all the ways my agency could improve," he says. "Now, I get to build agencies from the ground up, incorporating all those lessons I learned the hard way."

Edwin's secret sauce? His nursing background. "When I'm helping a new agency to get started, I'm not just thinking about meeting regulatory requirements. I'm thinking about how to make the owner's job easier, how to make the nurse's job smoother and less taxing, how to ensure patients get the best care possible, and how to create a sustainable business model. It's like being the fairy godfather of Home Health, and I love every minute of it."

Last year, Edwin helped set up dozens of new home health agencies. "The best part," he smiles, "is when I visit these agencies months later and see them thriving with systems, I helped them to create. The bonus is always a happy staff, satisfied patients, and owners making a profit while providing quality care. And let me tell you, my consulting fees for these projects aren't small. They've allowed me to pay off my student loans and take my family on our first real vacation in years."

So, what do you think? Ready to be the architect of patient-centered home health care? Every frustration you've experienced, every workaround you've created, and every "if only" you've muttered under your breath – is valuable insight that can help your clients build better home health agencies. It's time to take that wealth of knowledge and turn it into a consulting business that not only pays well but also shapes the future of healthcare delivery in your community. The personal satisfaction when you hear from a client that their license was approved is nothing short of pure joy. The thought of not having to be the one who has to worry when the caregivers and nurses call out is sheer bliss!

Administrative Services: Turning Paperwork into Profit

Alright, my fellow nurses, let's talk about something that might make some of you groan: "Administrative Services". But hold onto your stethoscopes, because we're about to turn those mundane tasks into money-making machines. In this category, we've got:

- Medical billing and coding consulting

- Credentialing services
- Healthcare data analysis and reporting

We're going to zoom in on credentialing services, because if there's one thing that can make or break a healthcare provider's career (and paycheck), it's proper credentialing.

Credentialing Services:

Your Ticket to the Big Leagues of Healthcare Administration

How many times have you had to update your own credentials, chase down references, or wait anxiously for your privileges to be approved? Well, imagine being the person who makes that process smooth as butter for other healthcare professionals. That's what a credentialing consultant does, and trust me, it's a service that's in high demand.

As a credentialing consultant, you can:

- Manage the entire credentialing and privileging process for healthcare providers
- Ensure compliance with accreditation standards and regulatory requirements
- Develop and implement credentialing policies and procedures
- Develop, set-up and implement credentialing processes/systems for new providers
- Conduct primary source verification

- Prepare files for credentialing committee review
- Assist with reappointment and renewal processes.

Why Nurses Excel at This:

You understand the importance of credentials in healthcare settings. You're familiar with various healthcare roles and their required qualifications. You're detail-oriented (all those orders you had to read, decipher and execute at a moment's notice, never forgetting a word or task) You know how to navigate complex healthcare systems and bureaucracies

Getting Started:

- Familiarize yourself with NCQA, Joint Commission, ACHC, CHAP and other relevant credentialing standards
- Consider getting certified as a Certified Provider Credentialing Specialist (CPCS) or a Certified Healthcare Human Resource (CHHR) professional designation.
- Develop a deep understanding of credentialing software and databases
- Network with medical staff offices, healthcare administrators, and independent practitioners

- Start by offering your services to small practices or local agencies

The Perks:

- High demand (every healthcare provider needs credentialing)
- Potential for remote work
- Steady income with opportunities for growth
- Satisfaction of helping healthcare providers practice to their full potential

The Challenges:

- Dealing with time-sensitive deadlines
- Managing large volumes of detailed information
- Staying updated on changing regulations and requirements

Veronica, a former Long-Term Care MDS specialist, who now runs a thriving credentialing consultancy says: "I used to dread the credentialing process for my own renewals," she laughs. "Now, I'm the go-to person for healthcare providers who want their credentialing headaches to disappear."

Veronica's secret weapon? Her nursing background. "When I'm working on a provider's application, I'm not just filling out forms. I understand the critical nature of each credential, the importance of timely approvals, and the stress providers feel during this process. I can speak their language and anticipate potential issues before they arise."

Last year, Veronica helped over 100 healthcare providers get credentialed or re-credentialed. "The best part," she says with a grin, "is the relief in their voices when I tell them their application is approved. And my consulting fees have never been a question. This career shift has allowed me to create a flexible schedule that lets me enjoy my life on my own terms while still bringing in what I did when working in the office 40 hours a week and sometimes more if I choose to." Thats the point of shifting right? Having a Choice?!?

So, what do you think? Is Credentialing fairy godmother (or godfather) to stressed-out healthcare providers your calling? Every frustration you've experienced with paperwork, every eyeroll at bureaucratic red tape, every sigh of relief when your own credentials finally came through – that's all valuable insight that can help you streamline this process for others. You know what to look for. You know what's missing and what to ask, because you know what everything should look like. There is no "Healthcare HR specialty "in college. Can an HR specialist do this? Sure. Do they have critical thinking skills? Your experience? Nope. Something to definitely think about.

It's time to take that wealth of knowledge and turn it into a business that not only pays well but also helps healthcare providers focus on what they do best – caring for patients. The satisfaction of knowing you've helped a doctor, nurse practitioner, or fellow RN clear the final hurdle to starting their dream job, That's priceless. And the best part? No more night shifts, no more missed family dinners, and no more scrubs (unless you want to wear them while working from your home office, of course!).

The mind shift needed to understand that everything a nurse does, every single task can be commoditized, is profound. A price tag can be placed on it all. And you can specialize in any of them. Gone are the days of having to be everything to everyone in order to keep your head above water. Mental health and quality of life become very important when you think about the fact that you may have only 10 years in retirement before you are physically unable to "enjoy life" the way you used to. Why can't we have careers we love and a life that truly is filled with joy?

But here's the real kicker – the skills you've honed as a nurse aren't just valuable in healthcare settings. They're superpowers in the business world. Your ability to remain calm under pressure, to communicate complex ideas simply, to juggle multiple priorities – these are the very skills that high-paid consultants spend years trying to develop.

So, I want you to do something for me. Tonight, when you're lying in bed, possibly dreading your next shift, I want you to close your eyes and imagine a different future. A future where your nursing knowledge is your ticket to freedom, not your ball and chain. A future where you are valued not just for your ability to show up, but for your unique insights and expertise.

Imagine a world where your years of experience aren't just lines on a resume, but the foundation of a thriving business. A world where you're not racing against the clock to finish your charting but setting your own schedule. A world where you're not just surviving but truly thriving.

This isn't a pipe dream. It's a reality that nurses all over the country are creating for themselves right now. And you know what? They're not superheroes. They're nurses, just like you, who dared to see their skills in a new light.

The Big Picture:

Everything You Know is Billable

That moment you sigh and think, *"There has to be another way"* That's a business waiting to be built.

You don't have to become a CEO with a team of 50.

You just have to package what you already know and offer it as a service.

You've taught, explained, trained, fixed, and solved your way through every role. Now it's time to let that experience work for *you*.

So tonight, before bed, ask yourself: "What am I doing every day that someone else would pay to have done well? What do I love doing that other people procrastinate with because their not good at it, or just plain hate doing it? This is the key to understanding that people & businesses will pay someone to do it.

Then ask:
"What do I want my next chapter to look like?"
Because you, my friend, are not just surviving
healthcare anymore.
You're ready to lead it on your own terms.

Scan to Access Tools for Chapter Thirteen

Chapter 14: Innovative and Emerging Opportunities

It's time to put on your innovator hats. Not just to "think outside the box," but to redesign the box entirely. We're about to dive into a world where your nursing expertise isn't just valuable, it's revolutionary. But before we jump in, let's clear the air on a few things.

No, technology will not replace nurses. It's not even close. Nothing replaces human connection, clinical intuition, and fast decision-making you bring to the table. Let's just settle that now.

When we talk about innovation in nursing, I want you to expand your lens. This isn't about developing new charting software — though that would be a win, too. This is about creating healthcare systems, tools, and solutions that transform care at its core.

For far too long, nurses have been stifled and dismissed when it comes to technological innovation. Any ideas really. You're on the frontlines of healthcare. You already know where healthcare fails and where it thrives. That insight isn't just useful — it's the foundation of your next chapter.

Innovation doesn't belong to someone "smarter." It belongs to someone who knows how things work, and how they could work better. That's you.

Here's where the magic really happens: It's time to start thinking like the "powers that be." What keeps hospital CEOs up at night? What are the pain points for healthcare administrators? What makes Owners cringe when they hear about it? When you can answer questions and provide solutions, that's when you strike gold.

You have information and insights that IT companies and healthcare consultants would kill for. You understand the day-to-day realities of healthcare delivery. You know where the systems break down and where they shine. You know the strengths and weaknesses of the current systems. This knowledge makes you a potential disruptor in the healthcare space.

In this chapter, we're going to explore a range of innovative opportunities where nurses like you are making waves. From AI and machine learning to revolutionary approaches in healthcare administration, we'll look at how nurses are driving innovation far beyond traditional roles.

So, open your mind to the possibilities. Let go of any preconceived notions about what nurses can or can't do in the world of healthcare innovation. Because I'm telling you, the future of healthcare isn't just nurse-led – it's nurse-innovated.

Are you ready to see just how far your nursing skills can take you in the world of healthcare innovation?

Let's dive in and explore the exciting frontier of nurse-led innovation!

Technology in Healthcare: The Nurse's Role

Now that we've set the stage, Let's start with one of the biggest arenas of disruption: **healthcare technology**. Spoiler alert: It's not just about being an end-user anymore.

Healthcare IT Consulting: From User to Designer

All those times you've muttered under your breath about the clunky Electronic Health Record (EHR) system you're forced to use, and every time you've cursed an EHR at 3AM, you've been diagnosing a broken system. What if, instead of complaining, you built the solution?

As a nurse IT consultant, you bring something invaluable to the table: real-world experience. You know what works at 3 AM when you're juggling multiple patients and what falls apart when the system crashes during shift change. This insight is pure gold for healthcare IT companies.

Take Christina, for example. After 7 years in the Hospital and 10 years as a Hospice Nurse, Christina transitioned into healthcare IT consulting. "I used to complain about our EHR all the time, then I took the time to learn it and understand what its weaknesses were." she said. "Now, I'm part of the team designing a system that actually makes sense for the healthcare staff. You cannot imagine the incredible satisfaction when I see my ideas implemented and I know I'm making life easier for nurses everywhere."

Telemedicine Setup and Support:

Bringing Healthcare to the Digital Age

If the pandemic taught us anything, it's that telemedicine is here to stay. We've moved beyond the basics and now face higher expectations. Almost every provider now sees setting up an effective telemedicine program as essential. But who's going to develop and implement these complex systems? Providers rely on IT professionals, but successful integration into healthcare depends on understanding the fundamentals. That's where nurse entrepreneurs are making their mark.

As a telemedicine consultant, you can help healthcare providers:

- Set up user-friendly telehealth platforms
- Train staff on effective virtual patient interactions
- Develop protocols for remote patient monitoring
- Ensure compliance with state and federal telehealth regulations

Mark, a former home health nurse, now runs a successful telemedicine consulting business. "I saw firsthand how telemedicine could transform home health care," he explains. "Now, I help agencies across the country implement telemedicine programs that improve patient care and staff efficiency. It's the perfect blend of my nursing experience and my love for technology."

The Intersection of Nursing Expertise and Tech Innovation

Here's where things get really exciting. Tech companies are starting to realize that they need nurses involved in every stage of healthcare technology development. From conceptualization to testing to implementation, nurse innovators are becoming an integral part of the process.

Imagine being part of a team developing:

- AI-powered triage systems that actually understand the nuances of patient assessment
- Virtual reality programs for patient education that make complex medical concepts easy to understand
- Wearable devices that not only track vital signs but interpret them in a clinically meaningful way

The possibilities are endless, and nurses are uniquely positioned to bridge the gap between cutting-edge technology and practical healthcare applications.

You don't need to be a coding wizard to make an impact in healthcare technology. Your nursing expertise, combined with a willingness to learn and innovate, is your superpower. Whether you're interested in consulting, product development, or implementation, there's a place for you in the world of healthcare tech.

So, the next time you find yourself frustrated with a piece of healthcare technology, don't just complain – start thinking about how you could make it better. Because who knows? Your idea could be the next big thing in healthcare innovation.

AI and Machine Learning in Healthcare: Your Nursing Knowledge, Amplified

Let's talk about the buzzwords that are taking the healthcare world by storm: Artificial Intelligence (AI) and Machine Learning. Now, before you start picturing robots taking over hospitals, let's get one thing straight – AI in healthcare is all about amplifying human expertise, not replacing it. And guess what? Your nursing knowledge is the secret sauce that can make AI truly revolutionary.

AI: Your New Sidekick, Not Your Replacement

Think of AI as the world's most efficient intern. It can process vast amounts of data, spot patterns, and make suggestions. But it needs your nursing expertise to understand the context, make nuanced decisions, and provide that human touch that's so crucial in healthcare.

Where Nurses Fit in the AI Revolution

You might be thinking, "I'm not a tech expert. I have trouble with my iPad. My seven-year-old showed me how to work certain apps on my phone. How can I contribute to AI development?" Here's the thing – you don't need to be a coding wizard to be at the forefront of AI in healthcare. What you do need is your nursing experience and insights. Here's how you can make an impact:

1. Identifying Opportunities: You're on the front lines. You know where the bottlenecks are, where errors commonly occur, and where better decision support could make a difference. These insights are invaluable for AI developers.
2. Designing Solutions: Your understanding of clinical workflows can be integral in shaping AI tools that actually work in real-world healthcare settings.
3. Training AI Models: Your expertise can help ensure that AI systems are trained on

relevant, high-quality data that reflects the realities of patient care.

4. Implementation and Feedback: Who would be better at guiding the rollout of AI tools and provide crucial feedback than the nurses who will be using them? (That's a novel idea, isn't it?)

Real-World AI Applications in Nursing

Let's look at some exciting areas where AI is making waves in healthcare, with nurses leading the charge:

1. Clinical Decision Support

Imagine an AI system that can analyze a patient's vital signs, lab results, and medical history in real-time, flagging potential issues before they become critical. Nurses are helping develop these systems, ensuring they align with real-world clinical practices.

2. Predictive Analytics for Patient Care

AI can predict which patients are at higher risk for complications, readmissions, or specific health issues. Nurses are crucial in refining these predictive models, making sure they consider the subtle signs that experienced nurses recognize.

3. Administrative Task Automation

Have we had a discussion about revolutionizing healthcare administration? AI systems are being developed to automate time-consuming tasks like scheduling, documentation, and even coding for billing. Nurses are at the forefront, ensuring these systems actually save time and improve accuracy.

4. Personalized Patient Education

AI-powered systems can tailor patient education materials based on individual needs, learning styles, and health literacy levels. Nurses are helping design these systems, bringing their experience in effective patient communication to the table.

The AI-Powered Care Plan Revolution

Let's dive deeper into an area where AI could be a game-changer: Care planning and MDS assessments in long-term care.

Imagine an AI system that could:

Draft truly personalized care plans (not the generic ones we see now in most EHRs) but one that is based on a resident's comprehensive assessment and complete history. Ensure MDS assessments are accurate, compliant, and optimized for appropriate reimbursement. Continuously update care plans based on the residents' progress and changing needs.

Flag potential issues or opportunities for care improvement and documentation

This isn't science fiction, it's a real possibility. And nurses like you are perfectly positioned to help develop and implement such systems.

Your Next Steps in the AI Revolution

Ready to be part of the AI revolution in healthcare? Here are some steps you can take:

- Stay Informed: Keep up with the latest developments in healthcare AI. Follow healthcare tech blogs, attend webinars, or join online communities discussing these topics.
- Identify Problems AI Could Solve: Start noting down processes or tasks in your workplace. Once you understand the concept of AI and its potential, you can easily identify problems that could benefit from AI assistance.
- Collaborate: Reach out to tech-savvy colleagues or local tech meetups. Your nursing insights combined with their technical skills could spark innovative ideas.
- Consider Further Education: While you don't need to become a data scientist, some basic understanding of AI and data analytics can go a long way. Look for

online courses or workshops designed for healthcare professionals.

- Speak Up: If your organization is implementing new tech solutions, make sure you're part of the conversation. Your front-line experience is invaluable in ensuring these tools actually work in practice.

Do you realize the future of AI in healthcare isn't just about algorithms and data, it's about combining technological power with human expertise. And that's where you, with your nursing knowledge and experience, have the power to shape the future of healthcare.

So, are you ready to be at the forefront of the AI revolution in healthcare? Your nursing expertise could be the key to developing AI solutions that truly transform patient care.

The Financial Revolution:

AI as Your Path to Prosperity

Now, let's talk about something that you might not readily want to discuss as it goes against what "Nursing" is truly viewed as - the potential for significant financial rewards in the world of healthcare AI. We all know that nursing is viewed as an altruistic career. We work for patients. Everything centers on "for the patients". But some of us also know it can be lucrative; the concept of Overtime would be moot if not. Many of us have sacrificed countless evenings, weekends, and holidays for that extra pay. We've missed family dinners, kids' soccer games, precious moments with loved ones, first dates, hell ANY social life whatsoever all for the sake of financial stability or getting ahead.

But what if I told you that your nursing expertise, combined with AI innovation, could not only match but potentially well exceed your overtime earnings - all while giving you back your life?

Here's the exciting reality: The healthcare AI market is booming. "The global artificial intelligence (AI) in healthcare market was valued at $19.54 billion in 2023 and is expected to grow at a compound annual growth rate (CAGR) of 43.2% from 2024 to 2032, reaching $490.96 billion by the end of that decade." That's billion with a 'B'. And guess who's perfectly positioned to tap into this goldmine? That's right - nurses like you.

Consider this:

- AI consultants in healthcare can command fees ranging from $150 to $500 per hour.
- Nurses who develop successful AI applications or start AI-focused healthcare companies can see their earnings skyrocket into the seven or even eight-figure range.
- Even as employees in health tech companies, nurses with AI expertise are

seeing salaries that dwarf traditional nursing roles.

So, the care planning and MDS assessment AI we discussed? Imagine if you were the nurse who developed that system. You wouldn't just be improving patient care - you'd be revolutionizing an entire industry. And the financial rewards? They could set you up for life, or your family for generations.

But it's not just about the money. It's about creating a legacy. It's about developing solutions that could impact millions of patients and healthcare providers. It's about building a business that continues to generate income long after you've stopped actively working.

Think about it: Instead of selling your time and mental wellbeing for overtime pay, you could be investing your expertise into developing AI solutions that work for you 24/7. You could be the one calling the shots, setting your own schedule, and yes - making it home for dinner with your family.

This isn't a pipe dream. Nurses around the country are already making this leap. They're partnering with tech companies, founding startups, and consulting on AI projects. And they're not just making a difference - they're making a fortune.

So, the next time you're considering picking up that extra shift, ask yourself: Could this time be better spent developing the next big thing in healthcare AI?

Could your unique insights be the key to unlocking not just better patient care, but also the financial freedom you've been working so hard for?

Here are some actionable steps you can take to start your journey into healthcare AI:

- Educate Yourself:
    - Watch YouTube videos on AI. A couple of my favorites are The AI Advantage for everything AI and for learning some real basics and then in healthcare, there are Channels like "AI in Medicine" and "Healthcare Robotics" this will offer a great introduction.
    - Join Discord communities focused on healthcare technology and AI. Look for groups like "HealthTech Innovators" or "Nurses in Tech".
    - Read AI-focused healthcare blogs. Sites like "HealthcareITNews.com" and "AI in Healthcare" provide current insights and trends.

- Experiment with AI:
    - Try out open-source AI language models to get a feel for the technology's capabilities in healthcare scenarios.
    - Explore platforms like Google's Teachable Machine to

understand how AI can be trained on specific datasets.

- Network and Collaborate:
    - Attend virtual or local meetups on healthcare technology and AI.
    - Connect with tech-savvy colleagues or local startups working in Healthtech.

- Start Small:
    - Identify a simple process in your workplace that could benefit from automation or AI assistance.
    - Sketch out how an AI solution might work to address this issue.

Every AI revolution starts with a single idea. Your nursing expertise combined with AI knowledge could be the catalyst for the next big innovation in healthcare. The question is, are you ready to take that first step towards your AI-powered future?

Revolutionary Approaches to Healthcare
Administration: From Bedside to Boardroom

When we talk about nursing innovation, it's easy to focus solely on patient care. But what if I told you that some of the most groundbreaking opportunities for nurse entrepreneurs lie in an area many of us try to avoid - healthcare administration.

That's right. We're about to dive into the world of backend processes, reimbursement, and compliance. Stay with me here, because this is where the magic happens.

Shifting Focus: The Administrative Revolution

For years, nurses have been the ones grumbling about administrative inefficiencies. We've dealt with clunky systems, confusing paperwork, and processes that seem to be designed to make our lives difficult. But who is better at fixing these problems than the nurses who understand them inside and out?

The Reimbursement Revolution:
AI-Driven Coding and Billing

Let's talk about a pain point that affects every healthcare organization: reimbursement. Did you know that, according to recent studies, more than 50% of potential reimbursement is left on the table due to poor coding and reporting? That's billions of dollars that could be going towards better patient care, improved facilities, or (let's be honest) better staff salaries.

Now, imagine an AI-driven system, conceived and developed by nurses, that could optimize this entire process. This system wouldn't just code and bill - it would analyze every aspect of patient care, ensuring that all services provided are accurately documented, coded, and billed according to the latest regulations and contractual agreements.

The implications are staggering:

- Healthcare providers would be assured of receiving 100% of the reimbursement they're entitled to under their agreements.
- The human error factor in coding and billing would be virtually eliminated.
- Compliance with complex and ever-changing regulations would be automatic and consistent.
- Healthcare organizations could redirect resources from billing departments to patient care.

- The data gathered could provide invaluable insights into care patterns and resource utilization.

Compliance Automation: From Headache to Competitive Advantage

Compliance - it's the word that makes most healthcare professionals cringe. But what if, instead of being a burden, compliance could be a competitive advantage?

Enter nurse-led compliance automation. By combining your understanding of healthcare regulations with cutting-edge technology, you could develop systems that:

- Automatically updated policies and procedures based on the latest regulatory changes
- Provide real-time guidance & education to staff on compliance issues
- Generate comprehensive reports for audits and inspections

- Predict and prevent potential compliance issues before they occur

The Nurse Entrepreneur's Advantage in Administration

Because you may have never been an Administrator or Healthcare Business owner doesn't mean you don't understand all the rules and regulations. You think about those things AND are sure patient care is done correctly every single day. So, the secret is - that's exactly why you're perfectly positioned to revolutionize healthcare administration. You understand the day-to-day realities of healthcare delivery. You know how services are provided, documented and coded. You've seen firsthand the challenges of understanding and ensuring accurate reimbursement coding and maintaining compliance.

This insider knowledge, combined with innovative technology, could truly transform how healthcare organizations operate. And the best part? The potential for financial rewards in this space is enormous.

Getting Started in Administrative Innovation

Ready to dive into the world of healthcare administration innovation? Here are some steps to get you started:

- Identify Pain Points: What administrative tasks cause the most frustration in your current role? In the role of others around you? These are potential opportunities for innovation.

- Educate Yourself: Take courses in healthcare administration, coding, and compliance. Platforms like Coursera and edX offer a wealth of options.
- Network: Connect with healthcare administrators and tech professionals. Join professional organizations like the American Health Information Management Association (AHIMA) or the Healthcare Financial Management Association (HFMA).
- Start Small: Look for opportunities to improve administrative processes in your current workplace. Success in small projects can lead to bigger opportunities.
- Consider Partnerships: If you have a great idea but lack technical skills, consider partnering with developers or tech companies to bring your vision to life.

The next time you're frustrated with an administrative task, don't just complain - start thinking about how you could innovate to make it better. Your insights could lead to solutions that transform the entire industry, improving both patient care and the bottom line.

Are you ready to be the nurse who revolutionizes healthcare administration? The opportunity is there - Time to take it and improve your bottom line.

Digital Health and Wellness:
Nursing in the Virtual Age

Alright, let's talk about a field that's exploding faster than a busy ER on a full moon - Digital Health and Wellness. This isn't just about fancy gadgets or trendy apps. It's about leveraging technology to extend our reach as nurses, improve patient outcomes, and yes, potentially create thriving businesses.

Apps and Platforms:
Your Nursing Knowledge, Now Pocket-Sized

All those times you wished you could be there for your patients 24/7? Well, with health and wellness apps, you practically can be. And who is better at creating these apps than nurses who understand exactly what patients need?

Consider Rickey, a diabetes educator who turned app developer. "I was tired of seeing my patients struggle between appointments," he said. "So I created an app that helps them track their blood sugar, meals, and medication, and provides real-time education and support. It's like having a nurse in their pocket."

Opportunities in this space are endless:

- Chronic disease management apps
- Mental health support platforms
- Pregnancy and postpartum care apps
- Medication adherence tools
- Wellness and preventive health apps

The best part? You don't need to be a coding whiz to make this happen. There are plenty of app development platforms designed for non-technical founders. Your nursing expertise is the real secret sauce here.

Remote Patient Monitoring: Extending Your Reach Beyond the Hospital Walls

Remote patient monitoring is revolutionizing how we care for patients with chronic conditions. And guess what? Nurses are at the forefront of this revolution.

Nicholas, a former Telemetry Nurse who now runs a *remote* monitoring service for cardiac practices. "We use wearable devices to track patients' vital signs and symptoms," he explains. "Our nurse-led team analyzes the data and intervenes early when we spot potential issues. We've reduced hospital readmissions by 40% in our patient population."

As a nurse entrepreneur in this space, you could:

- Develop protocols for remote monitoring
- Create training programs for remote care nurses
- Design patient education materials for home monitoring
- Consult with healthcare organizations on implementing remote monitoring programs for many disciplines.

Virtual Nursing Education:
Sharing Your Knowledge, Changing Lives

Who says you need a classroom to be an educator?
With digital platforms, you can share your nursing knowledge with students and fellow professionals around the globe.

Tori-Ann, an experienced Hospice nurse, created an online course teaching specialized end of life and palliative care skills. "I was always training new nurses at work," she says. "I realized I could reach so many more by creating online courses. Now, nurses from around the world learn the most recent palliative care and end of life techniques from my videos and interactive modules. You'd be surprised at how much teaching others broadens your frames of reference and perspective. It took my career to the next level"

Consider these opportunities:

- Creating online courses for nursing students or continuing education
- Developing virtual simulation programs for skill practice
- Hosting webinars on specialized nursing topics
- Participating in Conferences as an educational speaker
- Creating a YouTube channel or podcast sharing nursing insights

Getting Started in Digital Health and Wellness

Ready to dive into this exciting field? Here are some steps to get you started:

- Identify Your Niche: What area of nursing are you most passionate about? That's likely where you'll find your digital health opportunity.
- Research Existing Solutions: Look at what's already out there. How can you improve upon it with your nursing expertise?
- Learn the Basics: Take some online courses in digital health, app development, or online course creation. Platforms like Coursera and Udemy offer great options.
- Network: Join digital health meetups or online communities. Connect with tech professionals who might become potential collaborators.
- Start Small: Begin with a simple project, like a health education blog or a basic wellness app. You can always scale up as you learn and grow.
- Seek Feedback: Test your ideas with fellow nurses and potential users. Their input will be invaluable in refining your digital health solution.

Your nursing knowledge is your power in the digital health world. Never underestimate the value of your experience. You understand patient needs, clinical workflows, and the realities of healthcare delivery in a way that tech professionals often don't. The hands-on, real-life experience that you bring to the collaboration adds a factor of authenticity to the developer's ability to create a truly useful product, which they wouldn't have been able to achieve without you.

So, the next time you wish for a better way to reach or educate patients, co-workers or the healthcare community, stop wishing and start creating. Your next big idea could be the digital health solution that transforms patient care and catapults you into a whole new career stratosphere.

What stops you from bringing your nursing expertise into the digital age? The virtual world is waiting for your real-world nursing wisdom. Let's make it happen!

Precision Medicine and Genomics:

Nursing at the Forefront of Personalized Healthcare

Nurses, it's time to dive into a field that sounds like it's straight out of a sci-fi movie but is very much our present and future: Precision Medicine and Genomics. Don't let the fancy terms intimidate you. At its core, this is about what we've always strived for – providing the right care to the right patient at the right time.

What is Precision Medicine?

Precision medicine is an approach that considers individual variability in genes, environment, and lifestyle for each person. In simpler terms, it's about tailoring medical treatment to the individual characteristics of each patient. And genomics? That's the study of all of a person's genes (the genome), including how those genes interact with each other and with the environment.

Now, you might be thinking, "That's great, but what does this have to do with nursing?" The answer is – Everything.

The Nurse's Role in Precision Medicine

As nurses, we're the ones who spend the most time with patients. We're the ones who notice the subtle changes, who hear the detailed family histories, who see how treatments affect different patients in different ways. This puts us in a unique position to contribute to and benefit from the precision medicine revolution.

Here are some ways nurses are making waves in this field:

- Genetic Testing and Counseling Nurses are increasingly taking on roles in genetic testing and counseling. Imagine helping a patient understand their genetic risk factors and guiding them through decisions about preventive care or treatment options.

- Pharmacogenomics: This is about understanding how a patient's genetic makeup affects their response to drugs. As a nurse, you could be instrumental in preventing adverse drug reactions and ensuring patients receive the most effective medications for their genetic profile.
- Patient Education: With your communication skills and clinical knowledge, you're perfectly positioned to educate patients about the implications of their genetic information and how it relates to their health.

- Research and Data Collection: Nurses play a crucial role in collecting detailed patient data that fuels precision medicine research. Your observations and documentation could contribute to groundbreaking discoveries.

Entrepreneurial Opportunities in Precision Medicine

Let's talk about business. The precision medicine market is exploding, expected to reach $119 billion by 2026. Here's how nurse entrepreneurs are carving out their niche:

- Genetic Counseling Services: Amy, an oncology nurse, started a virtual genetic counseling service. "I saw how overwhelmed patients were after receiving genetic test results," she says. "Now, I offer personalized counseling to help them understand their results and make informed decisions about their health."
- Precision Medicine Education: Samuel, a nurse educator, created an online course teaching healthcare professionals about pharmacogenomics. "There's a huge knowledge gap in this area," he explains. "My course helps nurses and other clinicians understand how to use genetic information to guide medication decisions."
- Precision Health Coaching: Imagine combining your nursing knowledge with precision medicine to offer ultra-personalized health coaching. That's exactly what Krista did. "I use genetic information, along with lifestyle and environmental factors, to create truly personalized wellness plans for my clients," she says.

- Precision Medicine Technology Some nurse entrepreneurs are partnering with tech companies and universities like UC Irvine Health to develop precision medicine tools. From apps that help patients understand their genetic risks to platforms that assist clinicians in making genetically informed treatment decisions, the possibilities are endless.

Getting Started in Precision Medicine and Genomics

Excited to explore this field? Here are some steps to get you started:

- Educate Yourself: Take courses in genetics and genomics. Many universities now offer online programs specifically for healthcare professionals.
- Get Certified: Consider certifications like the Genetics/Genomics Nursing Certification offered by the American Nurses Credentialing Center.
- Join Professional Organizations: Groups like the International Society of Nurses in Genetics (ISONG) offer great networking and learning opportunities.
- Start Small: Begin by incorporating genomics into your current practice. Could you start collecting more detailed family histories? Could you learn to better explain genetic test results to patients?

273

- Check out Big Pharma websites for new opportunities to get your feet wet in the industry. There are always opportunities for Nurses in Pharmaceuticals.
- Identify Opportunities: Look for gaps in patient care or education related to precision medicine. These gaps could be business opportunities.
- Collaborate: Consider partnering with genetic counselors, researchers or tech companies to bring your precision medicine ideas to life.

As a nurse, you bring a unique perspective to precision medicine. You understand not just the science, but the human element and how genetic information affects real people in real situations. Your ability to see a set of patients and objectively see the differing factors at just a glance is a skill PHDs lack.

How fascinating is this incredible healthcare revolution? Your nursing expertise, combined with the power of precision medicine, could not only transform patient care but also launch you into an exciting new career frontier. The future of personalized healthcare is here, and it's got nurse innovators written all over it!

Virtual and Augmented Reality in Healthcare:
Nursing in the Digital Dimension

Tech-savvy nurses, it's time to step into the future – or rather, bring the future into healthcare. We're talking about Virtual Reality (VR) and Augmented Reality (AR). Now, before you start thinking this is all fun and games, let me tell you – these technologies are revolutionizing healthcare, and nurses are at the forefront of this digital transformation.

VR and AR: More Than Just High-Tech Toys

First, let's break it down:

- Virtual Reality (VR) immerses users in a completely digital environment.
- Augmented Reality (AR) overlays digital information onto the real world.

In healthcare, these technologies are not just cool – they're game-changers. And guess what? Your nursing expertise is the key to making these high-tech tools truly effective in healthcare settings.

Training and Education: Welcome to the Virtual Classroom

Those clunky mannequins you practiced on in nursing school. Well, say hello to their high-tech cousins. VR and AR are transforming nursing education and training.

Kassandra, a nurse educator who developed a VR program for IV insertion training. "Students can practice as much as they want in a safe, virtual environment," she explains. "They gain confidence before ever touching a real patient. And the best part? I can create scenarios that might be rare in real life but crucial for nurses to know how to handle."

Opportunities in this space include:

- Creating VR simulations for rare or high-risk procedures
- Developing AR apps for anatomy and physiology education
- Designing VR scenarios for emergency response training
- Building AR tools for just-in-time training in clinical settings

Patient Care:

Bringing Comfort Through Technology

VR and AR aren't just for training – they're making waves in patient care too.

David, an oncology nurse, partnered with a tech company to create a VR program for chemotherapy patients. "Patients can put on a headset during their infusion and be transported to a calm beach or a peaceful forest," he says. "It has dramatically reduced anxiety and pain perception during treatments. The outcomes have been phenomenal"

Other exciting applications include:

- AR apps for patient education, showing how medications work in the body
- VR programs for physical therapy and rehabilitation
- AR-guided systems for vein visualization during blood draws
- VR experiences for pain management and distraction during procedures

Surgical Assistance:

AR in the Operating Room

While not all nurses work in the OR, it's worth noting how AR is transforming surgery – and creating opportunities for nurse entrepreneurs in the process.

Imagine AR glasses that can overlay a patient's MRI or CT scan directly onto their body during surgery. Or consider AR systems that can guide a surgeon's movements with unprecedented precision. Nurses with OR experience are invaluable in developing and implementing these technologies.

Getting Started with VR and AR in Healthcare

Excited to dive into this digital dimension? Here's how to get started:

- Educate Yourself: Take online courses in VR and AR development. Platforms like Coursera and Udemy offer great options but also investigate online programs with Universities like MIT.

- Experience It: Try out VR and AR applications yourself. Many VR arcades now offer healthcare-focused experiences. Laerdal Medical, Wolters Kluwer and the National League for Nursing (NLN) are collaborating to create a lifelike VR Nursing educational program as I write this book, so be on the lookout for that.
- Identify Opportunities: What processes in your nursing practice could be enhanced with VR or AR? Those are your potential innovation goldmines.
- Network: Join healthcare technology meetups or online communities. Connect with developers who might become potential collaborators.
- Start Small: Begin with a simple AR app, like a patient education tool. You can always scale up to more complex VR simulations as you learn.
- Seek Funding: Look into healthcare innovation grants or pitch your ideas to healthcare technology incubators.

The Nurse Entrepreneur's Advantage in VR and AR

You might be thinking, "But I'm not a tech expert!"
You don't need to be. Your nursing expertise is what sets you apart in this field. You understand the realities of patient care, the needs of healthcare providers, and the nuances of clinical settings.

This knowledge is crucial in developing VR and AR applications that are not just technologically impressive, but actually useful and usable in healthcare.

The most successful healthcare VR and AR applications aren't created by tech gurus alone — they're developed by teams that include healthcare professionals like you.

So, the next time you're in a patient's room, in a training session, or even in the OR, start looking at your environment with VR and AR in mind. How could these technologies enhance what you're doing? How could they solve problems or improve outcomes?

Your next big idea could be the VR or AR application that transforms a key aspect of healthcare. And the best part? You don't just have to imagine it — you can create it, bringing your nursing insights into the digital dimension and potentially launching a thriving business in the process.

The world of VR and AR healthcare innovation is upon us. I know this seems like a futuristic fantasy world and it may seem that way to you because you've been working so long and hard in a healthcare system that keeps trying to trudge along with the least amount of innovation possible to promote the idea of "saving money". To be completely clear, the digital frontier is wide open, and it absolutely needs nurse entrepreneurs like you to lead the way. Whether you want to start your own or collaborate with developers, the world is open to you. You can make virtual healthcare and education magic happen!

Emerging Fields for Nurse Entrepreneurs:

Pioneering New Frontiers

Alright, my innovative nurses, we've covered a lot of ground in this chapter, from AI and Precision Medicine to VR and AR. But we're not done yet. The world of healthcare is evolving at breakneck speed, and new opportunities for nurses are emerging all the time. Let's explore some of the cutting-edge fields where your nursing expertise could be the key to groundbreaking innovations.

Environmental Health and Sustainability in Healthcare

Climate change isn't just an environmental issue – it's a health issue. And nurses are uniquely positioned to lead the charge in making healthcare more sustainable.

Meet Marla, a former Med-Surg nurse who now runs a consulting firm helping hospitals reduce their carbon footprint. "I saw firsthand how much waste hospitals generate," she says. "Now, I help healthcare facilities implement sustainable practices that not only benefit the environment but also improve patient outcomes and reduce costs."

Opportunities in this space include:

- Education with the Joint Commission's "Sustainable Healthcare Initiative"
- Developing eco-friendly medical supplies and equipment
- Creating programs to reduce hospital waste and energy consumption
- Consulting on the health impacts of climate change
- Designing "green" healthcare facilities

Global Health Initiatives and Telemedicine

The COVID-19 pandemic showed us just how interconnected our world is when it comes to health. It also highlighted the potential of telemedicine to bridge gaps in healthcare access.

Consider James, a nurse practitioner who started a telemedicine platform connecting volunteer healthcare providers with underserved communities worldwide. "We're able to provide consultations, triage services, and health education to people who might otherwise have no access to healthcare," he explains.

Potential ventures in this area:

- Developing telemedicine solutions for remote or underserved areas
- Creating global health education programs
- Consulting on international health policy and disease prevention

- Designing mobile health clinics for disaster response

Telemedicine and Digital Health:

The Post-Pandemic Landscape

The COVID-19 pandemic has been a catalyst for rapid change in healthcare, particularly in the adoption of telemedicine and digital health solutions. As nurses, it's crucial to understand these changes and the opportunities they present.

Key Insights:

- Accelerated Adoption: The pandemic necessitated a swift transition to telemedicine to maintain social distancing and protect both patients and healthcare providers. This rapid adoption has overcome many previous barriers, including acceptance by patients and caregivers. This is impactful information when development previously was slowed by bureaucracy. Post Covid modalities have a quicker pace to fruition.
- In-Hospital Applications: Telemedicine isn't just for connecting with patients at home. It's also proving valuable within hospitals, allowing for consultations and monitoring while minimizing direct contact with infected patients.
- Mobile Health (mHealth): The integration of smartphones and wearable devices in healthcare has accelerated. These tools are

282

now being used for patient education, prevention, and management of conditions like atrial fibrillation. Remote

- Monitoring: Home ECG surveillance for COVID-19 patients and remote antiarrhythmic drug loading are just two examples of how telemedicine is enabling complex care at home. Interdisciplinary

- Approach: The success of telemedicine relies on collaboration between healthcare providers, technologists, and policymakers. Nurses are ideally positioned to bridge these fields.

Opportunities for Nurse Entrepreneurs:

- Telemedicine Implementation Consulting: Help healthcare organizations integrate telemedicine into their existing workflows.
- Patient Education Programs: Develop digital resources to help patients effectively use telemedicine and Mobile Health tools.
- Remote Monitoring Services: Create or manage services that use wearable devices and smartphone apps to monitor patients with chronic conditions.
- Telemedicine Training: Develop programs to train other healthcare providers in effective telemedicine practices.

- Digital Health Policy Advocacy: Use your frontline experience to influence policies that support the effective and ethical use of telemedicine.

The Future of Telemedicine:

While the pandemic has accelerated the adoption of telemedicine, the challenge now is to maintain this momentum. As nurse entrepreneurs, we have a unique opportunity to shape the future of digital health. Our clinical expertise, combined with an understanding of patient needs and healthcare workflows, makes us invaluable in developing and implementing effective telemedicine solutions.

Telemedicine isn't just about replicating in-person care through a screen. It's about reimagining healthcare delivery to be more accessible, efficient, and patient-centered. As nurses, we're not just adapting to this digital revolution – we're leading it.

Are you a part of this digital health transformation? Your nursing insights could be the key to developing the next breakthrough in telemedicine. Let's seize this opportunity to create a healthcare future that's more connected, more accessible, and more effective than ever before!

Wellness and Medical Tourism:
Nursing Beyond Borders

Here's a field you might not have considered: the intersection of healthcare, wellness, and tourism. As people increasingly travel for both wellness experiences and medical procedures, there's a growing need for experts who understand healthcare, hospitality, and the unique challenges of providing care on the go.

Nurse Story: Judy, a nurse entrepreneur who's redefined the concept of medical tourism with her innovative business model. Judy offers a range of services that showcase just how diverse this field can be:

- School Trip Nursing: Judy contracts with schools to provide on-site nursing care during field trips. She ensures students receive their daily medications and handles any medical emergencies that may arise, allowing schools to conduct educational trips with peace of mind.
- Private Concierge Nursing for Travelers: For individuals or families traveling with medical needs, Judy offers personalized nursing care. This service is particularly valuable for elderly travelers or those with chronic conditions who want to explore the world without compromising their health care.

- Same-Day Surgery Support: Recognizing that many patients travel for outpatient procedures, Judy provides pre- and post-operative care for those undergoing same-day surgeries away from home.

Judy's business exemplifies how nurses can leverage their skills to create unique, in-demand services that bridge healthcare and tourism. But the opportunities in this field extend even further:

- Wellness Retreat Programs: Nurses can design and lead health-focused retreats, combining their medical knowledge with wellness practices like nutrition, fitness, and stress management.
- Medical Tourism Consulting: Like Sarah, an oncology nurse we mentioned earlier, you could help hospitals create programs that cater to international patients, ensuring they receive culturally competent care.
- Travel Health and Safety Protocols: With your understanding of infectious diseases and public health, you could consult with travel companies or destinations on health and safety measures.
- Specialized Travel Experiences: Design travel packages for people with specific health conditions, ensuring they can explore the world safely.

The key to success in this field is leveraging your nursing expertise to address the unique health challenges that come with travel and tourism. Whether it's managing medications across time zones, preparing travelers for health risks in different environments, or ensuring continuity of care for those seeking medical treatments abroad, your nursing background is invaluable.

Moreover, this field allows you to combine your passion for healthcare with the excitement of travel and cultural exchange. It's an opportunity to expand your horizons while making a significant impact on people's lives.

To get started in this field:

- Identify Your Niche: Like Judy, think about unique ways to combine nursing with travel and tourism.
- Get Certified: Consider certifications in travel health nursing or international patient care.
- Network: Connect with travel agencies, schools, and international healthcare providers.
- Start Small: Begin with local clients or short trips before expanding to more extensive services.

As a nurse, you're uniquely qualified to ensure people stay healthy and receive excellent care, no matter where they are in the world.

Whether it's accompanying a school group on an educational adventure, supporting a patient through overseas surgery, or designing wellness experiences that transform lives, your skills as a nurse are your passport to an exciting career in wellness and medical tourism.

- Ready to take your nursing skills global? The world is waiting, and there are patients and clients out there who need your expertise to travel, heal, and thrive. Let's redefine what it means to be a nurse in our increasingly connected world!

Robotics and Human-Machine Interaction in Healthcare

Ok, before you panic, we are going to touch on robotics. But again, please know Robots will never take the place of Nurse. They will simply be the best assistant you ever had.

As robots become more prevalent in healthcare settings, there's a growing need for professionals who understand both nursing and robotics. So, once you're past your aversion, it's time to get skilled and educated on what they can do to make your job easier.

Take Kevin, a former surgical nurse who now works with a robotics company. "I help design robots that can assist in patient care," he explains. "My nursing background is crucial in ensuring these robots are actually helpful and not just cool tech gadgets that are clunky and get in the way."

Areas to consider:

- Consulting on the development of care robots
- Creating training programs for nurses working with robotic systems
  - Once you educate yourself, the best way to see the systems integrated is to create processes for those integrations. Who better to do that than you?
- Developing protocols for human-robot interaction in healthcare settings
- Designing robotic solutions for home healthcare

Biohacking and Human Enhancement

While it might sound like science fiction, the field of biohacking – using science and technology to improve human capabilities – is growing rapidly. And guess what? It needs the expertise of healthcare professionals like nurses.

Cheyanne Welton, also known as "the biohacking nurse" is a registered nurse, avid traveler, and known amongst the top 50 biohackers in the world. As a young child she faced several health issues like fatigue and depression, and later on mold toxicity and lyme disease. Cheyanne has spent nearly a decade studying with experts on the key to unlocking health. She has discovered that it all revolves around one thing. You are as healthy as your mitochondria. Cheyanne is passionate about bringing key insights on how to "hack" your mitochondria. Cheyanne has developed interesting "hacks" as she calls them including the Red-Light Therapy (anti-aging mask) and many more for sleep, light, mood, and detoxification.

Potential areas for Nurses to explore:

- Developing safe and ethical biohacking protocols
- Consulting on the healthcare implications of human enhancement technologies
- Creating education programs about the risks and benefits of biohacking
- Designing monitoring systems for individuals using enhanced technologies

Getting Started in Emerging Fields:

How excited are you about these cutting-edge opportunities? Who knew these opportunities were even available to Nurses? To get the ball rolling, here's how to dip your toes in:

- Stay Informed: Follow healthcare innovation news and attend technology and innovations in healthcare conferences.
- Network Broadly: Connect with professionals not just in healthcare, but in

tech, environmental science, tourism, and other related fields.

- Think Creatively: How can your nursing skills apply to these emerging fields? Your unique perspective could lead to groundbreaking innovations.
- Start Small: Begin with a blog, podcast, or small consulting gig in your area of interest.
- Collaborate: Many of these fields require interdisciplinary approaches. Don't be afraid to partner with experts from other fields.

As a nurse, you bring a unique combination of medical knowledge, practical skills, and a deep understanding of human needs. This makes you invaluable in these emerging fields where healthcare intersects with other disciplines and many other industries.

The point here though is to understand that the future of healthcare extends far beyond hospital / facility / direct patient care walls and Nurses have an opportunity to be at the forefront of these exciting new frontiers. Let your imagination run wild. Your nursing background, combined with your innovative spirit, could be the key to unlocking the next big breakthrough in these emerging fields.

Your Nursing Superpowers Unleashed:
A World of Possibilities

Wow! What a journey we've been on in this chapter.

From AI and genomics to virtual reality and wellness tourism, we've explored a universe of opportunities that you, as a nurse, are uniquely positioned to seize. I know we've thrown a lot at you, and your head might be spinning with all these possibilities. But here's the thing – that's exactly the point! My every intention with this book was to show you options and opportunities. If you now feel spoiled for choice, you now understand that if you choose to stay in direct patient care, it's because you are choosing to. If you get nothing else from reading this book, I want you to understand that there is a world of opportunity just outside your door. Your Nursing license is a key to a whole host of careers; you might not have ever fathomed.

The world of healthcare is transforming at lightning speed, and you are on the frontlines of this revolution. Your skills, your experience, your intuition – these are superpowers in the world of healthcare innovation.

Think about it for a moment. When you became a nurse, did you ever imagine you could:

- Develop AI systems that revolutionize healthcare on a global scale?
- Create virtual reality programs that transform medical education?

- Start a business that combines healthcare with global adventures?
- Pioneer new frontiers in genomics and personalized medicine?

Probably not. I won't even go into why Nursing Schools and Colleges don't enlighten their nursing students on how vast the Nursing Field truly is. But here we are, in a world where *ALL* of these opportunities (and so many more) are not just possible – they're waiting for nurses like you to jump in the pond and bring them to life.

Now, I'm not saying you need to rush out tomorrow and start a cutting-edge tech company (although if that's your dream, go for it!). What I am saying is this: Open your eyes to the possibilities. Let yourself dream again. That frustration you feel with a clunky hospital process could be the seed of the next big healthcare innovation. That idea you have for improving patient education could be the foundation of a thriving business.

Every groundbreaking healthcare innovation needs the insights of people who truly understand patient care. That's you. Your hands-on experience, your ability to connect with patients, your deep understanding of healthcare realities – these are invaluable in shaping the future of health and wellness.

So, as we wrap up this chapter, I want you to do something for me. Take a moment to dream. Imagine a healthcare future where your biggest frustrations have been solved, where patients receive the kind of care you've always wished you could provide, where your nursing skills are valued more than ever before.

Wanna hear the exciting part? You have the power to create that future. Whether it's through embracing new technologies, starting your own business, or pioneering new fields of care, you can be the change you want to see in healthcare.

You've spent your career taking care of others. It's now time to nurture that spark of innovation within you. The world needs your nursing superpowers more than ever — not just at the bedside, but in labs, in tech companies, in startups, and in boardrooms.

So, what's your next adventure going to be? Whatever it is, know this — your nursing background isn't just relevant, it's your secret weapon. The future of healthcare is bright, and it has 'nurse innovator' written all over it.

Are you ready to unleash your nursing superpowers and change the world? The adventure starts now. Let's make some healthcare magic happen!

Scan to Access Tools for Chapter Fourteen

Chapter 15

The Nurse Entrepreneur's Crossroads:

Reflecting, Reassessing, and Reimagining Your Future

Ok, it's time for a breather. I'm grabbing a margarita and my sunglasses and taking you all out on my sunny lanai with me. We're going to take a breath and take it all in before we move on to anything else. So, kick off those shoes, settle into a comfy chair, and let's chat.

Taking Stock: From Bedside to Boardroom and Beyond

Wow, what a journey we've been on, huh? When we started this adventure together, we talked about recognizing your incredible nursing skills and applying a business mindset to them. But I bet you never imagined just how many doors those skills could open.

We've explored everything from IV companies to Wound Care specialties, DME and Residential Assisted Living, AI and Genomics to Virtual Reality and Medical-Wellness Tourism. We've looked at how you can leverage your expertise in consulting, education, and even global health initiatives. And you know what? I'm willing to bet that most of your nursing colleagues have no idea that all these opportunities exist. Heck, I've been in this game for decades, and even I'm amazed at how many options are out there for nurses who want to spread their wings.

But here's the kicker — we've only scratched the surface. The world of nurse entrepreneurship is vast and ever-expanding. Your nursing superpowers are more valuable and versatile than you ever imagined.

I'm sure you're raising your eyebrows and looking at me and saying, "Laurie, this is all incredible, but it's also a lot to take in." You're absolutely right. That's why we're here, sipping our margaritas (or your beverage of choice — no judgment) and taking a moment to process it all.

Let's start at the beginning.

The Hidden Tolls:

Moral Injury and the Path to Change

Let's talk about something that's probably been the catalyst for you even considering a change. This has probably been simmering in the back of your mind throughout this whole journey — *why*. Why are you considering this transition? Why are you looking for alternatives to traditional nursing roles? They've served you so far. It's paid the bills.

For many of us, it goes deeper than just wanting to pay the bills. It's more than just a change of pace or a new challenge. We're dealing with something called *moral injury*. It's a term that might be new to you, but I bet the feeling isn't.

Moral injury is that deep, gut-wrenching distress that comes from having to work in ways that violate your ethical standards. It's not just burnout – it's a profound sense that you're unable to provide the care you know patients deserve because of systemic or corporate constraints.

Think about it:

- How many times have you had to discharge a patient before you felt they were truly ready, all because of insurance or bed availability issues?
- How often have you been forced to cut corners on care due to understaffing or time pressure?
- When was the last time you felt you could provide the level of care you know patients deserve without compromising your own well-being?

Each of these situations chip away at your sense of purpose and integrity as a nurse. Over time, this accumulation of moral compromises can lead to deep-seated distress, disillusionment, and a loss of faith in the healthcare system.

I am here to let you know – it's okay to acknowledge this. It's okay to say, "I don't want to be this kind of nurse anymore because it takes too heavy a toll on my spirit." This doesn't make you weak or uncommitted to traditional roles. It makes you human. It makes you someone who cares deeply about providing care while maintaining your own well-being. Now, let's not get it twisted. The ability to digest and take accountability for the fact that we continue to look aside sometimes, when we know damn well, we shouldn't, is something every nurse on earth lives with and goes to sleep knowing. Some of us have never mentioned or spoken about these things. This is the part of the job our family and friends don't see or understand. To be honest they could never conceive of the possibility. To them we are a virtuous entity. We care for the sick and disabled. We are above reproach in every way. And we'd like to keep it that way. So, we don't share.

As we sit here on the lanai, watching the Florida crimson sun dip lower in the sky, sipping a refreshing drink, I want you to take a moment. Breathe deeply. Acknowledge the challenges you've faced, the moral injuries you've endured. Apologize to yourself for not acknowledging your needs sooner and deciding we deserve better. No matter the "*Why*".

When Nursing Becomes Too Much to Bear

Something that doesn't make it into nurse recruitment brochures or heartwarming hospital commercials is the weight you carry home after your shift ends - the emotional burden that's invisible to the outside world but feels as heavy as lead to you.

You know that feeling when your phone buzzes with an invitation from a friend, and instead of excitement, you feel dread? Because you're a hospice nurse, and this week alone, you've watched four of your patients take their last breaths, held the hands of their grieving families, only to look at your schedule and see 4 new patients to welcome, who need your care and compassion. How do you explain to your friend that you can't make it to their birthday dinner because you're emotionally drained, trying to process the cycle of life and death you've witnessed?

Or maybe, you drag yourself home after a 12-hour shift that felt like 24. Your husband greets you at the door, excited to see you and eager to talk about dinner plans. But all you can do is burst into tears when he asks what you want to eat. Because how do you tell him that you're not crying over dinner choices, but because you had to serve your patients dinner in their beds tonight? There were only two CNAs for the entire evening shift, and despite your best efforts, you couldn't give your patients the dignity of a proper mealtime. The guilt, the frustration, the feeling of inadequacy - it all comes crashing down at that moment over a simple question about seafood or Italian. The look on your husband's face is now ingrained in your soul as just another part of your day you really shouldn't share with others.

This is the moral injury we are talking about. This is the emotional toll. It's not just about big, dramatic ethical dilemmas. It's about the small, daily compromises that chip away at your spirit. It's about knowing what good care looks like but being unable to provide it due to circumstances beyond your control. It's about carrying the weight of these compromises home with you, day after day, until you feel like you're drowning in an ocean of unmet needs and unfulfilled professional standards.

And let's be real - your family and friends, as much as they love you, often don't understand. They see a stable job, a respectable profession, and that overtime paycheck. They see the house, but they don't see the nights you lie awake, replaying the day's events, wondering if you could have done more. They don't feel the knot in your stomach when you think about going back for another shift, another week, another year of this emotional tug-of-war.

This is why the transition we're talking about is so important. It's not just about finding a new career path. It's about reclaiming your life, your emotional well-being, your ability to be present for yourself and your loved ones. To enjoy the fruits of your labor. To be happy about the career choice you've made.

Imagine waking up in the morning happy and having the energy to sing along with your kids on the way to carpool. Picture yourself attending a friend's wedding without the cloud of work stress hanging over you. Think about how it would feel to make dinner plans without the fear of last-minute call offs looming over your head. Or waking up on a Saturday and knowing you can go anywhere you want because there is no emergency in your business that can take you away from your plans.

This is what entrepreneurship can offer you. It's not just about business opportunities or financial gain. It's about creating a life where your nursing skills are valued, where your compassion doesn't come at the cost of your mental health, where you can make a difference without sacrificing your well-being in the process.

So, when we talk about transitioning to entrepreneurship, or non-traditional nursing roles, we're not just talking about changing jobs. We're talking about changing lives - starting with your own. We're talking about finding a way to honor your calling as a nurse while also honoring your need for balance, for joy and for a life outside of healthcare.

Acknowledging these feelings doesn't make you a bad nurse. It makes you human. It makes you recognize that to care for others effectively, you must also care for yourself. Sometimes, that means charting a new course - one that allows you to use your nursing skills in a way that fills you up instead of draining you dry.

For those of you who choose to stay at the bedside, I applaud you. Your dedication is admirable, and the healthcare system needs passionate nurses like you. But I implore you – please discuss these struggles with someone outside of healthcare. While your colleagues might be going through similar challenges, sometimes they're too close to the situation to offer the perspective and support you need.

All healthcare workers struggle, and sometimes they might find it hard to empathize when they're dealing with their own battles.

As we sit here, I want you to take a moment. Close your eyes. Breathe deeply. Take a sip of your beverage and imagine a future where your nursing skills are making a difference, but you're not carrying the weight of moral injury or emotional toll home with you. Imagine a future where you can be fully present for your family and friends, where your compassion isn't limited by corporate constraints, where your creativity and expertise are encouraged.

That future is possible. And we're going to explore how to make it your reality.

Embracing Change:

From Anxiety to Excitement

Now that we've acknowledged the challenges and emotional tolls of traditional nursing roles, we took a breather and took stock of where we are and where we're going. Let's shift our focus to the exciting journey ahead. Change can be scary, I know. The thought of leaving the familiar world of bedside nursing for the unknown territory of entrepreneurship or non-traditional nursing roles might feel like stepping off a cliff. But what if I told you that this cliff is a launchpad?

Change, my friends, isn't just inevitable it's an opportunity. An opportunity to grow, to redefine your impact, and to fall in love with your career all over again. Now, how can we transform that knot of anxiety in your stomach into butterflies of excitement?

First, let's address fear. It's normal to feel apprehensive about such a big change. You might be thinking, "Can I really do this? Am I cut out for this?" The answer is a resounding yes! I promise no one is better qualified for this than You. And, you're not starting from scratch. You're leveraging years of experience, critical thinking, problem-solving skills, and a deep understanding of healthcare operations. You've got this!

Now, let's reframe how we think about this transition:

- From Job Security to Career Control: Instead of relying on a single employer for your livelihood, imagine having multiple income streams and the ability to *choose* your projects, workloads and work schedules.
- From Burnout to Passion: Picture waking up excited about your work, knowing that you're making a difference on your own terms.
- From hands tied by Corporate Constraint to Creativity & Innovation: Think about having the freedom to implement your ideas without navigating layers of senior

leadership and opinions from people who have never done your job.

- From the never-ending Work-Life *Imbalance* to Flexibility. Envision a schedule that allows you to be there for your family, friends and finally for Yourself! Without guilt or having to ask permission is going to be bliss.

Embracing change doesn't mean abandoning your identity as a nurse. It means expanding it. You're not leaving nursing behind; you're pioneering new ways to apply your nursing expertise.

Let's address some common fears that might be holding you back:

- "I don't have any business skills." You've been using business skills every day in your nursing career. Managing resources, prioritizing tasks, communicating effectively, managing staff, planning and coordinating with different departments and outside vendors, these are business skills. The specific knowledge you need can be learned, just like you learned complex medical procedures. This part is simply a mind shift. A little learning but a true mind shift from working for someone else to working for Yourself. No one else to blame for failures, but no one to take the credit for your successes either. It's all YOU baby!

304

- "What if I fail?"

Let's pause for a moment and really think about this. Are you afraid to fail when you hold people's lives in your hands every single day? Hold on, let me wrap my head around that for a second.

Here's the truth: You're not afraid to fail. What you're truly afraid of is not knowing. Period. You're apprehensive about aspects of business that you haven't encountered before. But we can combat that.

We do what nurses do best: we go online or to a local college and learn what we need to, or we find someone who has the knowledge and partner with them to learn what they know or hire them! It's that simple. We are McGyver in scrubs. We always figure it out. Just like we're creating a business, there are businesses that focus on these aspects and have created services, consultants and mentors willing to help. From billing and coding experts to payroll and cleaning services. And you just might find a Gem of an office manager who has had their hands in every single department of a business and can be your savior on all thing's customer service, snail mail, email, office software, payroll software, PC setups, printer setups, and so much more. Just like you can spot a great PCT/CNA from a mile away, this will be the same thing. Trust your instincts. You've honed them through years of nursing, and they'll serve you well in business too. Your nursing career has already taught you how to adapt and problem-solve in high-stakes situations. Those same skills - assessing a situation, gathering resources, and taking decisive action - will serve you incredibly well in your new venture. So, instead of fearing failure, think of it this way: you're embarking on a new learning journey. And if there's one thing nurses excel at, it's continuously learning and adapting to new situations. You've got this!

- "I'll miss patient care." Who says you have to give it up entirely? Many nurse entrepreneurs find ways to incorporate direct patient care into their business models. Plus, by creating innovative healthcare solutions, you might end up positively impacting even more patients than you could at the bedside under someone else's management.

Embracing change is about opening yourself up to new possibilities. It's about recognizing that your nursing skills and experience are invaluable assets that can be applied in countless ways beyond traditional healthcare settings.

So, take a deep breath. Feel the excitement bubbling up inside you. You're not just changing careers - you're expanding your impact, reclaiming your time, and creating a life that aligns with your values and aspirations. The world is waiting for you, and it's full of opportunities you've only begun to imagine.

Every great journey begins with a single step. And you, my friend, are already taking steps. You're reading this book, right?

Overcoming Self-Doubt:

You Are More Than "Just a Nurse"

Now that we've addressed the fear of the unknown and reframed how we think about failure, let's tackle another common hurdle: self-doubt. How many times have you caught yourself thinking or saying, "But I'm just a nurse"? It's time to banish that phrase from your vocabulary because, there is no such thing as "just" anything. You are *Everything!*

Recognizing Your Unique Skills

As a nurse, you've developed a set of skills that are highly sought after in the business world.

- **Critical Thinking**: You assess complex situations and make decisions quickly. In business, this translates to strategic planning and problem-solving.
- **Communication**: You explain complex medical concepts to patients and families. This skill is crucial for operations, marketing, networking, and client relations.

- **Multitasking**: Juggling every task imaginable at one time. That's project management in action.
- **Adaptability**: Healthcare is always changing, and you've kept up. This flexibility is essential in the ever-evolving business landscape.
- **Empathy**: Your ability to understand and relate to others is key to building strong business relationships.
- **Attention to Detail**: Precision in day-to-day patient care, assessment skills and your degree of keen observation translate to financial management and quality control skills beyond anything anyone in business has ever seen. You don't miss a thing!

I'm going to entrench you into this mindset if it kills me. The skills you possess are innate. They come from a deep understanding of what healthcare should be. They come from millions of hours of learning, but also from observing and taking the time to understand.

There's a host of things I could say here, but it would diminish what you truly have accomplished so far. So please, take a moment to look at that list. Really look. Take it in, because the next time you're sitting in your car at the end of a shift, I want you to summarize how you used those skills in every single moment of the last 12-16 hours.

Bask in your ability. Soak it in. You do these things every single day without recognizing them because the environment you're in wants it that way. If you recognize your skills, you'll realize you can do them on your own. You manage. You schedule. You complete the tasks. You comfort and educate your patients and families (and sometimes the doctors as well). Take it in and really hold on to it. This is your power.

The Nurse Entrepreneur Advantage

Your nursing experience gives you a unique edge in the business world:

- **Industry Insight**: You understand healthcare from the inside out. This knowledge is invaluable for identifying gaps and opportunities in the market.
- **Credibility**: Your nursing experience, education and current licensure is instant credibility in health-related businesses.
- **Holistic Perspective**: Nurses see the big picture of patient care. This translates to a comprehensive view of business operations.
- **Ethical Foundation**: The strong ethical principles in nursing are a solid foundation for building a reputable business.

Challenging Imposter Syndrome

Feeling like a fraud? You're not alone. Many nurses-turned-entrepreneurs grapple with imposter syndrome.

Here's how to fight it:

- **Acknowledge Your Achievements:** List your accomplishments, big and small. You've already mastered one of the most challenging professions out there.
- **Reframe Your Thoughts:** Instead of "I don't know enough," try "I'm learning and growing every day."
- **Seek Support:** Connect with other nurse entrepreneurs. You'll find you're not alone in your doubts, and you can lift each other up.
- **Keep Learning:** Continual education boosts confidence. Take a business course, attend workshops, read widely.

When we talk about imposter syndrome, I'm not just speaking from theory – I'm speaking from experience. As an LPN who has never progressed to RN in my 30-year career, one of my very first positions was a Unit Manager of the first Medicare recognized "Alzheimer's Unit" in the country and now I'm a Certified Compliance Consultant with a nationally recognized Healthcare Consultant firm, I live with imposter syndrome every day.

I fight to be recognized as an expert in my accomplishments daily. But— those feelings of self-doubt don't negate my expertise or my potential.

In fact, those feelings are often a sign that you're pushing yourself to new heights.

We'll dive deeper into strategies for managing imposter syndrome later in the book, but for now, your value isn't determined by titles or traditional career paths. It's about the impact you make and the expertise you bring to the table.

Celebrating Your Expertise

- **Recognize Your Value:** Your years of nursing have given you insights that many would pay top dollar to acquire.
- **Share Your Knowledge:** Consider starting a blog, podcast, or social media account showcasing your expertise. Seeing the impact of your knowledge will boost your confidence. However, be mindful of who you share your dreams with. Not everyone in your current environment may be supportive. Choose your confidants wisely.

- **Mentor Others:** Nothing affirms your expertise like helping others learn from your experience.

- **Start Small:** Begin with a side project while keeping your nursing job. Each small success will build your confidence.
- **Network Strategically:** Attend meetups or join online communities related to your areas of interest. Surrounding yourself with like-minded individuals can be incredibly motivating. The key here is "like-minded." Don't limit yourself to your current work environment. Some colleagues may cheer you on, while others might express negativity due to their own fears or perceived inequities. Their issues are not your responsibility. As my mom used to say, "Misery loves company." But you have a choice. You can choose to succeed on your own path and enjoy your life, rather than staying in a situation that doesn't fulfill you just for the sake of familiarity. The adventure you choose is up to you.
- **Set Achievable Goals:** Break your big dreams into smaller, manageable tasks. Each completed task is a confidence booster.
- **Celebrate Small Wins:** Did you create a business plan? Launch a website? Land your first client or new job? Celebrate every milestone, no matter how small it seems.

Every successful entrepreneur started somewhere. Your nursing background isn't a limitation – it's your solid foundation. You've already proven you can handle one of the most demanding professions there is. You've saved lives, comforted the suffering, and navigated complex healthcare systems. If you can do all that, you can absolutely thrive as an entrepreneur.

So, the next time that little voice in your head says, "But I'm *just* a nurse," I want you to stand tall and respond, "I am a nurse, I am also a healthcare expert, a problem-solver, a critical thinker and a soon-to-be entrepreneur. I've got this!"

Envisioning Your Future:

From Dream to Reality

Now that we've addressed your fears, recognized your unique skills, and boosted your confidence meter, it's time to paint a picture of your future as a nurse entrepreneur. This isn't just daydreaming – it's the first step in turning your vision into reality.

1. **Visualize Your Ideal Day**: Close your eyes and imagine your perfect day as a nurse entrepreneur. What time do you wake up? Where do you work? What kind of tasks are you doing? Who are you helping? The more vivid this vision, the more motivated you'll be to achieve it.

2. **Define Your Impact**: Think about the mark you want to leave on healthcare. Are you developing innovative patient care solutions? Teaching other nurses? Improving healthcare systems? Your entrepreneurial journey should align with your deepest values and aspirations. Maybe you're thinking about how changing your career will positively affect the rest of your life. Your family and friend relationships. Your legacy. All these factors give you motivation to make the changes you need to.

3. **Set Concrete Goals & Timelines**: Break down your vision into tangible, achievable goals. What do you want to accomplish in the next month? Six months? Year? Five years? Writing these down makes them real and actionable.

4. **Identify Your Support System**: Who will be there to encourage and support you on this journey? Think about family, friends, mentors, and fellow nurse entrepreneurs. Surrounding yourself with positivity and support is crucial.

5. **Commit to Lifelong Learning**: Nurse Entrepreneurship is not different than Nursing in this area. You made this commitment when you became a Nurse. The healthcare and business landscapes are always evolving. Your commitment to continuous learning and growth doesn't change. The subjects that may diversify

314

your focus from Nursing and Healthcare to Business and Marketing as well. What skills do you need to develop? What knowledge gaps do you need to fill?

The nurse entrepreneurs you admire today once sat where you are — curious, cautious, and full of possibility – with a vision and the courage to pursue it.

Embracing Your Nurse Entrepreneur Identity

As we wrap up this reflective chapter, I want you to take a moment to embrace your new identity. This isn't about leaving nursing behind – it's about expanding what it means to be a nurse in today's world.

It's important to note that when we talk about taking control of your nursing career, we're not just talking about starting a business. While entrepreneurship is one path, it's not the only one. Taking control might mean transitioning to a different area of nursing, moving into healthcare technology, becoming a consultant, or any number of other possibilities we've discussed. The key is that you're making active choices about your career direction, rather than feeling stuck on a predetermined traditional path. Whether you decide to start a business, switch specialties, or innovate within your current role, you're taking the reins of your professional life.

You are more than "just a nurse." You are an innovator, a problem-solver, a caregiver, an educator and now, maybe an entrepreneur. Your nursing experience isn't a limitation; it's your foundation for any choice you make for your career.

Embrace the challenges ahead as opportunities for growth. See your fears as signs that you're pushing your boundaries and expanding your potential. Trust in the skills and resilience you've developed throughout your nursing career, they will serve you well on this new path.

Becoming a nurse outside of the traditional role isn't just about changing your career – it could be about changing healthcare for the better. You have the power to innovate, to improve patient care, to create solutions to problems you've seen firsthand. You're not just building a business; you could be shaping the future of healthcare.

As you stand on the brink of this exciting new chapter in your life, hold your head high. You've got the knowledge, the skills, and now the mindset to succeed as a nurse entrepreneur. The journey ahead may not always be easy, but I promise you, it will be worth it. So, take a deep breath, square your shoulders, and step confidently into your new role. The world of healthcare entrepreneurship is waiting for you, and it needs your unique perspective and expertise.

We've taken this moment to reflect, recharge, and reimagine your future as a nurse outside of the traditional roles set out for us. We've solidified our dream and made plans for what's to come. We've shifted our mindset and set goals. We've created a new vision.

What's next? You might be wondering about some of the practical aspects of making this transition - particularly when it comes to finances. How do you bridge the gap between your current nursing role and your entrepreneurial dreams? In the next chapter, we'll dive into strategies for maintaining financial stability while building your business, helping you turn your vision into reality.

This isn't the end of anything – it's just the beginning of your incredible journey. Let's make it happen!

Scan to Access Tools for Chapter Fifteen:

Chapter 16: The Transition:
Where Rubber Meets the Road

Alright, you've made it this far. Congratulations! We're standing at the edge of something big. You've decided to make a change, to step beyond the traditional boundaries of nursing, and I couldn't be prouder of you. This is where the rubber meets the road, where dreams start becoming reality.

Now, I know you're excited, but you're also terrified. "What if I'm making a mistake?" is probably running through your head. Let me stop you. Before you have a meltdown, Traditional Nursing isn't going anywhere. You have chosen a career that will *always* be there. While I'd love it if you leaped and never looked back, and were over the moon happy forever, just know that you're not going at it alone. That voice of doubt? It's normal. In fact, it's a sign that you're about to do something incredible. Every nurse who's ever made this transition has felt that same mix of excitement and fear. The key is what you do with those feelings.

This chapter is all about embracing your decision to change and preparing yourself - mentally, emotionally, and practically - for the journey ahead. We're going to talk about shifting your mindset from "*just a nurse*" to a healthcare innovator, entrepreneur, or whatever amazing role you decide to step into. We'll discuss practical strategies like side gigs and financial planning, but we'll also dig into the emotional side of this transition.

This isn't just about changing jobs. It's about redefining what it means to be a nurse in today's world. It's about taking control of your career and your life. And yes, it's going to be challenging at times. But I promise you, it's also going to be one of the most rewarding journeys you'll ever embark on.

So, are you ready to take that step off the ledge and into your new future? Don't worry, I've got your back. Let's do this together. In the QR code below you'll find *The Nurse-to-Entrepreneur Transition Map* it was created so you can orient yourself, find your footing, and move forward with clarity, no matter where you're starting from.

Scan to Access your Transition Map

The Nurse-to-Entrepreneur Transition Map

Where you are. What to expect. What to build next.

PHASE ONE: Realizing You're Ready

You've felt it — burnout, misalignment, or simply the whisper that something more is possible. This phase is about acknowledging what's no longer working and allowing yourself to imagine change without guilt.

PHASE TWO: Reclaiming What You Know You

are not "starting over." You are starting from a deep well of clinical expertise, emotional intelligence, and professional insight. This is where you begin to reframe your nursing skills as strategic, transferable, and powerful.

PHASE THREE: Designing Your Exit Strategy

This phase blends logic with courage. It's where you explore side gigs, map your timeline, assess your finances, and make small pivots that protect your energy and honor your future goals.

PHASE FOUR: Preparing Your Support System

You don't have to do this alone. Here's where you begin building emotional and logistical support — from family conversations to boundary-setting to find mentors and allies who understand the road you're on.

PHASE FIVE: Becoming the Leader of Your Next Chapter

This is the integration phase. The old story loosens its grip. You begin to see yourself as a strategist, a guide, a builder. You may still be working your day job — but the shift has already begun.

Shifting Perspectives: From Bedside to Beyond

Let's talk about something that might feel a bit uncomfortable at first: redefining who you are as a nurse. For years, maybe even decades, you've identified yourself primarily as simply a nurse. But you've been a bedside nurse. Your current position is direct patient care. You take care of sick and disabled people, in whatever arena that happens to be. Hospital, Nursing Home, Home Health, Hospice, Surgery etc... What you have taken on is the identity of what you've perceived as a "Nurse". It's your identity, your calling card, your superhero cape. But now? It's time to broaden that perspective.

As you embark on this transition, it's crucial to shift how you view your nursing experience. You're not leaving nursing behind — you're expanding what it means to be a nurse.

Recognizing Your Transferable Skills

Now to help shift your perspective, let's talk about something exciting: the treasure trove of skills you've accumulated as a nurse. These aren't just 'nursing skills', they're your professional currency. You've earned them through real-world challenges, high-stakes decisions, and the kind of experience no textbook could ever teach. In this next chapter, they're not just transferable, they're invaluable.

Let's break down some of your transferable skills:

- **Critical Thinking and Problem-Solving**: Every time you've assessed a patient, developed a care plan, or handled an unexpected crisis, you've honed these skills. In the business world, this translates to strategic planning and innovative problem-solving.
- **Communication:** You've explained complex medical concepts to scared patients, collaborated with diverse healthcare teams, and navigated difficult conversations. That's professional communication at its highest level. That's applicable in *any* field.
- **Adaptability:** Healthcare is always evolving, and you've kept pace. You've had no choice. Adaptability is one of the strongest assets in entrepreneurship and in leadership roles where change is constant.

- **Emotional Intelligence:** Your ability to read people, empathize, and manage emotions (yours and others') is invaluable in any people-centric role.

- **Project Management:** Ever coordinated care for multiple patients, juggling various treatment modalities, medications, diagnostics, resources, supplies and specialists? Congratulations, you're already a project manager!

- **Attention to Detail:** From medication administration and treatment protocols to patient counseling and, of course, charting your eye for detail is impeccable. This translates directly to quality control and process improvement in any industry.

- **Leadership:** Whether you've held an official leadership role or not, you've been leading and coordinating care, mentoring new nurses and have been a patient advocate. You can clearly make your voice heard.

- **Crisis Management:** You've handled life-and-death situations under pressure. That ability to stay calm and make quick, informed decisions is priceless in any high-stakes environment.

Now, here's your task: Take a moment to write down your top five nursing skills. Then, for each skill, think of a specific example of how you've used it in your nursing career. Finally, brainstorm how each of these skills could apply in your target field or role.

323

It's not about leaving these skills behind – it's about repackaging them for your new adventure. You're not starting from scratch; you're building on a rock-solid foundation of experience and expertise.

In the next section, we'll explore how to articulate these skills effectively as you network and pursue new opportunities.

Reflection Exercise:

Uncovering Your Hidden Talents

Take a moment to think about your typical day as a nurse. Now, let's reframe some of these everyday tasks into transferable skills:

1. Patient Assessment:
   - Nursing perspective: Checking vital signs, reviewing patient history and current symptoms
   - Business perspective: Data analysis, risk assessment
2. Patient Education:
   - Nursing perspective: Explaining medication regimens, side effects and expected outcomes
   - Business perspective: Client communication, training and development
3. Medication Administration:
   - Nursing perspective: Ensuring correct dosage, timing, and route

- Business perspective: Project management, quality control
4. Charting:
   - Nursing perspective: Documenting patient care, Compliance with regulations
   - Business perspective: Report writing, data management, compliance

5. Prioritizing Care:
   - Nursing perspective: Triaging patients, managing multiple cases
   - Business perspective: Resource allocation, strategic planning

Now it's your turn. Think of five tasks you perform regularly in your nursing role. Write them down, then try to reframe each one from a business perspective. What transferable skills can you identify?

The goal isn't to downplay your nursing skills, but to recognize how valuable and versatile they are in any setting. This exercise is about opening your eyes to the possibilities and learning to articulate your skills in a way that resonates beyond the healthcare field.

Now that you've started to reframe your nursing skills in business terms, let's talk about how to use this new perspective:

- Updating Your Resume: Instead of simply listing your nursing duties, highlight these transferable skills. For example, rather than "Administered medications," you might say "Managed complex treatment schedules, ensuring 100% accuracy in high-pressure situations."
- Networking: When you meet new people, don't just say "I'm a nurse." Try something like, "I'm a healthcare professional with expertise in crisis management and client education, looking to apply these skills in [your target field]."
- Job Interviews: Use specific examples from your nursing experience to illustrate these transferable skills. The STAR method (Situation, Task, Action, Result) works great here.
- Exploring Opportunities: As you look at job descriptions or business ideas, train yourself to spot where your nursing skills apply. You'll start seeing opportunities everywhere!

This is a skill you need to hone. The more you practice translating your nursing experience into business terms, the more natural it will become and the more confident you will be in your existing skills and experience. I can say this, and you can read this all day long, but putting it down on paper like this solidifies the concept. Seeing it for yourself makes this transition that much easier. You're not just a nurse – you're a highly skilled professional with a unique and valuable set of experiences. Realizing just how much you bring to the table gives you the ability to transition easily and confidently.

When you're building your business, the time commitment needed for traditional roles may stifle your ability to focus on your business. But you will of course need a way to maintain financial stability. So how can you do this without the full-time commitment of traditional nursing roles? This is where strategic side gigs come in, offering the perfect balance of income and flexibility.

Strategic Side Gigs:

Bridging the Gap

As you contemplate your transition from traditional nursing roles to entrepreneurship or non-traditional nursing careers, you're likely wondering how to make that leap without putting your financial stability at risk. This is where strategic side gigs come in. Let's be clear we're not talking about piling more work on top of your already demanding nursing schedule. Instead, these opportunities are about working smarter, not harder.

The idea here is to find opportunities that can maintain your financial stability while giving you the time and energy to build your business. It's about

327

making a strategic shift - moving away from your traditional nursing role and into positions that offer comparable pay but with more flexibility and less physical and emotional drain. This approach allows you to keep one foot in the nursing world while actively working on your entrepreneurial dreams.

Let's explore some specific opportunities that showcase this approach:

Home Health Care On-Call Positions:

The Weekend Warrior Option

Many Home Health Care companies offer "on-call" positions for both Scheduling and Supervisor roles. These opportunities can be a goldmine for nurses transitioning to entrepreneurship. Here's why:

- High Pay for Limited Time: These positions often pay 30 hours of work for a weekend shift, providing substantial income for an agreed upon time commitment.
- Flexibility: With weekend-only work, you have the weekdays free to focus on building your business.
- Utilizing Your Skills: These roles allow you to continue using your nursing expertise, keeping your skills sharp while you develop your venture.
- Networking Opportunities: Staying connected to the healthcare industry can

provide valuable contacts and insights for your business.

Think of it as flipping the script on the traditional side hustle. Instead of your business being the side gig, your nursing work becomes the side gig that supports your entrepreneurial dreams. This approach allows you to:

- Maintain a steady income stream
- Reduce the financial stress of starting a business
- Keeps you one foot in the nursing world while you grow your venture
- Creates a smooth transition from traditional nursing to the career you've always dreamed of.

Specialized Education and Training Services

Your nursing expertise can be channeled into education and training services, which often offer more flexible schedules and less physical strain:

- CPR and First Aid Training: Become certified to teach these essential skills to healthcare workers, teachers, or gym owners, daycare personnel and even corporate entities.
- Medication Administration Training: Many non-medical staff in various settings (schools, residential care homes etc.) need this training.
- Health and Safety Workshops: Offer these to local businesses or community organizations.

These opportunities allow you to set your own schedule, potentially earning as much (or more) than your traditional nursing role while freeing up time to work on your business.

One of the biggest advantages of these strategic side gigs is how they free up your weekdays for building your business. This isn't just about having more time it's about having the right time. By working weekends or off-hours, you open a world of opportunities during regular business hours:

- Networking: Attend industry events, conferences, or local business meetups that typically happen during weekdays. These connections can be invaluable for your new venture.

- Professional Meetings: Schedule meetings with potential clients, partners, or mentors during their regular work hours. This flexibility makes you more accessible and can accelerate your business growth.
- Business Development: Reach out to facilities, administrators, or other businesses during their operating hours. Being available during the '9 to 5' window can make you appear more established and professional.
- Administrative Tasks: Handle important business matters like banking, legal consultations, or government office visits during regular hours, avoiding the hassle of trying to squeeze these in during lunch breaks or after a long shift.
- Learning and Development: Attend workshops, seminars, or courses that can enhance your business skills, many of which are offered during standard business hours.

By aligning your work schedule with the business world's rhythm, you're not just freeing up time you're positioning yourself for success. This strategy allows you to fully immerse yourself in the entrepreneurial world during the week while maintaining financial stability through strategic weekend work. It's about working smarter, not harder, and giving your new venture the best chance to thrive.

For those of you still questioning whether this is feasible. Let me just mention there are opportunities I'm sure there are opportunities you have never even thought of.

Take Nursing in Washington State for instance. Did you know there is something called *Nurse Delegation Consulting?*

Nurse Delegation Consulting exemplifies how you can leverage your nursing expertise in a more flexible, potentially less demanding role. In Washington State, Registered Nurses can contract with Home Health agencies as Nurse Delegation Consultants. In this role, you would:

- Assess whether nurse delegation is appropriate for specific cases.
- Train agency workers on the proper procedure for taking vital signs and the correct process for documentation

- Educate staff on how these readings relate to clients' medication needs.

This side gig allows the nurse to apply their clinical knowledge and teaching skills in a consulting capacity, offering their services on a 1099 contract basis. The key benefits are:

- Flexibility to schedule around business-building activities
- Potential to work with multiple agencies, diversifying income
- Less physical and emotional drain compared to traditional bedside nursing
- Opportunity to impact patient care quality in a different capacity

This is just an example of what we don't think of when we're deep in the trenches. We work, day in and day out. We're tired at the end of the day; the last thing we want to think about is Nursing. If we don't think about opportunities, how can we move from what we don't like to creating the career of our dreams? How many opportunities do you think you're missing out on right now?

The goal here isn't to work more hours or take on additional stress. It's about finding strategic opportunities that provide financial stability with more flexibility and less burnout risk. This approach gives you the breathing room to build your business, pursue your entrepreneurial goals, and gradually transition away from traditional nursing roles.

As you consider these opportunities, think about which ones align best with your skills, interests, and long-term goals. The right strategic side gig can be your bridge to full-time entrepreneurship, allowing you to pursue your dreams without sacrificing your financial security. Let's look at a few more ideas.

Telemedicine Triage Nurse

We've spoken about this opportunity previously, but it bears mentioning again. This opportunity allows you to work on your time schedule, from home, without the long commute or grueling hospital shifts. Telemedicine might be your answer. As a telemedicine triage nurse, you'll provide phone or video consultations, assessing patients' symptoms and advising on the appropriate level of care.

- Flexibility: Many telemedicine companies offer evening or weekend shifts, perfect for freeing up your weekdays for business-building activities.
- Skills Maintenance: Keep your clinical skills sharp while exploring your entrepreneurial path.
- Future-Proof: With the growing popularity of telehealth, this experience could be invaluable for your future ventures.

Imagine advising patients from the comfort of your home office, then spending your days networking or developing your business plan. It's the best of both worlds!

Health and Wellness Coach

If you're passionate about preventive care and holistic health, this could be your ideal transition gig. As a health and wellness coach, you'll leverage your nursing knowledge to guide clients towards healthier lifestyles.

- Build Your Brand: Start attracting clients who could follow you to your future business.
- Flexible Schedule: Offer coaching sessions around your existing commitments.
- Entrepreneurial Skills: Gain experience in marketing, client relations, and running a service-based business.

This role allows you to impact lives positively while laying the groundwork for your own wellness-focused business. Plus, those client testimonials? They'll be gold when you're ready to launch full-time.

Medical Writing or Health Content Creation

Got a way with words? Your nursing expertise makes you the perfect candidate for medical writing gigs. From patient education materials to blog posts for healthcare websites, there's a growing demand for nurses who can translate complex medical information into easy-to-understand content.

- Project-Based: Take on as much or as little work as your schedule allows.

- Remote Work: Write from anywhere, anytime.
- Portfolio Building: Create a body of work that showcases your expertise, perfect for attracting future clients or partners.

Imagine turning those charting skills into a lucrative side gig that could evolve into a full-fledged medical communications business!

Clinical Research Coordinator (Part-time or Contract)

If you've ever been curious about the world of clinical trials, this could be your chance to dive in. As a clinical research coordinator, you'll help manage trials, ensuring they run smoothly and ethically.

- Higher Pay Rates: Often offer better compensation than traditional nursing roles.
- Exposure to Innovation: Stay at the forefront of medical advancements.
- Valuable Connections: Network with pharmaceutical companies and research institutions.

This role not only provides a steady income but also positions you at the cutting edge of healthcare innovation – a great launchpad for future entrepreneurial ventures in the research or pharma space.

Healthcare Technology Consultant

With your frontline experience, you're in a unique position to advise on the implementation of new healthcare technologies. Tech companies are always looking for nurses who can bridge the gap between developers and end-users. In some cases, you can do educational videos and provide them to the tech companies for a fee. This would free up your schedule completely.

- Project-Based Work: Allows for flexible scheduling around your business-building activities.
- Lucrative Opportunities: Tech consulting often commands higher rates than traditional nursing roles.
- Future-Focused: Gain insights into emerging technologies that could inspire your own innovations.

Imagine being the go-to expert for hospitals implementing new EHR systems or tech startups developing the next big healthcare app. Your nursing experience could be the key to unlocking this exciting and profitable field.

Occupational Health Nurse (Contract)

Companies are increasingly recognizing the value of having a nurse on staff to manage employee health. As a contract occupational health nurse, you could provide these services on a part-time or prn basis.

- Regular Hours: Often follows a more predictable schedule than hospital nursing.
- Corporate Exposure: Gain valuable insights into the business world.
- Potential Clients: The companies you work with could become clients for your future business ventures.

This role allows you to maintain your clinical skills while dipping your toes into the corporate world – a perfect combination for an aspiring nurse entrepreneur.

Legal Nurse Consultant

Ever watched a courtroom drama and thought, "They really need a nurse's perspective here"? As a legal nurse consultant, you'll provide medical expertise for legal cases, bridging the gap between healthcare and law.

- Flexible, Project-Based Work: Take on cases as your schedule allows.
- Intellectual Challenge: Apply your nursing knowledge in a completely new context.
- Entrepreneurial Potential: Many legal nurse consultants go on to start their own successful consulting firms.

This role not only offers a fascinating change of pace but also opens doors to a whole new industry.

Who knows? You might find your niche at the intersection of healthcare and law!

These side gigs aren't just about maintaining income — they're about strategically positioning yourself for entrepreneurial success. Each one offers unique opportunities to build skills, make connections, and gain experiences that will be invaluable as you build your own business. So, which one sparks your interest? Your next big adventure could be just a side gig away!

Valuing Your Expertise:
The Power of Choice

As we explore these side gig options, it's crucial to keep one key point in mind: You are in control. These opportunities aren't about taking whatever comes your way. They're about strategically choosing positions that value your expertise and align with your goals.

Key Points to keep in mind:

- Set Your Terms: As a contractor or consultant, you have the power to negotiate your rates and schedules. Don't be afraid to ask for what you're worth.
- Choose Your Projects: You're not obligated to accept every opportunity that comes your way. Select the projects or positions that excite you and compensate you fairly.

- Create Your Ideal Schedule: One of the biggest advantages of these side gigs is flexibility. Design a schedule that allows you to balance income generation with building your business.
- Know Your Worth: Your nursing experience is invaluable. Work with clients and companies who recognize and appreciate your expertise.
- Comfort is Key: The goal here is to create a comfortable transition. Only take on work that provides enough compensation for you to feel secure while pursuing your entrepreneurial dreams.

This approach isn't just about finding any side gig – it's about finding the right side gig. One that respects your time, values your skills, and provides the financial stability you need to build your future.

You've spent years honing your nursing skills. Now it's time to apply those skills where they're most appreciated and where they'll best support your journey to entrepreneurship. You have options, and you have value. Never settle for less than you deserve.

Additional Flexible Nursing Opportunities:

Script Nurse

Lights, camera, action... and medical accuracy! As a script nurse, you'll work with TV shows, movies, or theater productions to ensure medical scenes are portrayed accurately.

- Exciting Environment: Get a behind-the-scenes look at the entertainment industry.
- Flexible Schedule: Productions often need consultants on a project basis, allowing you to choose your commitments.
- Unique Application of Skills: Use your medical knowledge in a creative context.

This role not only provides an interesting change of pace but also allows you to educate the public indirectly about healthcare issues. Plus, it's a great conversation starter for networking events!

Cruise Ship Nurse

Want to see the world while maintaining your nursing skills? Cruise ship nursing might be your ticket to adventure.

- Travel Opportunities: Visit multiple destinations while working.
- Concentrated Work Periods: Often involves contracts for a few days, weeks or months at a time, leaving you with

extended periods to focus on your
business.
- Diverse Experience: Deal with a wide
range of medical issues, from minor
ailments to emergency situations.

This option allows you to combine work with travel,
potentially providing inspiration for your
entrepreneurial ventures. Just imagine brainstorming
your business plan while overlooking the Caribbean!

Theme Park Nurse

If you love the idea of a fast-paced environment with a
touch of excitement, consider working as a nurse at a
theme park.

- Seasonal Opportunities: Many parks have
increased needs during peak seasons,
allowing you to align work with your
schedule.
- Unique Environment: Blend healthcare
with hospitality in a fun setting.
- Networking Potential: Connect with
professionals from various industries who
visit or work at the park.

This role can provide steady income during busy
seasons while allowing you to focus on your business
during off-peak times.

Weekend Event Staff Nurse

From music festivals to sporting events, many large gatherings require on-site medical staff. This could be a perfect weekend gig for a nurse entrepreneur.

- Choose Your Events: Pick the events that interest you or fit your schedule.
- Higher Pay Rates: Event work often comes with premium pay, especially for weekend and evening hours.
- Networking Opportunities: Connect with event organizers and other professionals, potentially leading to future business opportunities.

Imagine providing medical support at a major music festival one weekend, then using that experience to inform your healthcare startup plans during the week!

Seasonal Vaccination Clinics

Transparency moment: These aren't my favorite due to tighter scheduling and fixed pay rates, they're worth mentioning for nurses who might find them a good fit.

- Predictable Short-Term Work: These clinics typically run for a defined period, allowing you to plan around them.
- Skill Maintenance: Keep your clinical skills sharp with hands-on patient care.
- Community Impact: Play a crucial role in public health initiatives.

Although these positions might offer less flexibility than some other options, they can provide a reliable income boost during specific seasons, which could be valuable when you're starting a new venture.

These diverse options demonstrate that nursing skills can open doors to opportunities you might never have imagined. Whether you're drawn to the glamour of Hollywood, the excitement of travel, the thrill of theme parks, the energy of live events, or the satisfaction of public health initiatives, there's a side gig out there that can support your entrepreneurial journey.

As you explore these diverse opportunities, you might be wondering how to choose the right side-gig or how to make the most of these options. The key lies in understanding not just what you can offer, but what businesses truly need. Our discussion about business pain points in Chapter 9 highlights the concept and now you can see how it applies to your transition strategy and choice of side gigs. By aligning your skills with the pressing needs of healthcare businesses, you can position yourself for maximum impact and value.

Leveraging Business Pain Points in Your Transition

As we explore these exciting side gig opportunities, it's crucial to understand the bigger picture of healthcare business needs. Every healthcare organization faces challenges that keep their administrators awake at night - we call these 'business pain points.' We spoke about them in Chapter 9. While you might not have encountered these directly in your bedside role, but indirectly you've probably been on the receiving end of a call from an administrator that called you and offered you double pay for a shift because they were down in staff numbers. Understanding pain points can be your secret weapon in choosing the perfect side gig and positioning yourself for success as a problem-solver, instead of just a jobseeker. Let's dive into how you can leverage these business pain points to guide your transition strategy and maximize your value in the healthcare market.

Identifying High-Value Opportunities:

Look for side gigs that directly address known healthcare pain points
Example: If you know staffing is a major issue, your weekend warrior option becomes even more valuable. Your ability to sweet-talk someone to work when they've already said no to the scheduler is worth every dime the agency is paying you. You could make the difference between a business being profitable or not.

Communicating Your Value:
When negotiating contracts or rates, frame your
services in terms of the problems you solve
Example: As a nurse delegation consultant, emphasize
how you help agencies to add services they can profit
from, how your contract helps maintain compliance
and improve care quality as well.

Choosing Strategic Side Gigs:

- Prioritize opportunities that allow you to
  gain insight into business operations and
  pain points

This knowledge will be invaluable as you develop your
own business

- Set Competitive Rates:

Don't undervalue your expertise - businesses are
willing to pay to solve critical problems
Research market rates, but also consider the unique
value you bring as an experienced nurse

- Develop Your Business Idea:

Use your side gig experiences to identify unmet needs
or persistent pain points in healthcare
These insights could form the basis of your future
business venture

By understanding and addressing business pain points,
you're not just finding a flexible source of income -
you're positioning yourself as a problem-solver and
value creator in the healthcare industry. This mindset
will serve you well as you transition from traditional
nursing roles to entrepreneurship.

However, choosing the right side-gig and understanding business needs are just part of the transition journey. As you embark on this exciting path, it's crucial to prepare yourself emotionally and practically for the changes ahead. Let's explore how you can build the resilience, confidence, and support system you'll need to thrive in your new role as a nurse entrepreneur.

Emotional Preparation:

Embracing Your Evolution as a Nurse

As you embark on this exciting journey to transform your nursing expertise into new opportunities, it's crucial to prepare yourself emotionally for the changes ahead. This transition isn't just about changing your job description – it's about expanding your identity as a nurse and leveraging your skills in innovative ways.

Addressing the Guilt and Identity Shift

Many nurses struggle with feelings of guilt when considering a move away from traditional bedside roles. Let's address these common concerns:

Patient Care Concerns: You might worry that by moving to a non-traditional role, you're no longer directly helping patients. By leveraging your expertise in new ways, you have the potential to impact patient care on a broader scale.

Colleague Considerations: Leaving your work "family" behind can be tough. Know that your transition might inspire others to explore new paths or even create opportunities for them in the future. This is all about choices. Everyone has their own choice to make. You deserve to do what's best for you and so do they. Expanding Your Nursing Identity: For years, your identity has been tied to traditional nursing roles. It's not only okay but exciting to expand this identity. You're still a nurse, just one who's choosing to apply your skills in innovative ways. This transition changes nothing about the core beliefs of being a nurse. How you provide care is the only difference. You are and always will be a Nurse no matter the path you decide to take.

Valuing Self-Growth: There's often an unspoken expectation that nurses should always put others first. Pursuing new opportunities isn't selfish – it's a way to grow professionally and potentially increase your impact on healthcare.

Strategies for Addressing These Feelings:

Reframe Your Impact:
You're not leaving nursing; you're expanding your influence on patient care and in healthcare.
Practice Self-Compassion:
Treat yourself with the same kindness you show your patients.
Visualize Your "Why"
Focus on how your new path could positively impact healthcare in unique ways.
Stay Connected:
Find ways to maintain connections with your nursing community, even as you transition.

Dealing with Fear and Uncertainty

Transforming your expertise into new opportunities can be both exciting and scary. Here are some strategies to manage these emotions:

Acknowledge your fears:

Write down what you're afraid of. Is it the unknown? Learning new skills? Naming your fears can often reduce their power over you. The documentation of your stumbling blocks will be the muscle you flex when you look back at all you've achieved.

Reframe your thoughts:

Instead of "What if I can't do this?", try "How can I apply my nursing skills to this new challenge?" You'll be so surprised how much your nursing skills apply to other areas of business.

Practice mindfulness:

Techniques like meditation or deep breathing can help you stay grounded when uncertainty feels overwhelming.

Seek support:

Connect with nurses who have successfully transitioned to non-traditional roles. Their experiences can provide valuable insights and reassurance. You are welcome to join the "No More ScrubsTM Community" of like-minded Nurses for support and insight on your transition journey. You'll find the link in your QR code at the end of the chapter.

Focus on your transferable skills:

Remind yourself of the many skills you've developed as a nurse that are valuable in various settings.

Building Resilience and Confidence

As you transform your nursing expertise, building resilience will be key. Here's how you can strengthen this crucial trait:

Set small, achievable goals: Each success, no matter how small, builds confidence. Maybe it's learning a new skill relevant to your desired role or making a new professional connection, creating your business plan or business logo.
Celebrate your progress:
Acknowledge each step forward in your transition journey.
Learn from setbacks:
View challenges as learning opportunities rather than failures.
Practice positive self-talk:
Replace "I'm just a nurse" with "I'm a skilled healthcare professional with valuable expertise."
Develop a growth mindset:
Believe in your ability to learn and grow. Your nursing background has equipped you with adaptability now it's time to apply it to your career evolution.
Remember your "why":
Keep your motivation for exploring new opportunities at the forefront of your mind. Write it down and revisit it often.
Take care of yourself:
Maintain healthy habits. Good self-care is crucial for emotional resilience during times of transition.

Transforming your nursing expertise into new opportunities is a journey of professional growth. It's okay to feel a mix of excitement, fear, and uncertainty. What matters is that you recognize the value of your nursing background and the myriad ways it can be applied beyond traditional roles.

Your nursing career has already proven that you're resilient, adaptable, and capable of handling complex situations. Now, it's time to apply those same strengths to your career evolution. By addressing these emotional challenges head-on, you're not just preparing for a new role – you're growing as a healthcare professional and expanding the very definition of what it means to be a nurse in today's world.

In the next section, we'll discuss practical steps you can take to make your transition smoother and more manageable. Are you ready to turn your aspirations into concrete plans? Let's explore the many ways you can transform your nursing expertise into exciting new opportunities!

Practical Steps for Transition:

Charting Your Course

Now that we've addressed the emotional aspects of your career transition, it's time to get practical. Let's break down the process into manageable steps to help you transform your nursing expertise into exciting new opportunities.

Creating a Transition Timeline

Assess Your Current Situation:

- Evaluate your financial stability
- Consider your current job satisfaction and stress levels
- Reflect on your skills and identify areas for growth

Research and Explore:

- Investigate potential career paths that interest you
- Network with nurses who have transitioned to non-traditional roles
- Attend workshops or webinars about alternative nursing careers

Develop New Skills:

- Identify skills needed for your desired role
- Create a learning plan (online courses, certifications, etc.)
- Set aside dedicated time each week for skill development

Build Your Professional Brand:

- Update your resume and LinkedIn profile
- Start a professional blog or portfolio showcasing your expertise
- Engage in industry discussions on social media or forums

Plan Your Exit Strategy:
Decide if you'll transition gradually or make a clean break
If gradual, plan how you'll balance your current job with preparation for new role
If leaving immediately, ensure you have adequate savings or a financial safety net

Setting Realistic Goals and Milestones

The SMART criteria when setting goals:
Specific, **M**easurable, **A**chievable, **R**elevant, and **T**ime-bound.

Short-term Goals (3-6 months):

- Complete a relevant online course or certification
- Attend two networking events in your desired field
- Secure an informational interview with someone in your target role

Medium-term Goals (6-12 months):

- Gain practical experience through volunteer work or a side project
- Build a professional website showcasing your expertise
- Secure a mentor in your desired field

Long-term Goals (1-2 years):

- Transition fully into your new role
- Establish yourself as a thought leader in your new field
- Achieve a specific income target in your new career

These timelines and goals are flexible. Adjust them based on your personal circumstances and progress.

Building Your Support System:

Your Career Transition Dream Team

Transitioning to a new career path can feel lonely, but it doesn't have to be. Building a strong support system can make all the difference in your journey.

Importance of Mentors and Like-minded Peers

Finding a Mentor: Look for someone who has successfully made a similar transition
Utilize professional associations or alumni networks
Don't be afraid to reach out — many professionals are happy to mentor

Joining Peer Groups: Seek out online communities of nurses exploring non-traditional roles
Attend meetups or form a local group of nurses interested in career transitions
Participate in mastermind groups focused on career development

Leveraging Professional Associations:

Join associations related to your target field
Attending conferences and workshops to expand your
network
Volunteer for committees to gain leadership
experience

Navigating Relationships During Career Transitions

Communicating with Family and Friends:

Explain your motivations for the career change
Be patient – it may take time for them to understand
and support your decision
Set boundaries if needed to protect your time and
energy

Managing Work Relationships:

Decide how and when to inform your current
employer
Maintain professionalism throughout your transition
Consider how you can leave on a positive note,
preserving relationships

Cultivating New Professional Relationships:

Network strategically in your target field
Offer value in your interactions – share your unique
nursing perspective

Follow up and nurture new connections regularly

Embracing the Journey:
Growth Through Change

As you embark on this exciting journey of transforming your nursing expertise, the path may not always be straight or smooth. Embracing the challenges and celebrating the victories along the way is crucial for long-term success and satisfaction.

Accepting Challenges as Growth Opportunities

Reframe Setbacks:

View obstacles as chances to learn and improve

Ask yourself, "What can I learn from this experience?"
Use challenges to refine your goals and strategies

Develop a Growth Mindset:

Believe in your ability to learn and adapt
Embrace the discomfort of trying new things
Seek feedback and use it constructively

Practice Resilience:

Develop coping strategies for stressful times
Maintain perspective – remember your "why"
Seek support when needed, it's a sign of strength, not weakness

Celebrating Small Wins Along the Way

Acknowledge Your Progress:

Keep a "wins" journal to track your achievements, no matter how small. Share your successes with your support network. Reflect regularly on how far you've come.
Reward Yourself:
Set up a reward system for reaching milestones
Take time to enjoy the journey, not just the destination
Use celebrations as motivation for the next goal

Pay It Forward:

Share your experiences to inspire other nurses. Offer support to those just starting their transition journey. Contribute to the broader conversation about evolving nursing careers

Conclusion:
Your Nursing Expertise, Reimagined

As we wrap up this chapter on transitioning from traditional nursing roles, let's recap the key points:

We've explored a variety of strategic side gigs that can provide financial stability while you build your new career. We've discussed how to leverage your understanding of business pain points to choose the right opportunities and maximize your value.We've emphasized the importance of valuing your expertise and choosing roles that respect your skills and time.

We've addressed the emotional challenges of a career transition, including guilt, fear, and identity shifts. We've outlined practical steps for creating a transition timeline and setting realistic goals and milestones. We've stressed the importance of building a strong support system, including mentors and like-minded peers.
We've encouraged embracing the journey, accepting challenges as growth opportunities, and celebrating small wins along the way.

This transition isn't just about changing jobs – it's about reimagining your nursing career *on your own terms*. The strategies and insights we've discussed are your bridge to a career you enjoy. A strategically chosen path will allow you to explore new possibilities while maintaining your financial stability and leveraging your valuable nursing expertise.

Your nursing skills are valuable far beyond the bedside. It's time to reimagine what's possible and create a career that truly fulfills you. The healthcare world needs your expertise, your compassion, and your innovative spirit in various roles and settings.

Your nursing experience gives you unique insights into healthcare challenges. Combine this with your growing business acumen, and you'll be well-equipped to offer solutions that healthcare businesses truly need and value.

The power is in your hands to select the roles that value your skills, provide the flexibility you need, and offer compensation that makes you comfortable as you transition into your new career. The world is full of possibilities – it's up to you to choose the path that best supports your dreams!

As you stand at this exciting crossroads, you might be wondering, "What's next?" Well, it's time to turn your vision into a concrete plan. In our next chapter, we'll dive into the nuts and bolts of building your nurse entrepreneur's business plan. We'll explore how to translate your unique skills and ideas into a viable business model, set achievable goals, and create a roadmap for your success. We're taking your career transformation from concept to reality. Get ready to put your nursing expertise into working in ways you might never have imagined!

Scan to Access Tools for Chapter Sixteen

Chapter 17: Building Your Nurse Entrepreneur Business Plan

Welcome to the exciting world of business planning!

Whether you're dreaming of launching your own healthcare venture or transitioning to a non-traditional nursing role, having a solid plan is your first step towards success. In this chapter, we'll guide you through the process of creating a business plan that transforms your nursing expertise into exciting new opportunities.

But don't worry – we're not just going to throw a bunch of business jargon at you and expect you to figure it out. Instead, we'll walk you through each step, showing you how to translate your valuable nursing skills into language that resonates in the business world. We'll use three main examples throughout this chapter to illustrate key points:

A nurse starting a Medical Beauty Business

A nurse transitioning to a Healthcare Technology role
A nurse launching a Healthcare Compliance Consulting business
These diverse scenarios will help you see how the principles we discuss can apply to various career paths and business models. These are just examples – the skills you'll learn here can be applied to any nursing-related business or career transition you're considering. Let's start building the foundation for your exciting new future!

Translating Nursing Skills to Business Language

As a nurse, you've developed a powerful set of skills that are highly valued in the business world – you just might not realize it yet. Let's start by breaking down some common nursing skills and seeing how they translate to business terms:

Nursing Task	Skill Demonstrated	Business Translation
Created complex care plans	Critical thinking, outcome planning	Strategic service design or program development
Trained new staff on protocols	Communication, leadership	Team onboarding or curriculum building
Documented care with precision	Attention to detail, compliance awareness	Risk mitigation and quality assurance

Now, let's look at how we might describe these skills in business terms for our example scenarios:

Medical Beauty Business: As an experienced nurse, I've developed strong client assessment skills, allowing me to quickly identify and address individual needs. My background in patient education translates directly to clear, effective client communication, ensuring each client fully understands their treatment plan and expected outcomes."

Healthcare Technology Role: "My nursing experience has honed my ability to navigate complex systems and prioritize critical tasks, skills that are essential in fast-paced technology environments. I'm adept at translating clinical needs into practical solutions, bridging the gap between healthcare providers and tech developers."

Healthcare Compliance Consulting: "Years of ensuring adherence to healthcare regulations have made me an expert in risk management and quality control. My experience in interdisciplinary collaboration allows me to effectively communicate compliance requirements across all levels of an organization, from frontline staff to C-suite executives."

Exercise: Take a moment to refer back to the list of your top five nursing skills. Now, try reframing each one in business terms. How might these skills apply to your dream business or ideal non-traditional role?

In the next section, we'll explore how to incorporate these reframed skills into your resume and professional bio, setting you up for success in your new venture.

Resume and Professional Bio Guidance

Now that you've identified your transferable skills, it's time to showcase them in your resume and professional bio. The key is to highlight your nursing background while emphasizing how it prepares you for your new role or business venture. You'll reuse this language everywhere: websites, proposals, emails, etc.

Resume Tips:

- Lead with a strong professional summary that outlines your nursing expertise and how it applies to your target role or business
- Use action verbs that resonate in the business world: "managed," "implemented," "optimized," "strategized"
- Quantify your achievements where possible (e.g., "Reduced medication errors by 30% through implementation of new tracking system")
- Include relevant certifications and continuing education, especially those related to business or your target field

Example for Healthcare Technology Role: "Results-driven nursing professional with 10 years of experience, seeking to leverage clinical expertise and technology skills to improve healthcare IT systems. Proven track record of implementing new technologies, reducing errors, and enhancing patient care through data-driven solutions."

Professional Bio Tips:

- Start with a compelling hook that captures your unique value proposition
- Briefly outline your nursing background and how it informs your current pursuits
- Highlight key achievements and skills relevant to your new direction
- End with a forward-looking statement about your goals or vision

Example for Healthcare Compliance Consulting: "Jane Doe is a healthcare compliance expert with 15 years of nursing experience across various healthcare settings. Combining her deep understanding of clinical operations with a passion for regulatory adherence, Jane helps healthcare organizations navigate complex compliance landscapes. Her innovative approaches have helped numerous facilities achieve and maintain regulatory compliance while improving operational efficiency. Jane is committed to elevating healthcare standards through effective, practical compliance solutions."

Communicating Your Value

Being able to articulate your value clearly and concisely is crucial, whether you're pitching to potential clients, interviewing for a new role, or networking with industry professionals.

Developing Your Elevator Pitch: An elevator pitch is a brief, persuasive speech that sparks interest in what you do. Here's a simple formula:

1. Who you are
2. What you do
3. Who you serve
4. What makes you unique
5. Call to action

Example for Medical Beauty Business: "I'm Sarah Johnson, a registered nurse with a decade of experience in dermatology. I've launched 'BeautyMD', a medical aesthetics clinic that combines cutting-edge beauty treatments with the safety standards of a medical practice. We serve clients looking for effective, nurse-administered beauty solutions. Unlike traditional spas, our treatments are backed by my extensive medical knowledge and commitment to patient safety. I'd love to show you how we're revolutionizing the beauty industry – can we schedule a quick call to discuss further?"

This pitch would be effective because:

1. It clearly identifies Sarah's background and credentials, establishing trust.
2. It succinctly explains the unique value proposition of BeautyMD.
3. It highlights the target market and what sets the business apart from competitors.
4. It ends with a clear call to action, inviting further engagement.

Your elevator pitch should be tailored to your specific audience and adaptable to different situations. Practice it until it feels natural and authentic to you.

Business Plan Components

Now, let's dive into the core components of a business plan. Whether you're starting a business or transitioning to a non-traditional role, thinking through these elements can help clarify your path forward.

Executive Summary:

This is a brief overview of your entire business plan. Although it comes first, write it last.

Key elements:

- Business concept
- Goals and vision
- Target market
- Unique value proposition
- Financial highlights
- Team overview

Example of an Executive Summary for Healthcare Compliance Consulting: "Compliance Pro Consulting leverages 15 years of nursing and regulatory experience to provide top-tier compliance solutions for healthcare organizations. Our mission is to simplify compliance, reduce risk, and improve patient care. We target small to medium-sized healthcare providers who struggle with staying up to date with changing regulations. Our unique approach combines clinical insight with regulatory expertise, offering practical, implementable solutions. With projected revenue of $500,000 in year one and a lean, experienced team, we're poised to become a leader in healthcare compliance consulting."

Company Description:

This section provides detailed information about your company and what makes it unique.

Key elements:

- Mission statement
- Company structure
- Nature of the business
- Industry and target market
- Competitive advantages

Example of a Company Description for a Medical Beauty Business:

"BeautyMD is a nurse-led medical aesthetics clinic that bridges the gap between traditional beauty treatments and medical-grade procedures. Our mission is to provide safe, effective, and personalized beauty solutions backed by medical expertise. As a limited liability company (LLC), we operate a brick-and-mortar clinic staffed by licensed nursing professionals. We serve the growing market of health-conscious consumers seeking advanced beauty treatments. Our competitive edge lies in our unique combination of medical knowledge, cutting-edge treatments, and a commitment to patient education and safety."

Market Analysis:

This section demonstrates your understanding of your industry, target market, and competition.

Key elements:

- Industry description and outlook
- Target market characteristics
- Market size and growth potential
- Competitive analysis
- Regulatory environment

Example for Healthcare Technology Role:

While this isn't a business plan, conducting a personal market analysis can be valuable:

"The healthcare IT market is experiencing rapid growth, driven by increasing digitization of health records, demand for improved patient care, and regulatory requirements. There's a particular need for professionals who can bridge the gap between clinical knowledge and technological expertise. Key players in this space include major EHR vendors and health tech startups. The role I'm targeting requires a unique combination of nursing experience and tech savvy, which aligns perfectly with my background."

Organization and Management:

This section outlines your business structure and the key members of your team.

Key elements:

- Organizational structure
- Management team profiles
- Board of directors or advisors
- Ownership information

Example for Healthcare Compliance Consulting:

Compliance Pro Consulting is structured as an S-Corporation. The management team consists of:

Jane Doe, RN, BSN (Founder and CEO): 15 years of nursing experience with a focus on regulatory compliance
John Smith, JD (Legal Advisor): Healthcare law specialist with 20 years of experience
Sarah Johnson, MBA (Operations Manager): 10 years in healthcare administration

We also have a board of advisors including a former state health department official and a healthcare IT security expert."

Services or Products:

Describe what you're selling or what services you're offering in detail.

Key elements:

- Detailed description of products or services
- Benefits to customers
- Competitive advantages
- Development stage (if applicable)
- Intellectual property status (if applicable)

Example for Medical Beauty Business:

"BeautyMD offers a range of nurse-administered aesthetic treatments including:

1. Advanced skincare treatments (chemical peels, microdermabrasion)
2. Injectable treatments (Botox, dermal fillers)
3. Laser therapies (hair removal, skin rejuvenation)
4. Personalized skincare consultations and product recommendations

Our competitive advantage lies in our medical approach to beauty, ensuring safe, effective treatments tailored to each client's unique needs. All treatments are performed by licensed nursing professionals, setting us apart from traditional spas."

Marketing and Sales Strategy:

Outline how you plan to attract and retain customers or, in the case of a job transition, how you'll position yourself in the market.

Key elements:

- Market penetration strategy
- Growth strategy
- Channels of distribution
- Communication strategy
- Sales strategy

Example for Healthcare Compliance Consulting:

Compliance Pro Consulting will use the following strategies to attract and retain clients:

1. Content Marketing: Regular blog posts and white papers on compliance issues
2. Speaking Engagements: Presenting at healthcare conferences and webinars
3. Networking: Actively participating in healthcare industry associations
4. Referral Program: Incentivizing current clients to refer new business
5. LinkedIn Outreach: Targeted outreach to decision-makers in healthcare organizations

Our sales process will involve initial consultations to assess client needs, followed by tailored proposals for our services."

Financial Projections:

This section outlines your financial plan and projections.

Key elements:

- Income statements
- Balance sheets
- Cash flow statements
- Break-even analysis
- Funding requirements (if seeking investment)

Example: While detailed financial projections would be too extensive to include here, you should prepare realistic forecasts based on market research and your planned operations. For a job transition, consider how your move might impact your personal finances and career earnings potential.

Your business plan is a living document. It should evolve as your business grows or as you refined your career transition goals. In the next section, we'll discuss how to apply business plan thinking to non-traditional role transitions.

Applying Business Plan Thinking to Non-Traditional Role Transitions

While we've focused primarily on business planning, these principles can be equally valuable when transitioning to a non-traditional nursing role. Let's explore how to apply this thinking to your career transition:

Personal SWOT Analysis:

Just as a business analyzes its Strengths, Weaknesses, Opportunities, and Threats, you can apply this to your career transition:

- Strengths: Your unique skills, experiences, and qualities
- Weaknesses: Areas where you need improvement or additional training
- Opportunities: Emerging trends or needs in your target field
- Threats: Potential obstacles or competition in your new career path

Example for Healthcare Technology Role:

Strengths: Clinical experience, understanding of healthcare workflows

Weaknesses: Limited formal IT training

Opportunities: Growing demand for clinically trained IT professionals

Threats: Rapidly evolving technology landscape

Define Your 'Product':
In this case, you are the product. Clearly define what you're offering to potential employers or clients:

- Your unique combination of skills and experiences
- The problem you can solve
- The value you can add to an organization

Identify Your Target 'Market'
Research and identify:

- Companies or organizations that need your skills
- Job titles or roles that align with your goals
- Industry trends and growth areas

Develop Your Marketing Strategy
Consider how you'll position yourself in the job market:

- Networking strategies (both online and in-person)
- Personal branding (LinkedIn profile, personal website, etc.)
- Continuing education or certifications to enhance your appeal

Financial Planning
While not a business per se, career transitions often have financial implications:

- Potential changes in salary or benefits
- Costs associated with additional training or certifications

- Savings needed to support you during the transition

Set Milestones and Goals

Just as a business plan includes projections and goals, set clear milestones for your career transition:

- Short-term goals (e.g., complete a relevant certification within 6 months)
- Medium-term goals (e.g., secure an entry-level position in your new field within a year)
- Long-term goals (e.g., advance to a senior role within 5 years)

By applying these business planning principles to your career transition, you can approach your move to a non-traditional role with the same strategic thinking and preparation as an entrepreneur launching a new venture.

Conclusion:

Whether you're planning to start your own business or transition to a non-traditional nursing role, the process of creating a business plan can be an invaluable tool in your journey. It forces you to think critically about your goals, your unique value proposition, and the steps you need to take to achieve success.

The most important part of building a business plan isn't the final document. It's the thinking you do while creating it. As you work through each section, you'll clarify your vision, anticipate challenges, and begin making decisions that reflect where you're truly headed. This isn't something to outsource. You need to understand the steps yourself so you can spot obstacles before they hit and adjust with confidence. Your plan is a living document, one that will grow and evolve as you do.

As we conclude this chapter, take a moment to reflect on how far you've come. You've learned to translate your nursing skills into business language, craft compelling resumes and elevator pitches, and think strategically about your future. You're well on your way to transforming your nursing expertise into exciting new opportunities.

In the next chapter, we'll explore strategies for marketing your new nursing business or promoting yourself in non-traditional roles. Get ready to learn how to showcase your unique value to the world!

Nursing to Business Language Quick Reference

1. Patient Assessment → Client/Market Analysis "Evaluating and understanding client needs and market conditions"
2. Care Planning → Strategic Planning "Developing comprehensive plans to achieve specific objectives"
3. Patient Education → Client Communication/Training "Effectively conveying complex information to stakeholders"

4. Medication Administration → Quality Control/Process Management "Ensuring accurate, timely delivery of critical services"
5. Triage → Resource Allocation "Prioritizing tasks and distributing resources effectively"
6. Documentation/Charting → Data Management/Compliance Reporting "Maintaining detailed records and ensuring regulatory compliance"
7. Interdisciplinary Collaboration → Cross-functional Team Leadership "Coordinating diverse teams toward common goals"
8. Crisis Management → Problem-solving Under Pressure "Making effective decisions in high-stakes situations"
9. Patient Monitoring → Performance Tracking "Continuous assessment and evaluation of key metrics"
10. Care Coordination → Project Management "Orchestrating multiple components to achieve desired outcomes"
11. Patient Advocacy → Client Advocacy/Relationship Management "Representing and protecting client interests"
12. Skills Training → Professional Development "Building and maintaining expertise in key areas"
13. Protocol Implementation → Process Implementation "Establishing and maintaining standardized procedures"
14. Risk Assessment → Market/Business Risk Analysis "Evaluating potential challenges and developing mitigation strategies"

15. Quality Assurance → Performance Optimization "Ensuring consistent delivery of high-quality services"

Chapter 18 Marketing Your Nursing Business: Sharing Your Gifts with the World

The very first time you put on your scrubs and stood in the mirror and placed your nursing school pin on your badge. The feeling of butterflies and the excitement? Nervously saying to yourself, "Can I really do this?" "Am I really ready?" You're probably feeling that same nervousness right now about your new journey. Here's the thing - you've been marketing yourself your whole nursing career. Every time you've built trust with a patient, collaborated with a difficult doctor, or mentored a new nurse, you've been marketing. You just called it something else. Now we're going to help you take those same skills and use them to share your unique gifts with the world.

Reframing Marketing for Nurses:

You're Already an Expert (You Just Don't Know It Yet)

Think about your last shift. I bet somewhere in those 12 hours, you walked into a patient's room and immediately sensed something was off. Maybe it was the way a family member wouldn't meet your eyes, or how your patient's hands were fidgeting with the blanket. Without a word being spoken, you knew exactly what to do next - whether that meant asking the family to step out, pulling up a chair for a heart-to-heart, or simply adjusting your approach to put everyone at ease.

That's what we call: *marketing gold.*

You see, while you've been focused on vital signs and medications, you've actually been mastering skills that marketing executives spend years trying to develop:

- Reading subtle body language
- Picking up on unspoken needs
- Building trust in high-stakes situations
- Communicating complex information in understandable ways
- Knowing exactly when to push forward and when to pull back

Every time you had to explain a complicated procedure to an exhausted patient at 3 AM you did it as if it was the first time you did it that day, right? How you instinctively know whether to lead with statistics or stories, whether to draw pictures or use analogies, whether to involve family members or have a one-on-one conversation?

That's not just patient education - that's sophisticated audience analysis and message crafting.

How about when you've had to get a buy-in for a new treatment plan from a skeptical patient? The way you anticipate concerns before they're voiced, address fears before they're expressed, and build confidence through education and empathy? Congratulations - you've been doing high-level sales and marketing all along.

Let's talk about something every nurse has mastered: the art of pre-framing. You know that moment when you're about to start an IV, and before the patient can even voice their anxiety, you're already saying, "You might feel a small pinch, but I'll be as gentle as possible, and it'll be over before you know it"? That's not just good patient care - that's an expert-level marketing strategy right there. You're addressing concerns before they become objections, building trust through transparency, and setting expectations that you know you can exceed.

Or consider how you handle shift change report. In those few precious minutes, you have to:

- Quickly assess what information is most critical
- Package complex data into digestible chunks
- Tailor your communication style to your audience
- Ensure your key messages are received and understood
- Build credibility with your colleagues

Sound familiar? That's because it's exactly what successful marketers do every single day.

But here's where nurses have an edge that traditional marketers would kill for: authenticity. In a world where consumers are increasingly skeptical of marketing messages, your nursing background gives you something priceless - genuine credibility born from real-world experience. When you talk about healthcare solutions, patient needs, or system improvements, you're not speaking from theory - you're speaking from thousands of hours of hands-on experience.

Think about it:

- When you recommend a product or service, it's because you truly believe it will help
- When you identify a problem, it's because you've seen it firsthand
- When you propose a solution, it's because you know exactly what works on the front lines

This isn't just marketing - this is mission-driven communication with purpose and heart. And in today's market, that's more valuable than any marketing degree.

The Mindset Shift:

From Nurse to Marketer

Now, I know what some of you are thinking: "But I hate selling! I became a nurse to help people, not to push products!" Here's the truth: good marketing isn't about pushing anything. It's about:

Understanding people's needs (just like you do with patients)

Offering genuine solutions (just like you do every shift)
Building trust through expertise and empathy (your superpower!)
Following up to ensure satisfaction (hello, rounding!)

The only real difference? Instead of doing this one patient at a time, you're now expanding your reach to help more people through your new venture. Whether you're starting a consulting business, launching a healthcare product, or offering specialized services, you're still doing what you've always done - making a difference in people's lives.

Let's put this into practice. How do you approach a new patient admission?

You:

1. Review their history before entering the room
2. Make a genuine connection in those first crucial moments
3. Assess their immediate needs
4. Establish trust through expertise and empathy
5. Create a plan that addresses their specific situation

Now, let's look at how this exact same process works in marketing your business:

1. Research your target market before reaching out
2. Make authentic connections through networking and outreach
3. Listen to potential clients' pain points
4. Build trust by sharing your relevant expertise
5. Offer solutions tailored to their needs

You are using the Skills You Already Have

Think about some of your most challenging patient interactions. Maybe it was explaining a complex diagnosis to a frightened family, or helping a resistant patient understand why they needed to change their habits. You did this:

- Found the right words to make complex concepts simple
- Read the room to gauge understanding and emotional readiness
- Adjusted your approach based on what you were seeing
- Knew exactly when to push forward and when to step back
- Built trust through consistent, honest communication

You've just described the core skills of content marketing, client relations, and brand building. The only difference now is that instead of doing this in scrubs, you might be doing it in a business suit (or let's be real - maybe in your home office wearing yoga pants, because who doesn't love working from home?).

From Task-Based to Value-Based Communication

Here's another shift in perspective that might help. Think about how you document your nursing care. In the early days of your career, you probably focused on tasks: "Administered medication." "Performed wound care." "Completed patient education."

But as you grew more experienced, you learned to document the value and outcomes: "Patient demonstrated understanding of new medication regimen." "Wound showing signs of healing with decreased drainage." "Patient verbalized commitment to lifestyle changes."

This same shift applies to marketing your business. Instead of just listing what you do, you're communicating the value you bring and the outcomes you create. You're not just "offering consulting services" - you're " helping healthcare organizations optimize staffing efficiency while maintaining quality metrics." Or "reducing costly staff turnover through effective systems implementation". Or "improving regulatory compliance while streamlining operational costs". Or "implementing solutions that increase productivity and reduce liability exposure". Make sense? These translations of your nursing expertise into business language are your key to opening doors, because now you're speaking directly to what keeps healthcare executives awake at night: their bottom line.

From Task-Based to Value-Based Communication:
A Different Way of Thinking

I know this might feel like a huge mental leap. For years - maybe decades - your value has been measured by how many patients you could handle, how many tasks you could juggle, how many fires you could put out with minimal resources. The system has trained you to think in terms of "more is better" - more patients, more tasks, more responsibility.

Let's pause for a moment and really acknowledge this: That mindset, while necessary for survival in traditional nursing roles, doesn't serve you in your new venture. In fact, it might be holding you back from seeing your true value.

Think about your most meaningful moments as a nurse. Was it when you managed twelve patients flawlessly? Or was it when you had time to really make a difference for one patient - when you spotted that subtle change that prevented a crisis, or when you took the extra time to teach a family member how to care for their loved one?

Those moments of impact - that's value-based thinking. And here's the beautiful thing: As an entrepreneur, you get to define what value looks like. You're no longer bound by metrics designed for

hospital productivity& profit. Instead, you can focus
on:

- The depth of impact you create
- The quality of solutions you provide
- The lasting changes you help implement
- The relationships you build
- The problems you solve

This shift takes time, and that's okay. Start small. Next time you're tempted to list all the tasks you can perform, try instead to describe how your expertise makes a difference. Instead of "I can handle multiple projects," try "I help healthcare organizations create lasting, positive change."

Your value isn't in how much you can do - it's in the unique perspective and expertise you bring to every situation. You're not just offering services; you're providing solutions that can transform healthcare delivery, improve patient outcomes, or make other nurses' lives better.

The Trust Factor

And let's talk about something nurses understand better than almost anyone else - the importance of trust. In nursing, trust isn't just important - it's essential. Your patients trust you with their lives, their dignity, their most vulnerable moments.

You've learned how to earn and maintain that trust through:

- Consistent, reliable care
- Clear, honest communication
- Demonstrated expertise
- Genuine empathy
- Unwavering professionalism

These exact same principles apply to marketing your business. Your potential clients need to trust you with their:

- Business goals
- Professional reputation Time and resources
- Hope for improvement Investment in your services

Building Your Marketing Foundation: Start Where You Are

Let's go back to that first day. You clocked in, fresh and new on the unit. You are expected to know every protocol, master every piece of equipment, and have memorized every medication. Instead, you started with the basics, built your confidence, and gradually expanded your expertise. Even though everyone expected you to know it all, you found ways to learn and grow while keeping your patients safe.

Here's the good news: Unlike that first day of nursing, you actually get to control the pace of building your business and marketing presence. You don't have to be everything to everyone on day one. In fact, trying to do too much too fast can dilute your impact and burn through your resources.

Your First Marketing Asset:

Your Network

Think about all the connections you've made throughout your nursing career. Not just the obvious ones - dig deeper:

- The supply rep who always helped you find what you needed in a pinch
- The IT person who actually answered your calls about the EHR
- The administrator who listened when you proposed a solution to a unit problem
- The physician who trusted your assessment skills
- The case manager who helped you navigate difficult discharges
- The other Nurses and techs who worked alongside you who know your work ethic and trust you implicitly.

These aren't just names in your phone - they're people who've seen your problem-solving abilities in action. They know firsthand how you handle challenges, how you communicate, and most importantly, how you get things done even in less-than-ideal circumstances.

Each Connection Has Value

These professional relationships aren't just about potential business - they're about understanding needs from different perspectives:

- Supply reps know purchasing pain points
- IT staff understand technology implementation challenges
- Administrators face regulatory and efficiency pressures
- Physicians seek reliable partnerships
- Case managers navigate complex system issues

The Art of Professional Outreach

Start with simple, authentic connections: "Hey Sarah, I know you moved to Tampa General last year. I'd love to hear how they're handling their documentation challenges. I'm working on some solutions in that space."

Notice this approach:

- Shows genuine interest in their experience
- Mentions a specific problem area
- Introducing your new focus naturally

Building Your Core Message

How did you learn to give report efficiently? You learned to lead with what matters most. Marketing works the same way:

Instead of: "I offer healthcare consulting services" Try: "I help hospitals reduce documentation errors by 40% through streamlined processes"

Your message should include:

- The specific problem you solve
- For whom you solve it
- The measurable impact
- How you're uniquely qualified to do it

Choosing Your Marketing Channels

Not all marketing channels are created equally in healthcare. Focus on where decision-makers are actually looking:

- LinkedIn for professional connections
- Healthcare industry publications
- Professional associations
- Industry conferences
- Targeted email campaigns

Digital Presence Basics

Your website and online profiles should reflect healthcare's priorities:

- Clean, professional design
- Clear focus on outcomes
- Relevant certifications/credentials
- Case studies/success metrics
- HIPAA compliance emphasis

Marketing Materials That Work

Create resources that provide actual value:

- Implementation guides
- Regulatory compliance checklists
- Process optimization templates
- ROI calculators
- Training protocols

The Follow-Up Formula

Use your nursing assessment skills in follow up:

- Document interactions
- Track responses
- Adjust approach based on feedback
- Maintain professional boundaries
- Keep communication focused on value

Measuring Marketing Success

Track metrics that matter:

- Qualified leads generated
- Proposal concerning conversion rates
- Client satisfaction scores
- Project completion metrics
- Referral sources

Building Credibility

Establish expertise through:

- Speaking engagements
- Published articles
- Industry Partnerships
- Client testimonials
- Case studies

Marketing isn't about pushing services - it's about connecting solutions to problems. You've spent your nursing career doing exactly that. Now you're just doing it on a larger scale.

Common Marketing Pitfalls to Avoid

1. Trying to be everything to everyone
2. Undervaluing your expertise
3. Using clinical language with business audiences
4. Neglecting to follow up
5. Focusing on features instead of outcomes

Marketing on a Budget

Start smart with:

- Professional LinkedIn profile
- Basic website
- Business cards
- Case study portfolio
- Networking event budget

Your First 90 Days of Marketing

Week 1-4:

- Define your service offering
- Create basic marketing materials
- Update professional profiles
- List key connections

Week 5-8:

- Begin targeted outreach
- Attend industry events
- Create valuable content
- Track responses

Week 9-12:

- Follow up on initial contacts
- Refine your message
- Build case studies
- Plan for next quarter

You already have the skills. You've been solving problems, building trust, and delivering results your entire nursing career. Now you're just packaging those skills differently.

The key is to start where you are, use what you know, and build from there. Your nursing experience isn't just relevant - it's your secret weapon in understanding and solving healthcare's biggest challenges.

Marketing Tools and Resources

Throughout this chapter, we've discussed various marketing strategies and approaches. To help you implement these ideas, we've created a suite of practical tools available through our companion website and workbook:

Marketing Quick-Start Tools (via QR code):

- Core Message Builder Template
- Network Contact Tracker
- Basic 90-Day Marketing Planner
- LinkedIn Profile Optimization Guide

Additional in-depth resources available in the From Scrubs to Startups Workbook:

- Complete Marketing Strategy Planner
- Content Calendar Templates
- Client Follow-up Systems
- ROI Tracking Tools
- Case Study Templates

Scan the QR code at the end of this chapter to access your quick-start marketing tools and begin putting these concepts into action.

Now looking back at your first nursing shift and how overwhelming it felt to walk onto that unit, carrying not just your stethoscope but also the weight of responsibility on your shoulders, do you understand how far you've come? Stop and take that in. You are what you have always dreamt of being. It's time to share that with the world.

Marketing your new venture might feel just as daunting right now. But just like you learned to master nursing skills one shift at a time, you'll build your marketing presence one step at a time.

Throughout this chapter, we've uncovered how your nursing experience has already equipped you with powerful marketing skills:

- Your ability to read unspoken needs
- Your talent for building trust quickly
- Your skill at communicating complex information clearly
- Your instinct for knowing when to push forward and when to pull back

These aren't just nursing skills - they're your insider marketing superpowers. And unlike that first day of nursing where you were expected to know everything immediately, you get to control the pace of building your marketing presence. You get to decide how and when to share your gifts with the world.

As you move forward, keep the mindset that marketing isn't about pushing services or making sales pitches. It's about what you've always done as a nurse: identifying problems, offering solutions, and making a difference in people's lives. The only difference now is the scale of your impact.

In the next chapter, you'll meet nurses who've successfully made this transition. They started exactly where you are now - with expertise, determination, and maybe a few butterflies in their stomachs. Their stories will show you just how far your nursing skills can take you when you dare to dream bigger.

Your journey from being a nurse to being an entrepreneur is unique, but you're not on that journey alone. Take what you've learned here, start with one small step, and keep building. The world needs your solutions, your insights, and your unique way of solving healthcare challenges.

After all, you've already mastered one of the most challenging professions in the world. Marketing? That's just your next nursing skill to master.

Scan to Access Tools for Chapter Eighteen

Chapter 19: Nurses Who Dared:

Success Stories in Nurse Entrepreneurship

Throughout this book, we've explored the incredible potential for nurses to innovate, lead, and revolutionize healthcare from the bedside and beyond. We've delved into the unique skills and perspectives that nurses bring to entrepreneurship, and we've provided practical strategies and tools for turning those insights into action.

But the true power of these ideas lies in the real-life stories of nurses who have dared to forge their own paths. These trailblazers embody the spirit of the Nurse Entrepreneur, showing us what's possible when we combine clinical expertise with an entrepreneurial mindset.

In this chapter, we'll dive deeper into the journeys of some of the remarkable nurses we've mentioned throughout the book. From Catie Strigen, the tech-savvy nurse bridging the gap between clinical care and innovation, to Alexis Holloway, the nurse aesthetics entrepreneur redefining patient care; from Ann Henning, the inventor solving everyday clinical challenges, to Ketinna, the home health *"Queen"* empowering others to succeed. These stories showcase the diversity and potential of nurse-led innovation.

We'll explore how Jennifer Myers, the remote nursing specialist, is reshaping the boundaries of nursing practice, and how Jodie Bellam, the creator of the Blue Hug showering aide, turned a patient care insight into a marketable product. We'll learn from Abigail Stanley, the legal nurse consultant who leverages her expertise in new contexts, and Stephanie Beggs, the nurse content creator building a community around education and empowerment.

Each of these nurses has a unique background, specialty, and business model, but they all share a common thread: they recognized an opportunity to make a difference, and they had the courage to pursue it. By digging into their stories, we'll uncover valuable lessons and inspiration that you can apply to your own transition journey.

As you read, give thought to these nurses starting exactly where you are now, with a passion for improving patient care, a wealth of clinical experience, and a drive to create change. Their journeys weren't always easy, but they persevered through challenges and learned invaluable lessons along the way.

So, get ready to be inspired, challenged, and motivated by these incredible stories of *nurses who dared*. Their experiences will reinforce the key concepts we've covered, provide tangible examples of what's possible, and hopefully spark some ideas for your own unique path.

Let's dive in and learn from these nurse entrepreneurs who are redefining what it means to lead in healthcare.

Jessica's Story:
Finding Happiness Beyond the Bedside

Jessica was a seasoned nurse with years of acute-care experience, admired for her dedication and reliability. Yet despite her outward success, inside, she felt increasingly drained, unsettled and undervalued. Her days were long, the shifts were emotionally exhausting, and Jessica found herself struggling to find a quality of life that included her family and friends. She consistently questioned whether this was truly the career she had envisioned.

The turning point came when Jessica made the bold decision to pursue a career that took her away from the hospital but not away from her patients. She knew she loved IVs and Infusion and was really good at it, but did not know if this was a "whole career". She quickly found out that infusion nursing truly was a thing. She transitioned to her new infusion nursing role even though the role is often dismissed by peers as "soft nursing." Despite facing skepticism and criticism, Jessica trusted her instincts. She recognized that her emotional and physical well-being, along with her personal happiness, deserved prioritization. Yaaay Jessica!

The shift to her new role wasn't easy initially, as she navigated negative perceptions and self-doubt. However, within months, Jessica found clarity: her new role not only allowed her to leverage her nursing expertise differently but also offered a drastically improved work-life balance. Jessica experienced genuine happiness in her nursing career.

Jessica shared openly on social media that her mind couldn't grasp what she had truly accomplished in the last year. She went on to highlight moments she could never previously enjoy—extended summer visits from her grandchildren, frequent one-on-one dinners with her children, and sharing precious once in a lifetime moments she would never have had the opportunity to do in her previous roles. Finally, she had the space to nurture herself and her family relationships.

Now empowered by her experience, Jessica actively creates content online, dedicated to showing other nurses the potential and possibilities that lie beyond traditional nursing roles. Her message is clear and resonant: Nursing doesn't have to feel draining or limiting; happiness and career satisfaction are achievable when you dare to redefine what your Nursing career looks like.

Nursing isn't confined to facility corridors and bedside roles alone. Each nurse you're meeting here has found a unique individual path. They've found the courage to embrace uncertainty, prioritize their personal happiness, and redefine success *on their own terms.* As you read these stories, let their courage inspire you to explore your own journey. Let them remind you that your skills, passion, and potential are too valuable to remain unfulfilled. Allow their stories to drown out the naysayers and forge ahead.

Abigail's Story:
Bridging Clinical Expertise and the Legal Field

Abigail was a skilled nurse working in a facility doing long 12 hour shifts just like you and me. One day she and other co-workers were gathered in a break room saying goodbye to a Veteran Nurse who was leaving the facility for a new role. That veteran nurse looked directly at Abigail and said "Abbi you'd be a great legal nurse". Abbi knew nothing about Legal Nursing or how to become one. She didn't even know it was a "thing". She quickly discovered her new passion in Legal Nurse Consulting, combining her clinical knowledge with the intricate world of law. Initially drawn to this niche by curiosity and a desire for professional growth, Abigail soon realized the immense potential her nursing expertise offered outside traditional clinical settings.

Transitioning into legal nurse consulting was transformative for Abigail. She found renewed excitement and deep satisfaction in her work, enjoying the analytical challenges and flexibility this specialty provided, not to mention the value of her expertise she had not ever experienced in healthcare. Abigail's newfound enthusiasm motivated her to help other nurses who felt stuck at the bedside, just as she once had.

Today, Abigail not only excels in her career but is passionate about mentoring other nurses. Through her platform, legalnursesecrets.com, Abigail offers a free masterclass to empower fellow nurses to confidently

402

enter the field of legal nurse consulting, helping them to redefine their professional lives and reclaim career satisfaction.

Mary's Story:

Innovation Through Compassion and Creativity

Mary, an Oncology Pediatric Nurse, blended compassion with creativity when she authored "Butterfly Pig," a children's book promoting self-love, advocacy, and inclusion. Her experiences at work inspired her to create a unique medical device designed for stuffed animals, transforming daunting medical procedures into empowering, playful experiences for pediatric patients.

Mary's innovative devices significantly reduced medical anxiety, enabling children to understand and actively participate in their care. Through her dual roles as nurse and entrepreneur, Mary demonstrates the powerful potential nurses have to innovate and improve patient outcomes beyond traditional clinical roles.

Today, Mary continues to inspire nurses and healthcare providers, reminding them that impactful entrepreneurship can flourish from everyday clinical insights and heartfelt creativity.

Jeannie's Story: Pivoting from Burnout to Professional Empowerment

Jeannie Nguyen, an experienced acute-care nurse of twelve years, reached a breaking point due to burnout and exhaustion. Recognizing that continuing along the same path wasn't sustainable, Jeannie made a pivotal decision to leave behind her bedside career.

Leveraging her clinical expertise, she successfully transitioned into the medical sales industry, discovering a renewed sense of professional purpose and passion. Driven to support other nurses facing similar burnout, Jeannie became a Certified Professional Coach, empowering nurses to see their clinical skills as assets in diverse and fulfilling careers beyond traditional nursing.

Today, Jeannie coaches' nurses through career transitions, openly sharing her own journey and emphasizing the vast potential awaiting nurses beyond bedside role

Embracing Your Power to Transform Healthcare

As we close this chapter, I want you to take a moment, yes - right now, to reflect on the stories we've shared and the journey we've embarked on together. Just as if we were sitting comfortably in a cozy living room, glasses of wine in hand, we are discussing not just the future of healthcare, but *your* future within it.

You've seen how nurses like Jessica and Abigail stepped beyond the traditional confines of nursing to redefine what healthcare can look like when driven by those who know it best—*nurses like you*. These stories aren't just tales of success; they're beacons, illuminating the path for you to step out on and forge that career you worked so hard for.

Why consider this path? Why step away from the familiarity and security of traditional nursing roles? The answer lies not just in the desire for a better work-life balance or more fulfilling professional experiences, though these are significant. It lies in something much deeper: the chance to reclaim control over how healthcare is delivered.

Imagine a healthcare system where decisions are not dictated solely by the bottom line but crafted with care and insight by those at the heart of patient care. Picture nurse-led clinics, wellness centers, and consultant agencies that prioritize patient outcomes and community well-being because they are led by people who have spent years in the trenches on the front lines, who have held hands, wiped tears, and listened to fears.

But let's be honest, stepping into the unknown can be daunting. The security of the hospital floor, the predictability of shifts, even the camaraderie among colleagues. Leaving these behind can feel like a huge leap. But let's pause for a moment, what's your demeanor at work right now? Are you truly safe? Do you feel stable? And most importantly... are you happy? If everything was perfect in your world, would you even be reading this book? Think about these questions, not just in passing, but really let them sink in. It's easy to keep moving through the motions day in and day out, but it takes courage to stop and ask yourself if this is really the path you want to continue on.

Every time a nurse steps into a role of greater influence and autonomy, the system shifts slightly towards a more compassionate, effective ecosystem. And who better to lead this charge than someone who understands both the profound challenges and the unmatched rewards of caring for others?

You possess skills that are incredibly valuable, not just in patient care but in leadership, innovation, and entrepreneurship. You have the power to not only imagine better ways of delivering healthcare but to make those visions a reality. It's not about discarding your nursing identity; it's about expanding it, stretching it to include 'entrepreneur', 'leader', 'innovator'.

So as we finish our wine and this conversation, I want you to hold onto the sense of possibility we've nurtured together. The road may be uncharted, but it's ripe with potential. And you're not alone. The community of nurse entrepreneurs is growing, filled with people who once stood where you stand right now, filled with questions but brimming with passion.

Take the stories of those who *dared to dream* as your armor and their lessons as your guide. Step forward with the knowledge that your journey could inspire the next generation of nurses to look beyond the bedside and see a world of opportunities.

The future of healthcare is not in the hands of faceless corporations; it's in the hands of caring, driven, and insightful individuals like you. It's time to rise, not just for yourself but for the betterment of all those you aim to heal. Let's make your career the best it can be—one adventure at a time.

Scan to Access Tools for Chapter Nineteen

Chapter 20: Embracing Your Nurse Entrepreneur Journey

As we settle into this moment of calm, I want to commend you for the bravery and curiosity you've shown simply by opening this book. You've embarked on a journey that requires you to question the familiar, to wonder if there's more to your professional life than the routine you've grown accustomed to.

Reflect for a moment. How do you feel each day when you step into work? Safe, valued, satisfied? Or do you find yourself yearning for something different, something more? If your days at work were truly fulfilling, would you be seeking answers in these pages? These aren't just idle questions; they are seeds from which new beginnings grow.

Choosing to explore a path beyond traditional nursing isn't about discarding your past; it's about embracing the full potential of who you are. Your experiences in nursing, marked by compassion, resilience, and acute insight, have uniquely positioned you to forge change, not only in your life but in the healthcare system itself.

This chapter isn't just about thinking outside the box. It's about realizing that maybe, just maybe, the box never really existed. You've always been capable of more than you were taught. Now, it's time to let yourself believe it.

Let's explore what it means to step into nurse entrepreneurship, where the challenges of today's healthcare environment intersect with your capacity to innovate and transform. As we journey through this chapter, allow yourself the grace to consider a future where you are not only a nurse but a pioneer, a leader, an innovator. This transition requires careful planning, yes, but it also demands something of even greater importance—your belief in the possibility of change.

The Catalysts for Change:

Addressing Systemic Issues in Healthcare

As we turn our discussion towards the deeper challenges of the nursing profession, it's important to recognize the systemic issues that many of us face daily. These aren't just hurdles; they are profound motivators for seeking new paths that offer more than just financial rewards. So many nurses I speak to feel the same way, overworked, underappreciated, and absolutely unsafe

Nurse Safety and Violence:

It's a harsh reality that violence in healthcare settings is on the rise at an alarming rate. Have you ever been threatened at work? It throws you, right? The place where you go to care for others turns into a scene where you're the one needing protection. This untenable situation is driving many nurses to seek environments where their safety and dignity are prioritized. It's no longer worth the long hours and mediocre pay. This is about our lives and our livelihood.

If we're honest, navigating this every day takes its toll, not just physically but mentally. When you're constantly on guard, wondering when the next outburst will occur, it's hard to focus on providing the care your patients need. It's exhausting.

Now, imagine a different scene. Picture a place where you feel safe, where the environment is shaped by your values and your understanding of care. Imagine creating a work setting tailored by you, for you. Sound good? This is where entrepreneurship can step in as a light at the end of a very dark tunnel. By stepping into a nurse-owned, nurse-led business, you can create a safer, more controlled setting where you can practice without fear. Entrepreneurship isn't just about taking control of your professional life; it's also about safeguarding your personal well-being and creating a space where you and your colleagues can thrive without fear.

Burnout and Mental Health: The chronic stress from high patient loads, long hours, and the emotional weight of nursing leads to burnout. Burnout impacts mental health and job satisfaction profoundly. It's more than the physical exhaustion of long shifts or the emotional drain from constant caregiving. Burnout infiltrates every aspect of your life, often forcing you to compartmentalize your emotions just to make it through the day. Have you noticed its toll on your relationships outside of work? It's tough, arriving home mentally checked out, isn't it? Think about how many times over the last year you've had to sit silently in your car for 20 minutes before you could face going inside, just to avoid exposing your loved ones to the trauma of your day. You suppress those feelings, put on a smile, and pretend everything is fine.

This emotional distancing can create a profound sense of isolation. It's challenging to share these experiences because you might feel that others won't understand or you might wish to protect them from the harsh realities of your work. This often exacerbates the difficulty in connecting with family and friends. You might find yourself missing out on life's precious moments because you're either too exhausted or too overwhelmed by work-related stress. It's a vicious cycle. Emotional disconnect leads to more stress, which deepens the sense of isolation.

Imagine breaking that cycle. Picture yourself stepping into a role where you call the shots—where your time and your emotional energy are yours to manage. Owning your own business or working for yourself opens up a world where you can fully engage, not just with your career but with all aspects of your life. It's about reclaiming your ability to be present, to truly connect with those around you, and to actively participate in your own life.

Entrepreneurship isn't just a career change; it's a lifestyle change. It offers the freedom to integrate work with your personal values and relationships, creating a fulfilling balance that nurtures all areas of your life, not just your professional achievements.

Moral Injury: Have we spoken about moral injury? It's

when you
know what's right for your patients, but you're caught
in the web of hospital policies or administrative
pressures. It's soul-sucking. Starting your own venture
means you get to make the rules. It means doing the
right thing is no longer an act of rebellion, but just a
normal day at work.

Economic Disparities:

Finally, let's talk about money. Ever wonder why
there's such a gap between what you earn and what
those at the top of the chain take home? Well, you're
not the only one. What if you could set your worth?
Nurse entrepreneurship is not just about making a
living; it's about making a life that rewards you fairly.
Isn't it time you got paid what you're truly worth? If
we haven't spoken about anything in this book, I have
drilled down that in any arena of nursing, Nurses need
to understand and demand their value.

So, as we sit here, sharing this moment, we think
about these things.

You didn't just make it to the end of this book — you
made it through a season that tried to convince you to
give up. You kept showing up. You kept caring. And
now, you've done the bravest thing of all: you've
picked up this book and allowed yourself to imagine
something different.
That vision you're holding on to, it's not a fantasy.

It's the future. And you don't have to build it alone. In the final chapter, I'll share why I created No More Scrubs™ and why the next part of your story might just be the most powerful one yet.

Scan to Access Tools for Chapter Twenty

Chapter 21 A Letter from the Author: No More Scrubs™ and What Comes Next

Join me on my lanai in Florida again, won't you? The sun is setting, casting that beautiful golden pink cotton candy glow across the sky. Grab a seat, let me get you a glass of wine? Sweet Tea maybe? Can you feel the warm breeze? It's carrying away the weight of your day. As we settle in, let's talk about what's keeping you at the bedside. Yup, I know you're swirling your drink and gazing at the sunset, trying to justify it in your mind. Job Security? Or maybe it's the "sunk cost bias" where you think that you have to continue with something because of all the time and energy you've invested even if it's no longer beneficial to do so. Or maybe it's simply fear of the unknown.

I hear you. I've been there. I had a 13-year-old son to take care of when my husband passed away from COPD at age 39. Believe me the fear is real. Somewhere, somehow, we have to move out of survival mode. So, when do we get to thrive? When do we get to celebrate our earned experiences and accomplishments? We've worked hard to get where we are.

The Crossroads We All Face

Every nurse reaches a crossroads at some point.
That moment when you realize something needs to
change. Maybe it came for you when you sat in your car
before a shift, willing yourself to go inside. Or perhaps
it was when you missed another family milestone
because you couldn't get your shift covered. Or worse.
when a patient or family member crossed a line, and
somehow you were made to feel it was your fault.
These moments force us to ask difficult questions:
Is this really what I signed up for? Is this worth the toll
it's taking on my life, my health, my relationships? What
else could I be doing with my nursing knowledge?
Here's what I want you to know, from one nurse
to another: This crossroads isn't a sign of failure. It's
an invitation to growth.

My Own Journey:

Finding My Path Beyond the Bedside

Let me share something personal with you. When
I started exploring opportunities beyond traditional
nursing, I felt like an imposter. Who was I to think I
could succeed outside the structured environment of
healthcare organizations? What if I failed? What would
my colleagues think?
But I knew I needed to try. So, I started by placing
myself in proximity to nurses who were doing what I
wanted to do. Nurses who were thriving outside
traditional roles. I observed. I listened. I asked
questions. I volunteered for projects that would give me

exposure to the skills I needed. Did you catch that? I didn't wait until I had it all figured out. I didn't wait for permission. I just started moving in the direction that felt right. Even though I was in deep bias because I had been told my entire career that no matter what I was always only going to be *just* an LPN.

There were plenty of stumbles along the way. Times when I questioned my decision, when I missed the predictability of my old role. But each small success built my confidence until eventually, I could look in the mirror and see not just a nurse, but a nurse entrepreneur. Someone who was using her nursing expertise in ways I had never imagined possible.

And if I did it, an LPN who never got that RN degree everyone told me I needed, then you absolutely can too.

What's Really Holding You Back?
Let's get honest with each other. What's really keeping you tied to a system that may be depleting you?

Is it money? The steady paycheck is comforting, I know, But consider this: many of the nurse entrepreneurs you've read about in this book are making more than they ever did at the bedside, with greater control over their time and less physical and emotional drain. That steady paycheck is tied to a corporation that could downsize at any moment and cut you off without a moment's notice. Believe me, I know that firsthand. Do you think the Nurses at Mass General ever thought they'd be laid off? Of course not, the stability that once was "nursing" isn't hospital facility anymore. Will there always be sick and disabled people? Yes. Where you care for them or provide services for them is Your choice. Why not choose where you have control of the outcomes and the business strength?

Is it your identity? After years of defining yourself as a *nurse* in the traditional sense, it can be disorienting to imagine yourself doing anything else. But, you're not leaving nursing behind, you're expanding your idea of what it means to be a nurse.

Is it fear of judgment? This is a big one, and it's deeply valid. You might worry about how to explain your career shift to family members who watched you struggle through nursing school, or to colleagues who might see your departure as abandonment.

Here's what I've learned: those who truly care about you want to see you thrive. And those who judge your choices without understanding your reality? Their opinions say more about them than about you.

The World Needs Nurse Innovators

When I look at healthcare today, I see a system crying out for transformation. We're the ones who see firsthand where the gaps are, where patients fall through the cracks, where processes break down. So why not be a vehicle of change?

Imagine a healthcare landscape shaped by those who've actually provide the care, who've held the hands of suffering patients, who've navigated broken systems while trying to do right by those in their care.

You might be thinking, "But I'm just one nurse. What impact can I really have?" Let me just tell you: It can be profound. Consider some of the nurses we've met throughout this book:

417

Abigail, transforming her clinical knowledge into a thriving legal nurse consulting business.

Mary, creating innovative products that make medical procedures less frightening for children. Jessica, finding joy in infusion nursing and inspiring others to redefine success. Each of them started exactly where you are right now, with expertise, with passions, with frustrations, and with a vision for something better.

The Moment I Knew

Many nurses who are considering leaving the bedside often ask, "when was the *moment* you knew?"

I didn't always have this clarity.
For a long time, I stayed quiet. Loyal. Careful.

To be completely honest I was just grateful to have a remote job in an industry I loved, and I thought if I just worked harder, stayed later, followed the rules, someone would finally see me.

But they didn't.
They saw my courage as a threat.

I wasn't even three weeks into building this when it happened. Eighteen days. That's all it took for someone to feel unsettled enough to report me to my CEO. Two months later my position was "terminated" due to downsizing. Coincidence? I guess it could be. lol

When my CEO (a non-healthcare MBA) found out I was using the word "consultant" when telling other nurses they had options, I was silenced.
And at first, I shrank. I questioned myself. I shut down a website and quieted my social media.

But then it hit me:

If 18 days of me speaking softly made them feel that unstable... what kind of power do, we *really* **have?**

That moment didn't break me, it built me.
Not because I was afraid.
But because I was finally *done*.

Done waiting for permission.
Done asking for a seat.
Done pretending I didn't already have everything I needed to build the table myself.

Taking the First Step

So, as we sit here watching the sunset, let me ask you:
What would your life look like if you took that first step toward nurse entrepreneurship?
Would you finally have time for those vacations you've put on hold because you could never get the PTO approval? Would you be present for family dinners without the cloud of exhaustion hanging over you?

Would you wake up excited about your day instead of dreading it? The beautiful thing about being a nurse entrepreneur is that you get to design a life that works for you. You get to set the terms. You get to decide what success looks like. And no, it won't be easy. There will be learning curves and moments of doubt. But having coached countless nurses through this transition, I can tell you with certainty, the hardest part is making the decision to begin. So, here's what I want you to do: **Start where you are.** You don't need to have it all figured out. Even small Steps move you forward. **Trust your circle.** Connect with other nurses who are on similar journeys. Their support and understanding will be invaluable. **Keep learning.** Your nursing education taught you how to be a lifelong learner. Apply that same curiosity to entrepreneurship. **Trust your expertise**. You bring a wealth of knowledge and experience that is incredibly valuable in countless contexts. **Be Patient with Yourself.** This transition is a journey, not an overnight transformation.

A Toast to Your Future

As the last rays of sunlight disappear and the stars begin to emerge, I raise my glass to you. To the nurse who dares to dream of something different. To the caregivers learning to care for themselves as well as others.

To the professional who recognizes their worth and refuses to settle for less.

The path of nurse entrepreneurship isn't for everyone. But for those who feel called to it, it offers the possibility of professional fulfillment, personal well-being, and the chance to make a difference on your own terms.

Whatever path you choose after reading this book, I hope you'll walk it with confidence, knowing that your nursing expertise is a foundation you can build upon in countless ways.

You're not alone in this journey. There's a growing community of nurse entrepreneurs ready to welcome you, support you, and celebrate your success.

I didn't set out to write a book and launch a movement. I wrote this book because I was heartbroken. Because I didn't know how else to reach nurses like me. The ones who couldn't breathe, couldn't rest, couldn't stay, but didn't know how to leave.

But as I wrote, the comments kept coming:

> "How do I actually do it?"
> "Where do I even start?"
> "What about money while I'm in between?"

And the truth hit me: This book isn't enough. That's when No More Scrubs™ was born. It's not a business. It's a reclaiming of your career, your voice, and your future. A safe space to build a new way of working. A nurse-built system that not only shows you how but gives you ways to earn while you figure it out. You've done the reflection. You've walked the hard road.

So, what do you say? Are you ready to turn your nursing expertise into the life you truly deserve?

Let's build it together.

Something no one can take from us.

Something that belongs to us.

I can't wait to see what you create!

Scan to Access Tools for Chapter 21

About the Author

Laurie Alves, LPN

Laurie Alves is a career-long nurse, educator, consultant, and creative force behind *From Scrubs to Startups*™. With over 30 years in healthcare from floor nurse to compliance manager to nurse entrepreneur She's lived the burnout cycle. And she's not here to teach from theory she's here to build what should've existed all along.

Laurie created this book for every nurse who has ever whispered, *"I can't do this anymore."*

Today, she helps nurses reclaim their time, income, and self-worth through education, business tools, and community inside the **No More Scrubs™ Vault** — a digital space where nurses are building legacies of their own.

Learn more at:

www.fromscrubstostartups.com
www.nomorescrubsvault.com

Resources & Links

Where You Go from Here

Follow the Movement

TikTok: @FromScrubsToStartups
Instagram: @FromScrubsToStartups

Download the Full Workbook

→ fromscrubstostartups.com/get-the-workbook

Scan to Get the Workbook

Enter the No More Scrubs™ Vault

→ fromscrubstostartups.com/vault

Scan to Unlock the No More Scrubs™ Vault

Share Your Story

Want to be featured in the next edition?
Tell us how this book impacted you.
→ fromscrubstostartups.com/nurse-story

Scan to Tell Us How This Book Impacted You